Studies in the Psychosocial

Series Editors

Stephen Frosh
Department of Psychosocial Studies
Birkbeck University
London, United Kingdom

Peter Redman
Department of Social Sciences
The Open University
Milton Keynes, United Kingdom

Wendy Hollway
The Open University
Hebden Bridge, West Yorkshire, United Kingdom

Aim of the series

Psychosocial Studies seeks to investigate the ways in which psychic and social processes demand to be understood as always implicated in each other, as mutually constitutive, co-produced, or abstracted levels of a single dialectical process. As such it can be understood as an interdisciplinary field in search of transdisciplinary objects of knowledge. Psychosocial Studies is also distinguished by its emphasis on affect, the irrational and unconscious processes, often, but not necessarily, understood psychoanalytically. Studies in the Psychosocial aims to foster the development of this field by publishing high quality and innovative monographs and edited collections. The series welcomes submissions from a range of theoretical perspectives and disciplinary orientations, including sociology, social and critical psychology, political science, postcolonial studies, feminist studies, queer studies, management and organization studies, cultural and media studies and psychoanalysis. However, in keeping with the inter- or transdisciplinary character of psychosocial analysis, books in the series will generally pass beyond their points of origin to generate concepts, understandings and forms of investigation that are distinctively psychosocial in character.

More information about this series at
http://www.springer.com/series/14464

Mihnea Panu

Enjoyment and Submission in Modern Fantasy

palgrave
macmillan

Mihnea Panu
Wilfrid Laurier University
Waterloo, Ontario, Canada

Studies in the Psychosocial
ISBN 978-1-137-51320-5   ISBN 978-1-137-51321-2   (eBook)
DOI 10.1057/978-1-137-51321-2

Library of Congress Control Number: 2016956119

Cover image © Eukariot Art Bureau (www.eukariot.com)

Printed on acid-free paper

This Palgrave Macmillan imprint is published by Springer Nature
The registered company is Macmillan Publishers Ltd.
The registered company address is: The Campus, 4 Crinan Street, London, N1 9XW, United Kingdom

Content

Content

1

The Bourgeois Returns

This text discusses the role played by fantasy and enjoyment in perpetuating the capitalist order and harnesses the historical and class charge of the term 'bourgeois' to its undertaking. More than 50 years ago, Roland Barthes was defining the bourgeoisie as 'the social class that does not want to be named' (Barthes 1972, 138). According to Barthes, bourgeois ideology functions by erasing the name 'bourgeois', thus transforming bourgeois reality into natural reality, into Nature (Barthes 1972, 141). But while critical theory, including the interwar modernist avant-garde, investigated the subjectivity they called 'bourgeois' with a sort of anato-mopathological minutiae, looking for the key to understanding and affecting the modern regime, the term is not often used in contemporary anti-capitalist analyses. It has been replaced, mostly, by structural analyses that focus on the 'middle class' or on the 'neoliberal' subject. The term 'middle class' is inadequate for an analysis of capitalist ideology because it is one of this ideology's active elements. In England, for example, the incognito of the bourgeois class was insured by its self-description as the 'middle class' (Moretti 2014). By spatialising its appellative, the bourgeoisie self-represents as an intermediate stratum, partly subaltern, and therefore is not responsible for the effects of capitalism. The suggestion

© The Author(s) 2016
M. Panu, *Enjoyment and Submission in Modern Fantasy*,
DOI 10.1057/978-1-137-51321-2_1

of spatial contiguity created by the terms 'low', 'middle', and 'high' also promises a potential for class fluidity not allowed by the old terminologies such as peasantry, proletariat, bourgeoisie, and nobility (Moretti 2014, 12). 'Middle class', then, participates in forging the bourgeoisie's mystique as a universal class that will eventually include everybody.

The signifier 'neoliberal'—which, unlike 'middle class', does carry critical valences—cannot perform the same tactical and analytical functions as 'bourgeois' because it fails to mobilise critically the genealogy of this subject. With its post-1970s connotations, 'neoliberal' misses the trajectory of a subjectivity—the bourgeois—devoted to liberal-capitalist ideology since its inception. Moreover, when using the concept 'neoliberal', it is tempting to exclude from analysis an important category of subjects: those who vociferously stand against neoliberal policies (marketisation and managerial control, privatisation of public resources, dismantling of welfare provisions and cutting down of public spending, aggressive pursuit and use of natural resources, pollution, etc.) while remaining passionately tethered to the colonial-capitalist dispositifs of enjoyment, even if it is in their organic, sustainable, responsible, and fair trade versions.

This book analyses capitalism starting from the play of enjoyment, identification, and desire—and not of rational interest, ignorance, education, or choice—because I believe that the unfruitfulness of our current anti-capitalist and decolonial tactics has to do with libidinal processes and not with reason as defined by the Enlightenment. At the moment, I do not think that one cannot radically question liberal-capitalism without engaging with issues of desire and enjoyment, without, in other words, analysing the mechanisms through which hegemonic fantasies condition our most private, cherished, and stubborn conducts, shaping the 'substance' of our 'being'. This analytical focus is exactly what I understand by a psychosocial approach, an approach that starts from a subject driven by mechanisms placed at another level than (self-)consciousness and rationality. Within this psychosocial conceptualisation, it is only in the realm of enjoyment (jouissance) that we might encounter anything resembling 'the truth of the subject', even if it is a truth shaped by elements that are contradictory, fleeting, and obscure to the subject herself. It will be seen that the instability and self-opacity of bourgeois subjectivity do not impede the bourgeoisie to thrive on the already mentioned promise that, one day, everyone will have access to the enjoyment so alluringly staged by the symbolic productions of Western capitalism.

While the present project aims to reactivate the symbolic weight accumulated historically by the signifier 'bourgeois', it also expands this signifier's range beyond the usual referents, the owners of the means of production for example. As the first two chapters detail, the term 'bourgeois' points to a constellation of psychological mechanisms specific to subjects formed in the post-war Europe and especially post-1990. However, while it makes claims about a contemporary European subject, this analysis does not aim for socio-historical exactness: its spatial-temporal frame defines a political focus rather than the specificity of its central object, 'the bourgeois'. My aim is to propose an apparatus for the critical investigation of contemporary liberal-capitalism, to the extent that this apparatus might help rethinking anti-capitalist tactics. As such, the precise spatial-temporal boundaries of bourgeois subjectivity are less important than this apparatus' ability to identify the symptomatic conducts supporting European liberal-capitalism. Thus, the term 'bourgeois' does not make either universal claims or strong claims for specificity, taking some critical distance from the understanding of social position in terms of a specific space, place, time, or class that drives 'either/or' sociological taxonomies. One might encounter bourgeois traits outside the territories mapped here. My onto-epistemological framework then, as suits a psychosocial approach, works with an overdetermined concept and its shifting libidinal charges, creating a tool that is fairly precise when discussing issues of fantasy and enjoyment but that otherwise remains ambivalent. My description of the bourgeois will navigate between current events and various genealogies of this subjectivity in manners that preserve this analytical fluidity.

I conceptualise 'Europe' as a symbolic production: 'Europe' as a global resonance chamber of resources, authority, power relations, knowledge, and violence, and 'Europe' also as the phallic signifier of our modern fantasies. When discussing 'Europe', then, I am not referring to an objective political-administrative, geographic, or historical entity and even less to the European Union, but to an ideal shaped by this already mentioned modern fantasy. And at this level of conceptualisation, there is no point in dissociating North America from Europe: as Sartre (2004, lviii) argued, North America is nothing but a 'super-European monster'.

I have also opted to describe the current order as 'modern' rather than 'capitalist' or 'neoliberal'. This is not because modernity is not capitalist: I agree with Fredric Jameson's (2002) argument that detaching these concepts from each other is politically and theoretically dubious. But this is because I regard 'modernity' as the ideological branch of capitalism or, more accurately, as the fundamental fantasy fuelling capitalism, an approach which makes visible interesting connections between the capitalist governing apparatuses and bourgeois enjoyment. That is, once we approach 'modernity' as a fantasmatic construction, we gain access to an analytical framework in which liberal-capitalist apparatuses are intractable only to the extent that the bourgeois subject invests them libidinally. Within this framework, as Chap. 3 details, the global mystique of bourgeois enjoyment can be understood not only in relation to the European colonial practices but also in relation to the seduction that the modern fantasy exerts on the very subjects it disqualifies from the status of modern.

The theory of subjectivity I propose makes use of concepts central to Lacanian psychoanalysis: the unconscious, of course, but also desire, jouissance, fantasy, ego ideal, disavowal, and identification. More accurately, it makes use of the way in which these concepts have been reshaped and put to work by various psychoanalytically inspired theories that address the question of who we are now and how we could experiment with affecting the elements of our being that we find unacceptable. At the same time, and equally importantly, any radical interrogation and transformation of the current liberal-capitalist regime must have a decolonial ethos. The two aspects are related: a true transformation of our reality, which involves experimenting with new modalities of being, desiring, and enjoying, passes through the obligatory decolonial moment of turning our backs on the Euro-bourgeois master and learning to avoid being interpellated by its look; of learning how not to mistake this look for the omnipotent gaze; and of learning how to give up the pleasures that submission to authority provides the bourgeois with. As many know by now, this is not an easy task: this book argues that one is bourgeois to the extent that one adopts a mechanism of self-preservation based on the refusal to recognise any event that threatens one's identification with authority.

I will be pitting Lacan-inspired work against equally crucial theoretical innovations coming from fields concerned with the same fundamental questions, but that remain attentive to the discursive effects of psycho-analysis. This means that psychoanalytical theory is not taken to be an objective lens through which one apprehends the truth of the social, but a libidinally charged discourse that reflects the anxieties and psychic investments of its producers and users. And, when dealing with a seductively universalist discourse like psychoanalysis, I think we should keep in mind Mary Ann Duane's (quoted in Fuss 1995, 36) insight that psychoanalysis, far from representing a universal science, functions as 'a quite elaborate form of ethnography, as a writing of the ethnicity of the white Western psyche'. The present work employs psychoanalysis as a tool for the investigation of the Euro-bourgeois psyche *and* as a compendium of the symptoms of its various producers. In other words, psychoanalysis is at the same time a useful instrument for the critical analysis of bourgeois order, one of the master discourses of modernity, and an explanation of bourgeois being and reality that reflects the fantasies of its authors. Thus, the blind spots of psychoanalysis map, to some extent, the framework of the modern fantasy in general.

The obvious example is the way in which psychoanalysis simultaneously imagines and obscures the relationship between race and sex/gender, and if using psychoanalysis for decolonial tasks, one needs to take seriously the idea that its racist-colonial logic is not simply an appendix of the Freudian theoretical body but subtends it in its entirety. The racialized 'primitive' is the figure, first invoked and then erased, that secures Freud's fantasy of a civilised European society, a 'civilized sociality that can seemingly exist and be (sexually) analysed independent of colonialism and racial problematics' (Eng 2001, 12). The issue being that, by ignoring the techniques of racial categorisation and regulation intrinsic to modern sexuality, the psychoanalytical theory of (hetero)sexual differentiation is complicitous with the hegemonic, unmarked whiteness that sustains both psychoanalysis and the current colonial-heterosexist regime (ibid. 13 and 139–142). As David L. Eng argues:

> ... the conceptualization of racial and sexual difference as if they were distinct categories of analysis is a false construction that serves the political power, economic interests, and cultural hegemony of a mainstream social order. We cannot isolate racial formation from gender and sexuality

without reproducing the normative logic domination that works to config-ure these two categories as opposed, independent discourses in the first instance. (Eng 2001, 19)

Chapters 3 and 4, respectively, further put to work psychoanalysis in its dual form, as both a symptom and a diagnostic of modernity, to discuss critical aspects of the contemporary dispositifs governing race and sex/gender, familism, and reproduction.

I will add that, however, this work's purpose is not polemical and that all throughout I have tried, with varying success, to take seriously Foucault's warning:

> … I think this serious and fundamental relation between struggle and truth … only dramatizes itself, becomes emaciated, and loses its meaning and effectiveness in polemics within theoretical discourse. So in all of this, I will therefore impose only one imperative, but it will be categorical and unconditional: Never engage in polemics. (Foucault 2007, 3–4)

In my attempt to escape the lure of polemical debate without abandoning a direct engagement with the discourses that currently have some weight in shaping reality, I bring to the fore the politico-theoretical points of convergence and disagreement in related intellectual productions only when this helps sharpen the analysis.

Dispositifs of Enjoyment

It is suitable to start by making clear my analytical premises, and this section will describe the events that inaugurate the bourgeois ego, desire, and enjoyment. I understand subjectivation as the process through which one becomes recognisable by the Other. And by 'Other' I mean a disem-bodied representation of the socio-symbolic structure, which assumes the function of governing the subject's social and libidinal fate. This is why, in the bourgeois subject's libidinal economy, this representation condenses a plethora of elements: authorities, institutions, language, discourse, the law, norms, symbolic codes, and so on.[1]

One of the central premises of the ontology adopted here is that 'the Other lacks', which is to say that the symbolic governing of (inter)subjectivity is not as firm as the subject imagines it to be. In fact, the Other's lack points out that there is nothing intrinsic in our symbolic structures (institutions, language, law, and norms) that allows them to stabilise meaning in a particular configuration or to reveal the ultimate truth of either subject or the social. The only thing that confers authority to such symbolic structures is the subject's libidinal investment in them and more precisely her desire to believe that these structures have the essential ability to speak the truth, to regulate, to prohibit, and so on. The lack condenses several levels of indeterminacy and most notably the incomplete nature of the symbolic order, its absence of a definitive, extra-linguistic referent, and its production of meaning through a system of relations between signifiers. This indeterminacy includes the processes that shape the ego, the unconscious, or desire and, at the level of subjective experience, means that the subject's ideal (e.g. 'man') is constructed through disavowed exclusions that return to destabilise it (e.g. 'woman'). It also includes the subject's formation under intersubjective conditions, most precisely in relation to the desire of the Other over which she has no control and which is unknowable. Irrespective of this conundrum of the lack, the Other remains the most significant figure in the subject's being.

Becoming recognizable by the Other is initiated by the person's insertion in an economy of signifiers (I/you, woman, daughter, white, Canadian, Jane, etc.). These signifiers govern the process of subjectivation by staking out a symbolic position that will become the subject's 'being'. Being created as a virtual position charted by names is not something any of us can control: this position represents a condensation point of desire, enjoyment, power, and knowledge produced before our symbolic/biological birth within the apparatuses that connect the family, the State, media, the medical profession, biological science, and a myriad other authorities. This 'alien' process of being named gains a much more intimate dimension for the subject once she[2] realises that these signifiers—Jane and so on—are related to the Other's desire. Once this connection becomes clear, the subject's effort to obtain the Other's love involves trying to assume said signifiers as 'that who/what I am'. This is because the basic question of desire concerns the desire of the Other, more precisely the relation between the Other's desire and my being:

> The original question of desire is not directly 'What do I want?', but 'What do *others* want from me? What do they see in me? What am I to others?' ... at its most fundamental, fantasy tells me what I am to my others. (Žižek 2008, 9)

At this moment, our most truthful being—desire and enjoyment—is tethered to the Other's desire, to becoming an ultimate object of desire or obtaining love, that is, obtaining definitive recognition for 'who/what we are':

> Insofar as lack is structured in fantasy, the subject's desire ... remains a desire for (phantasized) recognition – a desire to be desired or, better, loved by the Other. (Chiesa 2007, 163)

One's effort to become these signifiers that define her from the beginning (woman, white, etc.) so as to be recognized and loved is spurred by synergic pressures coming from various authorities, whose rites of institution constantly ask the subject to 'become what you are' (see Bourdieu 2003, 122). However, the process of 'becoming who we are' is doomed from the start: a gap always persists between one's 'names' (what one is supposed to be according to the symbolic taxonomies of her time and place) and one's 'being' (self-experience in all its guises—or, if you want, the Other's perception of the subject as the subject herself imagines it—which includes enjoyment, identification, unconscious processes, and desire).[3] At the ontological level, we can argue that this impossibility to close subjectivity, to become fully coincident with oneself, results from the already mentioned indeterminacies of signification. But at the libidinal level, the subject really cares about and it is perceived as a result of the Other's forever enigmatic and doubly elusive desire: not only can I never be certain of what the Other wants me to be (in order to give me the love I crave for), but also the Other itself, since lacking, has no access to this knowledge. In Lacan's (2004, 23) formulation, 'the Other concerns my desire to the extent that he lacks and to the extent that he doesn't know'.

Which, most disturbingly for the subject, means that the Other has no idea about the truth of desire[4] and therefore no answer to the burning question 'what do you want me to be?'

The knowledge of the Other's lack and of the impossible nature of the question of desire being highly disturbing, the main pre-occupation of the bourgeois will be to forget it and/or cover it up. However intense her efforts of masking it, though, the Other's lack persists as a deep anxiety, a sense that she is not quite what she is supposed to be: a clearly bound, self-transparent, and rational individual; a real woman; a mother; the apple of one's eye; loved and desired; and so on. This translation of the lack at experiential level is what Lacan calls castration anxiety.[5] It is this failure (or lack) of symbolic identity that determines the subject to concern herself with symbolic identification (McGowan 2013, 123–124), which in the modern order almost always results in processes of identifying with ideology and with authority.

The relationship to the Other's desire and to castration anxiety also shapes the subject's enjoyment (jouissance), an element that, as already argued, explains both the 'truth' of the bourgeois subject and the resilience of liberal-capitalism. As far as this analysis is concerned, enjoyment is the real currency of the liberal-capitalist economy. By jouissance I designate the intensities of affect that give one a reason to live. Such intensities can be experienced either as agreeable or as disagreeable (in Lacanian theory, jouissance often puts the subject at risk of self-destruction). Thus, they are not important to the subject because they are pleasurable, since they can as often be distress, guilt, or pain, but because they are the subject's most passionate moments of self-validation, the moments when the irresolvable dilemmas of subjectivity—recognition, lack, and desire—transform into experiences that seem to confirm the subject's existence as a coherent, unitary self, even if in irrational manners. It is for enjoyment that the subject lives and not for whatever professed rational reasons. And it is through its ability to mitigate the subject's unbearable relationship to the Other's lack that enjoyment, which can range from sex acts or consumption to neurotic symptoms, addiction, self-harm, or violent conducts like misogyny, homophobia, or racism, becomes the 'truth' of the subject. The intensities of jouissance give for a fleeting moment a semblance of structure and, even, solidity to 'being' by replacing the anxiety of lack with agonising passion;[6] they are therefore often obsessive-compulsive. Since they alleviate anxiety, even when they replace it with uncontrollable guilt, fear, panic, pain, self-obnubilation, phobia, hate, and so on, the bourgeois practices of enjoyment turn into repetitive, obsessive cycles, what psychoanalysis calls the 'drive' (I will return to a more in-depth discussion of the bourgeois drive and its relation to desire and jouissance in the final section).

Thus, bourgeois desire is shaped by an unfathomable and impossible to ultimately possess desire of the Other; bourgeois identity in relation to a name that constantly fails to describe the subject's experience; and bourgeois ego in relation to an alienated, specular, Other image whose coherence is constantly revealed as illusory (I will discuss the processes of imaginary identification in more detail in the third chapter). Our desire for love or recognition needs to come to terms with the realisation that someone else than the subject, an external authority, governs the norms of this recognition (Butler 2005, 26–30). On one hand, this means managing a situation where, being shaped by relations with the Other's desire that are not necessarily available to conscious knowledge, the subject remains self-opaque and, moreover, haunted by this opacity (ibid. 20). And on the other, it means that the subject's desire is governed from the start. Desire, enjoyment, and fantasy (on which more below), while not identical, are aspects of the same process of managing castration anxiety and, in capitalism, are governed through the same technologies. When trying to understand the unwavering appeal of capitalism, we should therefore account for the subject's lifelong and intimate insertion in a kaleidoscopic network of governing apparatuses that promise to manage her castration anxiety; it is to this task that the present analysis commits itself.

The term 'governing apparatus' or *dispositif*, borrowed from Foucault (1980), can help one understand the smooth integration of the bourgeois' desire and enjoyment with the various technologies of the capitalist regime. For Foucault (1980, 194–196), a dispositif consists of heterogeneous relations between a plethora of elements—institutions; regulatory decisions; laws; administrative measures; scientific statements; philosophical, moral, and philanthropic propositions; and so on—that, in response to a governing necessity, make possible the strategic affecting of reality. Deleuze (1992, 160–163) further teases out the connections between the governing apparatus and the subject's imaginary and symbolic dimensions by redefining the former as 'machines that make one see and speak', in other words as machines that regulate what can be seen, thought, or spoken; what forms of being are available to the subject; and how the products of those forms of visibility, enunciation, and subjectivation are distributed within various social spaces. Giorgio Agamben (2009, 20) describes the apparatus in similar terms, as a machine for producing subjectivation, and while not engaging in the theorising of either desire or enjoyment (Agamben uses instead the term 'happiness'), he describes them as elements governed by the apparatus. Agamben's (ibid. 14–15) reading of Foucault is rather strange, to say the least, considering that he posits a field of human being he does not hesitate describing as a 'substance' that ontologically precedes the processes of subjectivation. This 'life substance' is, of course, an idea that Foucault's work on the subject, as well as the present work, unequivocally rejects; any fantasy of a 'life substance' that precedes social relations is, of necessity, an effect of these relations, that is, a retroactive effect of the symbolic order. However, if one glosses over its awkward separation between the apparatus and the 'substance of life' and its rather unnecessary extension of the list of contemporary dispositifs to virtually every aspect of life—cigarettes, PCs, and mobile phones—the relevance of Agamben's essay is that it includes the Other in this list of dispositifs, reminding one of Lacan's argument that 'life is an apparatus of jouissance':

> Not only, therefore, prisons, mad houses, the panopticon, schools, confession, factories, disciplines, juridical measures, and so forth ... but also the pen, writing, literature, philosophy ... and – why not – language itself ... (Agamben 2009, 14)

To make the dispositif into a sharper instrument, however, it is necessary to emphasise the libidinal dimension that is only hinted at in the various descriptions discussed above and to re-define the dispositif as a 'machine that makes one see, speak, fantazise, desire and enjoy'. Capitalist dispositifs produce and deploy constant flows of seductive images and symbols that connect one's desire and enjoyment with various forms of strictly regulated identification, recognition, and fantasising. In other words, the dispositif shapes the bourgeois' most intimate, and often most unfathomable by the subject herself, conducts. It is to a discussion of the role of fantasy and enjoyment in this libidinal economy that I next turn.

The Liberal Fantasy of Missing Bits

The fantasy's function is to alleviate the anxiety generated by the bourgeois' relation with the desire and the lack of the Other, and central to accomplishing this function is the fantasy's representation of lack either as non-existent or as temporary and mendable. In addition to creating a narrative in which the lack is revocable, the fantasy also provides the subject with a schema of objects and practices that promise to fill up the empty spaces opened by the symbolic structure with their 'positivity' (Žižek 2008, 7). As a result, the fantasmatic scenario makes bourgeois reality seem solid and coherent, thus operational and manageable by the subject. It is from fantasy, then, that we learn how to desire (ibid. 118) meaning that, far from representing some illusory escape from reality, fantasy is very much its foundation. Reality does not test our fantasies but realises them, constructing objects of desire to pleasurably pursue and ego-ideals to pleasurably identify with (Copjec 1989, 227–228). In the case of the modern subject, this fantasmatic narrative takes the specific form of a story of loss.

While the Other's desire—and therefore the subject's own—is impossible to fully know and satisfy, the fantasy represents this impossibility as the fact that the subject is 'missing' or 'has lost' something, initiating her endless search for an object that could change this situation, that is, that can fill the lack. This object, the object-cause of desire, is what Lacan designates as *objet a*.[7] In other words, fantasy represents the impossibility to close meaning, experienced subjectively as the anxiogenic impossibility to capture definitively the Other's love/recognition, as an essential object (*objet a*) that was lost and that, if retrieved, would make the subject complete. *Objet a* does not exist except as a retroactive effect of the symbolic order: the subject is not missing and did not lose anything crucial; on the contrary, she has been constituted as a desiring being through her relationship with the lack in the Other that she now represents a loss.

As Joan Copjec (1989, 235) argues, the subject's quest to find her true nature somewhere beyond language results from the absence of a linguistic transcendental signified, that is, from the fundamental uncertainty of language. This quest is nevertheless an intrinsic element of the bourgeois libidinal economy and depends on fantasmatically staging the subject's completeness after the lost object is retrieved, and the subject's wholeness before the loss happened (since we cannot fantasise that we have lost something unless we also fantasise that we were at some point without loss). Bourgeois fantasy, thus, represents lack as 'something personal missing', something that the subject can solve if she tries hard enough.

I can re-phrase it this way: Lacan argues that nothing misses in the Real, in the sense that one cannot have a spontaneous perception of 'what is not there' (see Fink 1999, 177). No perception of a missing object is possible unless this perception is governed by a normative grid of intelligibility in which that object should be present. This grid is the bourgeois fantasy, which, as Copjec's argument suggests, points the anxious bourgeois towards objects that transcend the socio-linguistic uncertainty of her being and that promise to reinstate the fullness of a 'state of nature'. That is, the narrative of a pre-discursive, pre-symbolic origin of the subject, the social and reality, especially in its currently popular variant of a lost bond with the natural (law, order, social relations, enjoyment, instinct, body, sex/gender, sexuality, etc.) is a trope of the bourgeois fantasy that proposes this 'lost fullness' as a cover-up for the structural incompleteness of the symbolic order. The trope of the 'natural', in other words, tries to provide with a stable external referent a symbolic order that operates exclusively through an internal system of differences and uses this fantasmatic anchor to stabilise structurally unstable identities. In the process, the bourgeois fantasy presents the voluntary submission to authority that characterises bourgeois enjoyment as an inexorable dictum of either nature or its opposite, civilisation.

Isn't this fantasy of a lost essential object a sort of personalised retelling of liberalism's own story of loss, initially formulated by Rousseau, Locke, or Hobbes and constantly restyled since, including in Freud's own fantasies of origin? This liberal narrative makes entry into sociality (qua social contract) depend on a forced or voluntary giving up of something precious, a natural foundation of selfhood—innocence, enjoyment, harmony, freedom, aggressiveness, violence, or evolutionary selfishness. In whatever variant, this founding liberal fantasy stages a natural 'thing' that 'society' has taken away and explains individual anxiety and dissatisfaction through this loss. The popularity of the 'repressive hypothesis'[8] among the bourgeoisie, including their fantasies of overturning bourgeois society through sexual liberation, is an offshoot of this fantasy of lost 'natural wholeness'. The mystical-psychological fads promising the retrieval of the true self that lies buried under the rubbish of social identity are another. Here we can mention the ever-popular discourses of natural (genetic) gender, sexuality, race, and personality; or the similarly popular discourses of therapeutic self-discovery. See, for example, the promise of Frederick Perls, inventor of Gestalt therapy, to restore one's 'original, undistorted and natural approach to life' and allow the individual to heal his dualism and recuperate his wholeness and integrity (in Rose 1999, 217–263), or the similar assurance of Art Janov (ibid.), creator of primal therapy, that his method will help the bourgeois subject achieve a life devoid of tension and characterised by an internal unity that allows one to be 'completely his own self'. His brand of therapy, Janov affirms comically paraphrasing Bourdieu, allows people to 'become themselves and stay themselves'.

As the above quote from Žižek suggests, the fantasy provides the subject with attainable objects that act as substitutes for the impossible *objet a*. In other words, the fantasy facilitates the transformation of the impossible Thing (*objet a* as Real) into a particular object or, more precisely, a string of objects. In Lacanian language, we could say that fantasy stages the subject's transcending of lack through recovery of the imaginary phallus.[9] Indeed, I think we can legitimately call 'phallic' the objects offered by capitalism as remedies for the subject's loss, since they stand in for an object that would help him transcend castration. Evidently, for an object to become phallic, it must be ratified by the dominant dispositifs that govern enjoyment and desire; only though this symbolic sanction can an object assume the ideal status that allows the subject to invest it libidinally. Phallic objects, in other words, are strictly governed. Therefore, the phallic object, despite standing in for something as ethereal as the Other's desire (which is what the bourgeois really wants), takes a mundane shape: beauty, sex, shoes, mobile electronic devices, Facebook likes, career, titles, an art collection, a strong publication record, a judge's wig, a male descendant, and so on. In other words, to the terrifying question 'how can I become an ultimate object of desire?' or, even, 'who am I (for the Other)?' the modern fantasy responds: 'buy that green pair of stilettos'; 'become a volunteer in Ethiopia'; 'learn to play the piano'; 'enjoy exotic food'; 'be informed about electoral politics'; 'send your child to art school'; 'participate in a demo for a good cause'; 'write a book'; 'do charity' or 'get a promotion'. It can, of course, get less prosaic: the positivist dream of a theory-free language, that is, the absurd fantasy of a language cleansed of the uncertainty of language, or more generally the dream of objective truth, is as much part of the modern fantasy of fullness and harmony as are the fascist or corporatist dreams of an organism-like society (see Lacan 2007, 29–69).

I will call the conducts resulting from this meticulous libidinal governing 'bourgeois habitus' and will discuss them in detail in the second chapter. For the moment, I will mention that one's immersion in said capitalist dispositifs through the family, kindergarten, school, media, entertainment, toys and games, and so on, all circulating puzzling and seductive messages about desirability and recognisability, makes one's relationship with the Other's desire a dynamic, multifactorial process and not something that we can decode by hypothesising about the subject's first years of life and about primary repression, as psychoanalysis too often suggests. And that, while the bourgeois experiences the anxiogenic processes of desiring, recognition, and identification as personal, the fantasies that try to answer the impossible question of desire are collective formations, shaped by procedures not immanent to any one subject and organizing wide symbolic spaces. How else could one explain, for example, that the bourgeois' most secret sexual fantasies are patterned enough to be organised in 'consumer-friendly' categories by the sex industry?

However, things are not that easy for the bourgeois: the difficulty of her position results from the fact that the modern fantasy is not coherent. On the contrary, it harbours at its core a conflict that splits bourgeois identifications and enjoyment, introducing additional forms of anxiety in this already tensed psychic space. The second chapter will expose the repercussions of this conflict and connect the psychic structure of the bourgeois subject with the resilience of liberal-capitalist institutions and enjoyment. I will dedicate the remainder of this initial chapter to a more in-depth discussion of my understandings of modernity as a fantasy and of the specific forms that enjoyment (jouissance) assumes in the case of the modern subject.

Modernity as a Bourgeois Fantasy

I can bring together the previous arguments about modernity, fantasy, and the bourgeois psyche into a slightly different tactical-theoretical assemblage: the fantasy governing the bourgeois' intimate libidinal processes is one and the same with the narrative construction I call 'modernity' or, more adequately, 'modern fantasy' (and henceforth I will use 'bourgeois subject' and 'modern subject' interchangeably). To understand the description of modernity as a fantasy and my suggestion that it governs the bourgeois subject's most intimate libidinal processes, we should recall that the fantasmatic narrative sutures one's psychic world, that is, provides it with a structure that is bearable, chronological, intelligible, and so on: it constitutes the frame 'through which we experience the world as consistent and meaningful' (Žižek 2008, 123).

Joan Wallach Scott (2011, 47–51) argues as well for a re-conceptualisation of history, more precisely of feminist history, as a fantasmatic scenario that sutures discontinuities, contingencies, accidents, and contradictions into a sequential order. Her account emphasises the extent to which this fantasmatic narrative makes any modern identity (e.g. 'woman') seem constant in time and often in space. The modern fantasy stabilises contemporary identities (e.g. gender/sex identity) by prompting the subject's retrospective identifications with the intransient fantasmatic figures it conjures ('woman'), thus controlling the sets of commonalities/differences (woman/man, white woman/non-white woman, and so on) through which this subject makes sense of the 'I' (ibid. 48–49).

The fantasy thus produces a meaningful reality by dangling in front of the bourgeois subject the promise of fullness and coherence and makes the fulfilment of this promise depend on the normative ways of imagining, desiring, and enjoying produced by the liberal-capitalist governing machines: you too can attain the fullness of being a "true woman", but only if you obey the various libidinal blueprints of (bourgeois) femininity. Which is to say that the modern fantasy and the capitalist dispositifs it incites govern bourgeois life in the intimate realms of recognition, identification,[10] dreams, and deliriums. The book's central argument is that modern governing intricately connects enjoyment and submission to authority, so that the bourgeois' cannot obtain enjoyment without loving authority and vice versa. While the following chapters will detail this argument, the rest of this section describes the overlapping of the master narratives that shape modern subjectivity: modernity and capitalism.

What are the broad premises and implications of this tactical-theoretical assemblage that, I suggest, makes visible the connections between capitalist dispositifs, the modern fantasy, and bourgeois enjoyment? To start with, that modernity is not a set of European historical events marking a primary rupture with traditional society. On the contrary, the meaning and the reality effects of 'rupture' and of 'traditional society' are products of the modern fantasy. This fantasmatic scenario places the emergence of European Enlightenment and of capitalism as the Copernican events of world history, the true birth of civilisation, and fortifies this conflation of civilisation with Europe by weaving together myths of origin (Egypt, Athens, Rome, Renaissance, etc.) and rupture (e.g. the supersession of the Dark Ages by reason) that not only construct the entities they talk about (Athens, Dark Ages, reason, etc.), but also place them as the nodal points of meaning of our age, in both personal and collective narratives. This is why, while the modern fantasy strongly encourages such quests, any attempt to locate temporally and spatially either modernity's original moment of rupture with tradition or this traditional society itself reinforces the taxonomies and power relations that make modernity and capitalism the violent colonial regimes we experience. The deceivingly universal notion of 'modern' we hold, in its intimate connection with the notion of primitive or traditional, is developed in synergy with the process of European colonial invasion; just like Freud's apparently universal notions of 'modern sexuality' or 'modern psyche' are developed in relation to the same figure of the 'primitive' (more on which in Chap. 3). The narrative of modernity cannot be detached from its formative relationship with colonialism without obscuring modernity's most important premises and effects, and the same is valid of psychoanalysis' relationship to colonialism and with the modern fantasy.

However, unlike psychoanalysis, the modern narrative of rupture with tradition is also one of continuous progression towards the fullness, that is, beyond lack, and maybe this is why, also unlike psychoanalysis, modernity cannot be re-interpreted in a manner that confers it radical anti-capitalist or decolonial tactical valences. The modern fantasy, including in its liberal-capitalist variant, is a hegemonic narrative regime that soothes anxiety by translating structural lack into the tale of humanity's golden age, purportedly driving us all to destination ('the end of history' or, in Kantian formulation, the adulthood of humanity) on the motorway of truth, progress, freedom, prosperity, and enjoyment. This narrative promises the end of conflict and of transformation when the world will be fully modernised or developed, that is, will become (like) Europe and promises the supersession of every subject's castration when he will become fully modern, that is, will become (like the) proper European bourgeois. It thus plasters over the glaring contradictions of this age, for example, the contiguity of the discourse of progress with colonialism and genocide; of the discourse of industrialism, technology, and prosperity with mass immiseration; of the discourse of democracy with autocracy, elitism, hereditary privilege, police States, and war; and of the discourse of universalism with those of natural difference and with structural racism, homophobia, misogyny, and so on.[11] Once we think of our reality as an endless development towards the 'end of history', we can justify any present violence or absurdity in the name of future fullness.

The modern fantasy I refer to operates through a couple of basic discursive technologies, at a minimum. Firstly, the myth[12] of teleological, linear, progressive modern history, that is, the understanding of history as ruled by laws that make humanity evolve from 'primitive' to 'civilised'. This is the technique allowing 'Europe' to stand in, metonymically, for 'civilisation' at every particular historical stage constructed by this myth. In other words, the modern fantasy establishes a metonymic relationship between progress and Europe, allowing Europe to signify fullness, or the supersession of lack; this is what we call 'Eurocentrism'.

Secondly, the myth of 'natural difference' between objects or, in other words, the myth that a natural, objective essence founds and explains each object of knowledge. This myth allows the modern fantasy's dichotomous constructions of sameness/difference, including race, gender, sexuality, and so on, to appear as reality itself, as Nature. It also establishes taxonomy as the principal truth-generating modern technology: we live in an era when knowledge is produced predominantly through processes of separation, classification, and hierarchising, according to increasingly diversified notions of 'difference'.

Irrespective of the particular form it assumes and the governing technologies it spurs, the modern fantasy always positions 'Europe' as a phallic signifier: as the signifier of fullness, of transcendence of lack, and of complete enjoyment. As a phallic signifier, Europe governs the modern symbolic economy by making any other signifier depend on its relationship, avowed or not, with Europe. At the same time, Europe itself is placed above the metonymic chain, as if its meaning is self-standing, independent of the relationship with any other signifier (this is the ideological makeup of the signifier that Lacan calls 'the One'). This process of 'phallicising' Europe (and, as the third chapter will show, of the European) explains why all forms of bourgeois enjoyment include in some form the relationship between 'modern' and 'primitive' or between 'developed' and 'developing' into their fundamental framework. All these models of enjoyment represent 'modern' or 'developed' as embodied by Europe and by the proper European bourgeois subject.

These, then, are the elements of the fantasy that teaches the bourgeois subject how to desire. And at this point, I can draw out fully the continuity between the modern fantasy and liberal-capitalism: the narrative of capitalism as retold by its devotees, including in its mundane, managerial form encountered in offices and boardrooms, is a version of the narrative of modernity told by its respective devotees—and a lot of bourgeois are equally devoted to modernity and capitalism. The liberal narrativising of capitalism is a retelling of the modern-colonial fantasy of rupture, with capitalism presented, just like modernity is since Enlightenment, as a fundamental restructuring of sociality, desire, and enjoyment, of subjectivity as well as of social relations. Like modernity, capitalism supposedly sets the subject free from all 'traditional', 'ethnic', or 'feudal' forms of being and social relations and allows him to regulate his life according to no other constraints, but the relations of production and the choices he makes within the impersonal confines of liberal governmental spaces. The avowed purpose of capitalism is thus to transform all subjectivities so that they can fully enjoy the freedoms of market contractualism, in the same way in which modernity ties all subjectivity and sociality to the necessities of progress.

In this scenario, capitalism is characterised by permanent change, by instability, and by constant and radical innovation and renewal. This narrative of a protean, ever-evolving capitalism is precisely what seduces certain academic leftists, who blame the failure of anti-capitalist tactics on the unparalleled capacity of this system to adapt and to co-opt. My argument goes in the opposite direction: liberal-capitalist modernity is structured by the desire for submission, by the bourgeois' enjoyment of fixed identities and ritual social relations, of comfort, predictability, and security. The dominant scenarios of capitalism and modernity, despite their apparent commitment to notions of growth, change, or progress, rely on an obsessive repetition where each and every narrative is contained by the same fantasmatic scenario (see Wallach Scott 2011, 51), and where social change results exclusively from the equally obsessive affluence/crisis cycles of capitalism. I will next turn to a discussion of the forms assumed by enjoyment (jouissance) within the modern fantasy.

Bourgeois Jouissance

The drive is usually described as an obsessive cycle that, while seemingly chasing an object, is in fact interested exclusively in the obsessive cycle itself. In other words, the jouissance produced by the circuit of the drive does not depend on attaining the drives' aim, which would be the satisfaction produced by possessing the drive's object; on the contrary, the subject starts enjoying the process of not attaining the drive's aim, the frustration of the drive. Moreover, too much proximity to the object runs the risk of removing its phallic aura and of exposing it as hideous, terrifying. There are various, and often contradictory, descriptions of the drive, but many of them emphasise the connections between drive and bodily or sexual enjoyment and the coincidence between the drive and the death drive. This last statement suggests that the jouissance produced by the drive is, like the death drive theorised by Freud, posing a risk to the subject's (symbolic and bodily) integrity. Following from this, most Lacanians theorise a strong dichotomy between desire and the drive in which desire acts as an antidote to the idiotic jouissance produced by the obsessive cycles of the drive or, the other way around, where the transgressive circuits of the drive disrupt the conservative symbolic confines of desire. In this dichotomous scheme, desire is initiated by and searching in vain for a missing object (*objet a*) that never was; while the drive does not search for a lost object but aims to enact the loss itself as a source of jouissance (see e.g. Žižek 2008, 328). The enjoyment of desire is permanently frustrated, while the enjoyment of the drive results from its repeated frustration. Thus, desire is of the negative, of the lost object, of the Other, and of fantasy, while the drive is of the positive, of satisfaction, and of the Thing (see Braunstein 2003, 102–115).

For the task of drawing a libidinal portrait of the bourgeois, however, it is more relevant to point out the similarities between drive and desire rather than to focus on their differences. Emphasising these convergences highlights the specificity of bourgeois jouissance as a form of managed risk, which sutures the dominant symbolic order rather than disrupting it. In order to describe this bourgeois jouissance, I will engage in a discussion that brings to the fore the identical ground of the drive and of desire as processes intrinsic to the realm of the symbolic/imaginary and that involves the subject's relationship to the desire of the Other and to fantasy. The drive is thus reconceptualised, not as a process opposed to desire, but as the obsessive, cyclical, and hopeless form assumed by desiring and enjoying in liberal-capitalism. The purpose of this discussion is to present bourgeois jouissance as nowhere nearly as risky for the subject as the death drive theory assumes; on the contrary, while there is some risk involved in bourgeois jouissance, it is a fully managed risk, in the sense that jouissance is performed under the protection of the modern governing regime and effects the suturing of this regime and of the bourgeois psychic economy.

While many Lacanians understand jouissance in relation to the body and sexuality, I (at the risk of being called a Jungian) see it crossing fields of experience that have no original sexual determination. Even when focusing on sexual forms of enjoyment, analysis needs to start from the premise that jouissance, be it of desire or of the drive, always belongs to the realm of the Other, to the symbolic/imaginary realm, and that there is no separation between the body and the symbolic or discursive orders. It is the symbolic order that makes possible bodily enjoyment, bringing to life 'dumb corporeal density' by segmenting the body into erotogenic zones (Dean 2000, 197 and 201). This process of linguistic animation of the dead flesh results in a fully symbolic body whose jouissance is also fully symbolic, plus, in the particular case of the bourgeois subject, in a fantasy of lost full jouissance. I will mention that talking about a fantasy of lost jouissance is not the same as talking about a 'remainder' of jouissance left after the subject's entry into language, as certain Lacanians do; the pre-symbolic, full jouissance to which the signifier 'remainder' alludes exists exclusively as a hypothesis conjured by the modern fantasy. The Lacanians who insist that through subjectivation the bourgeois acquires a 'surplus', 'residual', or 'remainder' jouissance imagine subjectivation as some form of dissection of 'natural' bodily jouissance by the scalpel of language, which takes away everything significant and leaves only a diagram of the body for the subject to enjoy. While the diagram is not an untrue representation of how bodily jouissance is produced in language, I find less fruitful the pre-supposition of a full, natural bodily jouissance that precedes it and would argue that, in fact, through subjectivation the bourgeois acquires a 'reminder' of full jouissance that is a fantasised memory. This should impede from the start any temptation to conceptualise the jouissance of the drive as resulting from some unmediated bodily sensation and the jouissance of the drive results from processes specific to the same imaginary and symbolic fields that shape the circuits of desire.

If jouissance is always of the symbolic/imaginary, then what are the similarities between modern drive and desire? Like desire, the drive is governed by fantasy; otherwise, it would permanently chase objects that are deprived of their phallic aura, that is, objects in their repulsive, Real form, which is absurd. No one can find an object worth pursuing unless that object has a phallic aura, symbolic, or imaginary, and only fantasy can bestow this aura on an object. Then, if the psychoanalytical definition of jouissance is that it always puts the subject at risk, it is exclusively the Other dimension of the drive that pushes the subject towards self-destructive modes of enjoyment. We should recall that jouissance is produced within the subject's relationship with the Other or, more precisely, revolves around her impossible to fulfil demand to be desired by the Other (see Jameson 1977, 367). What else can make dangerous activities pleasurable but their potential to make the self-desirable to the Other or to obscure the lack, even if for a fleeting and maybe final moment? What understanding or perception of death is there but the symbolic one? Thus, the jouissance of the drive is not so easily differentiated from the jouissance produced by desire: both drive and desire seem to compulsively enjoy the frustration of their aim. And the hypothesis that the death drive can be politically fruitful (Edelman 2004; McGowan 2013) needs further qualification since, I would argue, the bourgeois drive is not equipped to rupture the modern symbolic order. On the contrary, because strictly governed, the bourgeois drive re-confirms this order even while it seems to put the subject at risk.

Considering these points of convergence between drive and desire, it is probably more fruitful to represent the difference between them as one between form and content: if desire represents the fantasy-driven attempt to come to terms with lack by obtaining *objet a*, then the drive is the way in which, in everyday capitalist reality, desire settles for the enjoyment resulting from looping around phallic objects. And if the true aim of desire is to continue desiring, then in capitalism this aim is reduced to obsessively enjoying the dissatisfaction of the drive's loops. Drive, then, is the form in which the production of jouissance is designed and governed by capitalist dispositifs. Or, if you prefer, the drive is the form in which the capitalist symbolic economy of obsessive, paranoid-aggressive cycles of consumption/production shapes the subject's jouissance. Dean (2010, 9), starting from Foucault's lectures on liberal governing, makes a related point: the circuits of the drive that capture bourgeois enjoyment inside idiotic loops arise from the structural tension of liberal-capitalist dispositifs. More precisely, from the tension between the need to limit governing in the name of (market) freedom and the need to govern freedom so as to optimise the functioning of the market and to produce the population's well-being. This tension translates into the bourgeois' own conflict between freedom and danger, where liberal governing is supposed to insure at the same time her independence and her security. Today, liberal governing maintains the 'danger' element of this couple in a state of acuteness through technologies of 'permanent crisis' (Invisible Committee 2014). Trapped in this contradictory relationship to authority, bourgeois enjoyment cannot but circle around its own tail, taking the form we call drive.

The bourgeois drive yields jouissance from both the experience of loss and the promise of fullness. That is, the drive enjoys its failure to obtain or to be satisfied by the various phallic objects it pursues (experience of loss) and, at the same time, enjoys pursuing the lost object, the Thing for which the various phallic objects are stand-ins (promise of fullness). The mundane jouissance produced by bourgeois drives—say, the jouissance of buying a pair of shoes—always displays this double aspect. On one hand, this jouissance derives from the repressed knowledge that the new shoes will fail to fill the lack, thus making necessary a new purchase, a new loop of the drive (enjoying loss), and on the other, from the titillating promise of fullness, of having one's demand for love fulfilled once she attains the desirability promised by taking possession of the shoes.[13] Caught between loss and fullness, the bourgeois remains idiotically addicted to the process of buying, in other words to the plus/minus cycles of the drive. The interesting aspect of this looping is that, despite involving some element of risk for the subject, it seamlessly reproduces capitalist order. What is the risk involved by the drive and why is it not a threat to the system?

If, as argued, jouissance is by psychoanalytical definition risky, then we need to consider that risk-taking conducts produce various effects, from loss of one's framework for enjoying to reinforcing the dominant relations of power/knowledge. Jouissance can represent a risk because it goes beyond the pursuit of public good, of the well-being of the community (Braunstein 2003, 108) or because it exposes the lack, a rather different effect which destabilises not the well-being of the community but the community itself. One risk posed by the subject's practices of jouissance, and here I agree with the Lacanian doxa, is that of encountering the object of the drive—the person we lust over, say—as Real, meaning stripped of the (phallic) aura in which our fantasy drapes her/him: as a repulsive heap of flesh and pettiness. Another, no less threatening, is the risk of losing one's own phallic aura, the individuality, or agalma that, in the bourgeois fantasy, makes one uniquely meaningful and desirable to the Other. A third risk is realising that the Other is lacking, that there is no overall meaning to the symbolic order. All these forms of jouissance bring the subject dangerously close to the lack and thus to symbolic rupture. But I do not consider these forms of risk to be characteristic of bourgeois jouissance.

As already mentioned, the best example of bourgeois jouissance is the one produced by the obsessive cycles of production/consumption of liberal-capitalism that aim at nothing more than the circling itself and that are completely indifferent to their catastrophic social effects. Moreover, knowing about the deleterious effects of his conducts seems to increase the bourgeois' enjoyment. These capitalist drives are definitely a risk to the well-being of the community and, even, to the subject's being, without for this reason threatening liberal-capitalism. The risks involved in bourgeois jouissance confirm rather than challenge the law. Let me explain.

I have given above the example of shopping and argued that the jouissance produced by the shopping drive partly results from the bourgeois' unconscious knowledge that the object purchased will fail to satisfy. This, I was saying, means that the drive produces enjoyment out of the frustration of its aim, out of the encounter with loss: the bourgeois enjoys the repetitive process of shopping, rather than its results (i.e. rather than the possession of the object). More, the bourgeois enjoys the process of shopping *because* it fails in its aim of obtaining the Thing, which failure allows the bourgeois to unconsciously fantasise about re-engaging in another loop of the same shopping process even before the current loop is finished. At the same time, as also mentioned, the shopping fantasy yields jouissance by promising the Thing, but what I want to insist on is the unthreatening nature of the bourgeois enjoyment of loss. Enjoying the frustration of the drive's aim is potentially risky, since it involuntarily brings the bourgeois closer to realising the impossibility of attaining fullness through chasing phallic objects, which is a distressing realisation. However, while threatening to the self, this jouissance ratifies the dominant order, more, sutures it. And this is no small thing: the practice of shopping, even if dimly figuring the lack, props up the framework that guarantees bourgeois jouissance, that guarantees that the subject will be able to enjoy another cycle of shopping: capitalism. Thus, through his governed practices of jouissance, the bourgeois tends asymptotically towards an encounter with the lack only to keep one step away from it, precisely the step of the next run of the drive, of the next shopping spree. To phrase this slightly differently, managing the risk of bourgeois jouissance consists in never fully exposing the lack (in Other and subject), and this management is done in a feedback loop: the bourgeois enjoys as he was trained to do by the liberal-capitalist dispositifs, for example, by shopping; this enjoyment potentially challenges the narrative of personal fullness proposed by the modern fantasy since, at some level, shopping dissatisfies; however, the effect of shopping is to reinforce these dispositifs and therefore to confirm capitalism as natural; thus, shopping keeps the bourgeois away from the lack and safely obsessed with her familiar practices of enjoyment. Shopping keeps capitalism going, which keeps the subject's drive going. The threat to expose the lack, while present, is never real. The pleasurable fear and discomfort of bourgeois jouissance are thus reduced to the masochistic, if not necessarily conscious, thrill of having one's discomfiture ritualistically exposed through her behaviours: no matter how expertly done, shopping always fails to fulfil its aim, which is seizing the Other's desire. At the same time, like in a carefully scripted s&m game, the thrill is obtained with the knowledge that one is fully protected against any unexpected effects of his risky conducts by the same authority that makes the enjoyment possible (in this case, to repeat, the capitalist apparatuses of jouissance). As long as these processes continue, there is nothing in bourgeois jouissance that threatens the modern fantasy or capitalism.

To this mechanism of the drive, we need to add other customary forms of bourgeois jouissance, which hide symbolic failure by imaginarising it and projecting it on the subject's antagonist other. Racism, homophobia, misogyny, classism, and so on produce enjoyment by projecting this subject's castration on the other (non-white, gay, women, worker, and poor). The enjoyment derived from engaging in rituals that risk to expose one's identity as a put-on, as are for example gendered conducts—femininity and masculinity—has the same structure as that of shopping, feigning to threaten the symbolic order only to further strengthen the ideology of its 'naturalness'. And so does the enjoyment produced by bourgeois phobia, hysteria, or trauma[14]: while seemingly threatening to expose the ego as weak, lacking control, vulnerable, and undesirable, they in fact reiterate the uniqueness and individuality of the bourgeois ego (as expressed through his symptoms, trauma, and so on) and thus strengthen this ego and bourgeois reality (more on which in Chap. 2). Finally, the forms of phallic jouissance teased out of the bourgeois subject by the modern dispositifs through the prohibitions imposed on his drives—prohibitions on sexuality, on consumption and acquisition, on free time, and so on—also keep the subject at a safe distance from the lack. In fact, this prohibition to enjoy stands between the bourgeois and the ultimate risk of discovering that his fantasy of obtaining full jouissance or the Other's unconditional love is impossible.

The guarantee that one will not lose their identity as a result of these 'risky' conducts is the bourgeois symbolic law. The entire cultural production of capitalism is directed at re-suturing the symbolic order that gender, consumption, trauma, and so on threaten to expose as lacking and at making, again and again, the point that the Western performance of gender, trauma, or consumption is the fundamental characteristic of a proper modern subject, the most desirable subject possible. And if we assume, following Lacan, that her jouissance is unknown to the modern subject until it manifests itself in neurotic symptoms like guilt, remorse, confession, or penitence (Braunstein 2003, 108), then this catholic model of bourgeois jouissance as remorse and confession matches Foucault's (1990) own description of a modern society whose dispositifs are based on the model of confession, further charting a system in which being-qua-jouissance depends on the blessing of authority figures (president, priest, teacher, father, boss, therapist, scientist, coach, sergeant, coloniser, etc.). The risk that the bourgeois enjoys, then, is that of the catholic confession that titillates both sinner and confessor without disturbing God's law but, quite on the contrary, that depends on the normal functioning of this law to produce titillation.

Bourgeois enjoyment, far from threatening the symbolic, thrives on submission to a masculinised symbolic authority that refutes the idea that castration (or lack) represents the foundation of subjectivity and that incites the aggressive pursuit of phallic objects. The pursuits that characterise modernity, from the search for scientific truth to colonialism, are 'masculinist' endeavours that aim for phallic fullness; and anyone succumbing to the charms of this narrative becomes 'masculinised', that is, adopts patriarchal, castration-fearing, and phallus-chasing forms of jouissance. The list of Internet domains that sold for millions of dollars, as listed on Yahoo Canada Finance in , is a basic illustration of the forms in which capitalist apparatuses tease this macho drive: business.com; internet.com; sex.com; porn.com; diamond.com; beer.com; clothes.com; vodka.com; and insure.com.

The following chapter explores these operations using a device called the 'will-to-not-know' which, I propose, can usefully condense the traits of bourgeois subjectivity elaborated so far in operational form, further exposing the reasons for the resilience of the most destructive elements of modern reality.

Notes

1. Lacan uses the term 'the Other', which represents language and the symbolic, to also refer to the unconscious. The subjective representation of the Other obviously cannot access directly the repressed, but is influenced by it to a large extent.

2. An academic friend who kindly read an early version of this work was made quite uncomfortable by my use of the feminine pronoun to describe psychological traits that are unflattering, to say the least. She was right; the reversal of theoretical misogyny needs to be done more carefully than that. I have therefore opted in this text for the transgendering of the pronouns that indicate the category 'subject' and will be using both 'he' and 'she' fluidly, but according to a logic that tries to remain faithful to certain feminist principles. I do not make these principles explicit because they do not impinge directly on the logic of the argument; they might become evident to the reader at some other level.

3. This could be rephrased in more classical terms as the gap between the 'I' as subject of the statement and the 'I' as subject of the enunciation; or, even, as the gap between the signifier (name) and the signified (illusion of being) (see Chiesa 2007, 38 and 49).

4. This opacity of the Other's desire is the impenetrable element that the subject finds impossible to reduce to an imaginary double of herself and which persists as the traumatic kernel of the neighbour so often invoked by psychoanalysis (see e.g. Žižek 2004, 501).

5. As explained below (see note 9), I have decided to keep Lacan's adaptation of Freudian terminology, despite its bothersome inflexions for a feminist, because they reflect the ways in which our most intimate and personal fears are shaped by the patriarchal regime in which we live. It is only in a culture that places the penile as the core of desirability that the gap between one's name (e.g. 'man') and their experience (of forever failing to be a 'real man') is experienced as the supreme fear of losing the penis/phallus.

6. To those versed in Lacanian theory, it will be evident that, although my conceptualisation of jouissance is inspired by this theory, it puts it to work in a particular manner. The present analysis focuses on phallic jouissance, that is, on jouissance as governed, and considers the threat of being engulfed by the jouissance of the Other as the subject's fantasmatic production in response to this governing. In other words, the subject's search for the experience of an undifferentiated, overwhelming and self-dissolving jouissance beyond the signifier, even if often terrifying, is her attempt to escape the

symbolic and, therefore, is scripted by the fantasy of loss. What is important for the present discussion of jouissance, therefore, is that the subject aims towards the disappearance of the world through her jouissance (see Van Haute 2002, 219–227) *because* this momentary 'disappearance' makes anxiety and the lack disappear. These moments of 'loss of self' when the subject is engulfed by jouissance thus become the anchor for the subject's selfhood. What I call 'bourgeois jouissance' is therefore not a threat to subjectivity but its support.

7. What the subject really desires in the object is the kernel of the Real (*objet a*) wrapped in the subject's fantasy. The *objet a* has, for Lacan, both an imaginary and a real dimension, the latter discernable only after *objet a* has been 'imaginarised'. Thus, fantasy both puts the subject in contact with the Real lack in the symbolic and veils this lack through the imaginary dimension of *objet a* (Chiesa 2007, 142–143). At imaginary level, *objet a* can also be thought to represent the impossible to bridge gap between 'name' and 'being': '... *object petit a* [is] an impossible, formal object produced as the excess of a process or relation, a kind of gap that incites or annoys, the missingness or not-quite-rightness ...' (Dean 2012, 108).

8. The classic critique of the repressive hypothesis is that by Foucault (1990, 15–51).

9. The phallus is far from being an unproblematic concept in Lacan's theory. For present purposes, Žižek's (2006, 74) definition is a functional one:

> So one has to think of the phallus not as the organ which immediately expresses the vital force of my being, but ... as a mask which I put on in the same way a king or judge puts on his insignia – phallus is a kind of organ without a body which I put on, which gets attached to my body, without ever becoming its organic part, forever sticking out as its incoherent, excessive supplement.

However, Lacanian terms like 'phallic' might also be uncomfortable to use because they remind us of the intractability of the patriarchal law, of the pleasure modernity takes in classifying and ruling being in relation to penis, epidermal melanin, sexual desire, and so on.

10. Lacan (quoted in Stavrakakis 2007, 197) talks about the 'identificatory joy from which *jouissance* springs'.

11. There are several other contradictions in the way in which the bourgeoisie creates the fantasy of itself: the Weberian one between acquisitiveness and asceticism, for example, or the conflict between 'rationality' and the 'irrational'

impulses of capitalist accumulation, or that between capitalist accumulation and conservatism (see Moretti 2014, 5–6, 34–35, and 93–94).

12. Here, I draw on Roland Barthes' (1972, 117–129) myth as a symbolic operation that works to empty the signifier of history, of its contingency, and to present it in a manner that serves its ideological purpose which is transforming history into nature (Barthes 1972, 117–129). The myth is experienced by the myth-consumer as innocent speech, as a system of facts making the world appear as a 'harmonious display of essences' (Barthes, 131 and 142–143).

13. Thanks to Raluca Parvu who pointed out to me this ambivalence of the drive.

14. Trauma is considered in this book a characteristic conduct of the bourgeois subject, one of his main instruments of fake transgression, a form of risk-taking that remains oblivious to any social effects except for the narcissistic light in which it basks the subject.

References

Agamben, G. (2009). *'What is an apparatus?' And other essays*. Stanford: Stanford University Press.

Barthes, R. (1972). *Mythologies*. New York: Hill and Wang.

Bourdieu, P. (2003). *Language and symbolic power*. Cambridge: Harvard University Press.

Braunstein, N. (2003). Desire and jouissance in the teachings of Lacan. In J.-M. Rabaté (Ed.), *The Cambridge companion to Lacan* (pp. 101–115). Cambridge: Cambridge University Press.

Butler, J. (2005). *Giving an account of oneself*. New York: Fordham University Press.

Chiesa, L. (2007). *Subjectivity and otherness: A philosophical reading of Lacan*. Cambridge: The MIT Press.

Copjec, J. (1989). Cutting up. In B. Teresa (Ed.), *Between feminism and psychoanalysis* (pp. 227–246). London/New York: Routledge.

Dean, T. (2000). *Beyond sexuality*. Chicago/London: University of Chicago Press.

Dean, J. (2010). Drive as the structure of biopolitics: Economy, sovereignty and capture. *Krisis, 2*, 2–15.

Dean, J. (2012). *The communist horizon*. New York/London: Verso.

Deleuze, G. (1992). What is a dispositif? In T. J. Armstrong (Ed.), *Michel Foucault, philosopher* (pp. 159–166). New York: Routledge.

Edelman, L. (2004). *No future: Queer theory and the death drive.* Durham: Duke University Press.

Eng, D. L. (2001). *Racial castration: Managing masculinity in Asian America.* Durham/London: Duke University Press.

Fink, B. (1999). *A clinical introduction to Lacanian psychoanalysis: Theory and technique.* Cambridge: Harvard University Press.

Foucault, M. (1980). In G. Colin (Ed.), *Power/knowledge.* Brighton: Harvester Press.

Foucault, M. (1990). *The history of sexuality volume 1: An introduction.* New York: Vintage Books.

Foucault, M. (2007). *Security, territory, population: Lectures at the College de France, 1977–8.* Basingstoke/New York: Palgrave Macmillan.

Fuss, D. (1995). *Identification papers.* London/New York: Routlege.

Jameson, F. (1977). Imaginary and symbolic in Lacan: Marxism, psychoanalytic criticism and the problem of the subject. *Yale French Studies* No. 55/56, Literature and Psychoanalysis. The Question of Reading: Otherwise, 338–395.

Jameson, F. (2002). *A singular modernity: Essay on the ontology of the present.* London/New York: Verso.

Lacan, J. (2004). *Anxiety. The seminar of Jacques Lacan Book X.* Cambridge/Malden: Polity Press.

Lacan, J. (2007). *The other side of psychoanalysis: The seminar of Jacques Lacan Book XVII.* New York/London: W.W. Norton & Company.

McGowan, T. (2013). *Enjoying what we don't have: The political project of psychoanalysis.* Lincoln/London: University of Nebraska Press.

Moretti, F. (2014). *The bourgeois: Between history and literature.* London/New York: Verso.

Rose, N. (1999). *Governing the soul: The shaping of the private self.* London/New York: Free Association Books.

Stavrakakis, Y. (2007). *The Lacanian left: Psychoanalysis, theory.* Politics: Edinburgh University Press.

The Invisible Committee. (2014). *To our friends.* Semiotext(e).

Van Haute, P. (2002). *Against adaptation: Lacan's "subversion" of the subject.* New York: Other Press.

Wallach Scott, J. (2011). *The fantasy of feminist history.* Durham/London: Duke University Press.

Žižek, S. (2006). *How to read Lacan.* New York/London: W.W. Norton &Co.

Žižek, S. (2008). *In defense of lost causes.* London/New York: Verso.

Žižek, S. (2004). 'From politics to biopolitics....and back'. *Southern Atlantic Quarterly, 103*(2/3), 501–521, Spring/Summer 2004.

2

The 'Will-To-Not-Know'

There is one scene in Günter Grass' *The Tin Drum* (1999, 338–339) that makes a great preamble to this chapter's discussion of the will-to-not-know, the name under which I condense the mechanisms that allow the bourgeois to remain unmoved by the spectacle of violence. During Bebra theatrical troupe's wartime tour to the Normandy Atlantic Wall line of German defence, Oskar, Grass' main hero, and his fiancée compose a little sarcastic poem that sums up the situation of the German soldiers, and more generally of the liberal population in times of war. Despite living in concrete fortifications and among barbed wire, despite extreme violence and death becoming mundane events, the bourgeoisie continues to dream of landscaped gardens, refrigerators, and the happy hours bestowed by an electric plug. Even during the open display of atrocity, the poem concludes, the thought of comfort is like a drug, and the trend is towards the bourgeois-smug. The grotesque placing side by side of a homely list of bourgeois desires with the brutality of war is a classical avant-garde derision of the modern order. However, today's subjects could easily recognise themselves in a trend towards bourgeois smugness that equates being with fetishistic fantasies of comfort, refrigerators, and electric plugs. At the end of Grass' vignette, we are shown the Bebra troupe gluttonously devouring

© The Author(s) 2016
M. Panu, *Enjoyment and Submission in Modern Fantasy*,
DOI 10.1057/978-1-137-51321-2_2

an obscenely opulent picnic, while a group of nuns collecting crabs around the fortifications to feed the children in their kindergarten are massacred pre-emptively by the German forces. The troupe plays the gramophone loudly (*The Great Pretender* by The Platters) to cover the machine gun noise and, probably, the absurdity of the violence they witness. Their ability to pretend that this typical modern massacre is not happening depends on getting engrossed to the level of autism in the bourgeois comforts of music, food, chat, and play. Conversely, deriving enjoyment from these habits depends on one's ability to ignore that, in the process of producing bourgeois comfort, the modern dispositifs produce massacres.

It will be seen that the typical modern conducts that end up in the mortification and/or annihilation of others and sometimes of oneself are so resilient and addictive not because of ignorance, that is, lack of education, experience, knowledge, or information, but because the bourgeois extracts enjoyment from them. Obtaining enjoyment in this manner does involve a choice, but one that the bourgeois struggles to forget. The consequences for a politics of radical anti-capitalist transformation are important, since the will-to-not-know neutralises the customary liberal argument that modern evils are due to certain people's lack of education, an argument that the contemporary left eagerly imitates. While the purpose of this book is not to propose tactics, it is to signal that it is never soon enough for experimenting with new political-libidinal forms.

Modern Conflict

The previous chapter has argued that the modern fantasy manages the lack by staging a lost object (*objet a*) and by offering phallic objects as substitutes for it, thus promising fullness. This chapter continues the discussion by arguing that, because this fantasy is structured around a central antagonism, it fails to suture the bourgeois' lack tightly. Instead, it compels her contradictory identifications and convoluted libidinal loops that try to cover up these contradictions. These identifications and loops are governed through technologies whose more or less diverse forms hide their invariable logic and which constantly fold bourgeois jouissance back onto itself, bringing into being a bourgeois reality that appears very resilient to change.

Here are the two sides of this modern fantasmatic antagonism: on one hand, as a typology of desire and enjoyment, the bourgeoisie comes into being among discourses that contest metaphysical cosmogonies and truths, traditional hierarchies, and in-born privilege; in other words, among discourses that contest one's natural belonging to an objective social group. To feudalism's ontological fixity, the modern fantasy counterposes a 'free bourgeois' without categorical ontological determinations, whose subjectivity and position in social hierarchies are determined by her own (rational) efforts. According to its own cosmogonic myth, then, modernity emerges from a critical questioning of the social order that finds the law supposed to found this order to have no extra-discursive foundation.

Alenka Zupančič (2000, 23), for example, considers Kant's innovation to be the discovery of a modern subject deprived of substantial content, a creature whose most personal thoughts and desires are radically heteronymous. In Kant's texts as re-interpreted by Foucault (1984, 36), 'the critique is, in a sense, the handbook of reason that has grown up in Enlightenment; and, conversely, the Enlightenment is the age of critique.' For Foucault himself, modernity remains the 'philosophical ethos that could be described as a permanent critique of our historical era' and of ourselves (Foucault 1984, 39). Žižek (1991, 80) argues that '[the] leading motif of Enlightenment is, of course, some variation of the injunction "Reason autonomously! … Use your own head, free yourself of all prejudices, do not accept anything without questioning its rational foundations, always preserve a critical distance" …' The works of Hegel, Marx, Nietzsche, or Freud and the analytical genealogy they inspire—Heidegger, Wittgenstein, Sartre, de Beauvoir, Lacan, Foucault, and so on—argue, in various formats, that the socio-symbolic law is founded in nothing else but the letter of the law itself kept alive by the subject's desire for its command. More recently Laclau (Butler et al. 2000, 74) proposes a short story of twentieth-century intellectual thought where the crucial moment is the rupture between the dream of immediate access to the 'thing in itself' entertained by analytical philosophy, phenomenology, and structuralism (the 'thing' being the referent, the phenomenon, and the sign, respectively); and the moment of disintegration of this illusion of immediacy (Wittgenstein, Heidegger, poststructuralism/deconstruction).

In modernism, this exposure of the law as lacking any foundation beside its own proclamations, or as Lacan rephrases it, this revelation that God is unconscious, is usually represented as a moment of intense alienation. Here is Joseph Roth's description of modern theatre:

> Direction creates space. Now, there was no one to fill it, therefore the space was left dark, in the hope that the slender cone of light would rescue the human being. What an error! The human being was tied to a hole, and, trapped in the hollowness his own body had become, he stumbled through the night. (Roth 2004, 125–127)

Modernism transforms its anxiety about the loss of foundations into an obsession with the search for the New as supreme value[1] (see Jameson 2002, 121) that continues to haunt our popular culture. Fashion, art, media, or technology are obvious examples of this fetishism of the New. Even 'rebellious' subcultures incorporate this modernist anxiety—in the case of punk, say, anti-foundationalism takes the (naïve) libertarian form to: 'disobey authority, be yourself, fight against convention, live the way you want to', and so on. In any case, on this 'anti-realist' side of the modern fantasy, the subject's engagement in painful critical reflexivity remains her only source of bravery and dignity; on the contrary, the proper performance of bourgeois habitus becomes not only absurd, but also a shameful identity.

On the other hand, Nietzsche's statement 'God is dead' also implies that, while God might indeed be that, he won't for this reason so easily go away. And sure enough, there is another 'realist' narrative of modernity produced by some of the same protagonists, Kant, Hegel, Marx, or Freud, as well as by other enthusiastic contributors from Darwin to Einstein, Roy Bashkar, or Dawkins or disciplines like genetics and which brings God back in the form of a metaphysical order of being embodied in universal laws of nature or in ahistorical structures. This realist narrative founds truth and the good on unequivocal foundations: natural identities set to coincide with the name an object is given in the various modern taxonomies (e.g. woman, mammal, or carbon based). It is this second, realist version of the modern narrative that founds liberal-capitalist governing.

However, even the realist modern narrative has to deal with the fact that the death of God has been made public, meaning that from now on the big Other knows about it, as Žižek would put it. Liberal discourse might therefore include a variation on the narrative of the absence of transcendental foundations, but always in a form that neutralises its potential to disrupt bourgeois reality and that use it to re-suture this reality. Modernisation theories, for example, pretend to build on modernity's potential to disrupt all metaphysical assumptions only to re-inscribe the shaken foundations of the bourgeois world into a solid narrative of progress towards fullness. Thus, the modern fantasy of rupture is one of the tactics that covers the Other's lack and consolidates bourgeois reality by, paradoxically, pointing towards continuity: Europe's continuity with Greece, Rome, Renaissance, and generally civilisation and innovation; the rest of the world's persistence in its primitivism, stagnation, and irrationality; and the uninterrupted, Europe-led march of progress. Additionally, the network of modern dispositifs soothes Euro-bourgeois anxiety with the enjoyable spectacle of the disciplining or destruction of the 'primitive' subjects living outside the metropolis, further confirming the bourgeois order's natural stability, its status as the only order that can guarantee peace, happiness, and wealth. Some of these muscular discourses present modernity as nothing short of a global (bourgeois) revolution, without for this reason disturbing a hair on the head of bourgeois reality and of the authorities it inaugurates:

> Modernization is a *revolutionary* process. This follows directly from the contrasts between modern and traditional society. The one differs fundamentally from the other, and the change from tradition to modernity consequently involves a radical and total change in patterns of human life. (Samuel Huntington quoted in Driscoll 2004, 74)

The same tactic of soothing bourgeois anxiety by channelling it into aggressive colonial discourses shapes the United Nations development policy dogma, which posits the radical break with the past as the sometimes bitter pill that 'underdeveloped' countries in search of rapid economic growth have to swallow on their way to progress:

There is a sense in which rapid economic progress is impossible without painful adjustments. Ancient philosophies have to be scrapped; old social institutions have to disintegrate; bonds of caste, creed and race have to burst; and large numbers of persons who cannot keep up with progress have to have their expectations of a comfortable life frustrated (United Nations, Measures for the Economic Development of Underdeveloped Countries quoted in Driscoll 2004, 72)

Here, capitalist devastation becomes the inevitable hand of historical change, Europe the wise teacher that guides its children through the modern storm, and the 'pre-modern world' the fantasmatic construction that stabilises modern dispositifs in the comforting master/slave configuration. Thus, such modernisation discourses cover God's dead body with nomothetic stories of progress that cement Europe's phallic position, and deploy governing mechanisms that support bourgeois reality with the scaffolding of colonial-capitalist disciplines.

There is, at this point, a comment to be made on the pleasure with which contemporary theorists fond of the 'communist hypothesis' (on which more will be said in the final chapter) conflate the antirealist discourses of modernity and the ontological essence of contemporary capitalism. Žižek, for example, explains the historical rupture between the comfortable ignoring of contingency and the impossibility to ignore it any more as a result of the deterritorialised nature of contemporary global capitalism:

The passage from 'essentialist' Marxism to postmodern contingent politics (in Laclau), or the passage from sexual essentialism to contingent gender-formation (in Butler) or – a further example – the passage from metaphysician to ironist in Richard Rorty, is not a simple epistemological process but part of the global change in the very nature of capitalist society. (Žižek in Butler et al. 2000, 106)

Bruno Bosteels (2014, 61) concurs:

… there can be no doubt that the ontological themes of difference, multiplicity, event, becoming, and so on are the product of late capitalism as much as, if not more, they are its counteracting forces.

Despite the assurance displayed by these ontological verdicts, they are not as self-evident as they pretend to be. To start with, the genealogy of anti-realist discourses goes back to pre-World War II philosophical developments and farther into the 'pre-modern' eras, preceding the 'global change in the nature of capitalist reality' that Žižek invokes. The switch that Bosteels and Žižek refer to more realistically applies to the Marxian tradition's recent and uncomfortable engagements with anti-realist discourses. While such arguments dismiss anti-realism as nothing more than a capitalist ruse, a disciplinary effect of the metamorphoses of imperialism devoid of critical valences, their philosophical aggressiveness reflects the anxiety of the Marxist and liberal theoretical traditions about their loss of ontological absolutes, a very modern anxiety indeed. Bosteels (ibid., 62–63), for example, argues that capitalism has the admirable capacity to unmask the multiplicity hidden under any presence, and as such, all postfoundationalist discourses idiotically reiterate dominant capitalist structures, cancelling out critical reflection. Which critical reflection, we are left to deduce, is the prerogative of the sturdy Marxist axioms of dialectical materialism, base and superstructure reciprocal determinations, the proletariat and the bourgeoisie, the conflicts between forces and relations of production, and so on. Bosteels' argument, while dismissing anti-realism, exhibits the very modern admiration for capitalism frequently encountered in the writings of Marx-inspired authors, who seem to enjoy mistaking the obsessive repetitions of the modern regime for some sort of 'permanent revolution'. Bosteels (ibid.) charts this infatuation with capitalism's revolutionary potential in Marx himself as well as in Alain Badiou, for whom the dissolution of patriarchal, idyllic, feudal and traditional bonds, and hierarchies that capitalism enacts represents something we should welcome, the sign of capitalism's 'properly ontological virtue'. The similarities with the colonial discourses on modernity emitted by Huntington, the United Nations, and a virtually endless chorus of liberal-capitalist voices are not accidental. Despite being able to point out this affective investment in capitalism, Bosteels (63) himself argues that 'Transnational finance capital desubstantialises ontology even more thoroughly than the nineteenth century bourgeoisie would have dreamed. Flexibility, difference and innovation are on the order of dumb facticity today'; that one of the traits of capitalism is 'desacralising'; and that postfoundationalism is the 'spontaneous ideology of the late capitalism'.

I argue quite the contrary: capitalism sacralises hierarchy, identity, and essence. For the ones among us less swayed away by the charms of capitalism, what these theorists identify as the fluid, hybrid, and revolutionary traits of its late[2] period are in fact a paranoid rigidifying and intensifying of modern fantasy's typical rituals, not a tendency towards problematising hierarchies and identities and embracing the lack. Contemporary capitalism tenaciously defends realist-colonial ontologies through increasingly violent and militaristic deployments within and outside the Western strongholds. The entire structure of contemporary capitalism, including its most explosive aspects, is a symptom of the bourgeois determination that nothing fundamental should change. Misinterpreting this order's obsessive drive to defend the status quo for a tendency to permanently transform itself, as the globalisation theorists of the early 1990s also did, means succumbing to the seduction of capitalist advertising and mistaking the way in which the bourgeois regime imagines and represents itself for this regime's true enjoyment. Fittingly, I will discuss next the modern antagonism's impact on the bourgeois psyche, which shows how these technologies of 'perpetual change without any significant transformation' achieve an intimate, personal hold. It will be seen that anxiety pushes the bourgeois towards a definitive resolution of this realist/anti-realist antagonism that involves repressing one side of it, the dangerous side that threatens to expose the lack.

Enjoying Submission

Žižek (in Butler et al. 2000, 253–255) argues that unlike guilt, which stems out of the subject's fraught relation with the injunctions of the superego, anxiety stems out of the awareness that the Other is lacking (according to Žižek, guilt is a mask for anxiety). And when Lacan (1998, 41) argues that anxiety is 'that which does not deceive', I read it as a confirmation that anxiety 'sincerely' signals the bourgeois subject's ontic limit, the knowledge of the Other's lack that he cannot know without renouncing his customary jouissance. Referring to the same passage in Seminar XI, Badiou (2003, 43) confirms that anxiety is a form of Real overspill, and as such, 'it is necessary to channel anxiety's effect, since it destroys the adjustment to the repeatable' (ibid.). Anxiety disturbs the comforting cycles of the drive through which the bourgeois masks the lack and therefore is experienced as a threat to subjectivity that needs management. All this suggests that anxiety is an essential element in shaping the bourgeois libidinal economy, especially considering that the modern fantasy's narratives create the bourgeois subject as a very anxious one indeed.

My argument is that, in order to manage her anxiety, the bourgeois attempts to abolish the distance between herself and the dominant ideology; in the bourgeois fantasy, losing oneself in ideology is equivalent with abolishing the gap between name and experience. And losing oneself in ideology is performed by recognising the names (woman, Jane, Canadian, daughter, etc.) one was given by various symbolic authorities as representing that 'who she really is', and by forgetting that a choice to do otherwise, even if difficult, is available. This bourgeois technique of managing anxiety by submitting to the operations of realist ideology is metaphorically illustrated by Lacan's (2004, 6 and 22) story[3] of himself wearing a mask without knowing what it represents, while being approached by a giant female mantis. Here, the anxiety of not knowing if one is fatally disguised as a male mantis might be worse than the fear of knowing that you will be certainly killed. Not knowing how we stand in relation to the Other's desire, principally because we do not know what we are supposed to be for it—'I couldn't see my own image in the enigmatic mirror of the insect's ocular globe' as Lacan (ibid., 7) phrases it—is so anxiety-generating that we prefer the certain death of submitting to the fate that bourgeois authorities prescribed us. This submission is what Bourdieu, in an already mentioned formulation, also describes as fate, and interestingly, he also compares it with a form of death:

> 'Become what you are': that is the principle behind the performative magic of all acts of institutions. The essence assigned through naming and investiture is, literally, a fatum ... All social destinies, positive or negative, by consecration or stigma, are equally fatal – by which I mean mortal – because they enclose those whom they characterize within the limits that are assigned to them and that they are made to recognize. (Bourdieu 2003, 122)

This is the death of pretending that my being has a definite kernel and that I know precisely what this kernel is (e.g. a man or a woman) and of pretending that this authority-certified 'kernel of being' is exactly what the Other wants to see when looking at me. From this perspective, what Marcuse (2002, 12–14) calls 'one dimensional thought', the bourgeois aspiration to merge with the ideological command has less to do with the rampant technological progress of capitalism and more with the subject's desire to preserve the enjoyment that capitalism provides.

Ideological interpellation thus involves two steps,[4] the first a relation of domination in Foucault's (1982) understanding of the term, for example, one is born into an already set position as 'man' or 'French', and the second a power relation when the subject is seduced into accepting that he is indeed a French man. As already mentioned, this two-step dance of ideology suggests that one's decisive libidinal choices are not made in the first five years of life, as psychoanalysis often argues, but throughout one's life and through complex processes of adjustment and readjustment within the liberal-capitalist dispositifs. Reworking Althusser's (2008) scenario of the ideological operation, Judith Butler (1997, 107) also argues that the grounding condition for the success of ideology is the subject's second submission to the law. In Butler's (ibid. 107 and 111) analysis, one turns and faces the law when interpellated because one has had a prior interaction with the law and therefore understands that there are important gains in responding to this roll call, gains that he greatly desires. The reason for one's 'passionate expectation of the law' (129) that makes him turn around and rush towards it is the 'compelled consequence of a narcissistic attachment to one's continuing existence' (ibid. 113), the subject's deep desire to hang on to the 'I' that the law bestows on him (108). This two-step ideology is chillingly illustrated by Julio Cortázar's short story *Second Time Around* set in the years of the military dictatorship in Argentina, where a group of secret police agents convokes various citizens to a discreet house location, takes their information, and lets them return home only to summon them again sometime later. It is when they return, without being forced, once more to the house that they 'disappear' and are most probably tortured to death.

The desire for authority, for the law, or for losing oneself into realist ideology is a historical constant of a bourgeois class who, once the contradictions of the modern fantasy become apparent, quickly mutates from a 'revolutionary' class into a class desiring the immutability of feudal order. For example, Moretti (2014, 113–116) argues that, once the contradictions of the bourgeois socio-cultural dominion become evident during the Victorian age, the bourgeois becomes ashamed of himself and loses his 'style' and legitimacy. The early bourgeois cultural paradigm of pragmatism, efficiency, toil, honesty, and empirical rationalism is abandoned in favour of the exalted sentimentalism of the aristocratic regime, visible in the luridness of neogothic architecture and the rapprochement to the Ancien Regime classes (ibid. 160). From then on, this group hides its capitalist ventures under the veils of revamped aristocratic symbolism and loses its political, moral, and cultural identity and ascendancy. In the terms used here, this demonstrates the definitive victory of the realist side of the modern fantasy.

The rewards of submission are, however, great by bourgeois standards: once one accepts his name as a metaphysical substance, that is, accepts that the bourgeois symbolic law is one and the same with the natural law, he is protected both from ontic declassing and from the modern duty of contesting any given order, since only a fool would contest natural laws. In different terms, the second-time submission to the ideological regime that brings him into being offers the bourgeois the (illusory) promise of full jouissance if he persists in his already familiar patterns of intrasymbolic enjoyment. With the addenda that after his second submission, the modern subject loses hope of ever understanding himself without the gaze of the master that names him:

> ... a Master is a Master only in so far as I, his subject ... contain somewhere deep in myself agalma, the secret treasure that accounts for the unique character of my personality – a Master becomes a Master by recognizing me in my uniqueness. (Žižek 1994, 172)

That means that the bourgeois cannot seriously attack liberal-capitalist dispositifs without endangering his enjoyment: 'One cannot criticize too far the terms by which one's existence is secured' (Butler 1997, 129). Following the law has nothing to do with its truth and/or good and everything to do with its ability to regulate enjoyment.

Submission does not arrive as a voluntaristic event; there is no precisely identifiable moment when the subject is faced, Matrix-like, with the choice between 'yield!' and 'rebel!' or between 'knowledge' and 'ignorance'. The knowledge she needs in order to rebel, the bourgeois already knows, and she has her reasons to refuse it. The subject refuses to know what she already knows because, during the libidinal rituals she performs within the capitalist networks, she develops a very intimate relationship with the modern fantasy and the various authority figures it enthrones. At each cycle of the drive, the bourgeois glimpses the choice to refuse the jouissance it produces, and repudiates it. This economy of desire can be grasped if we re-conceptualise choice as happening at a level of thought we try to forget about, and enjoyment as something that we need to take responsibility for even when we are not conscious of the operations that produce it. The key to this economy is accepting that '[one] is always responsible for one's position as a subject' (Lacan quoted in Fink 1999, note 17, 238). That the bourgeois knows about this necessity to assume responsibility and about the Other's lack is demonstrated by the guilt she experiences in relation to her conducts (remember that guilt masks anxiety). This guilt is present even in situations when the modern ideology itself tells the bourgeois that she 'could not have done otherwise', that her enjoyment was pre-ordained by ineluctable, natural laws (Jacques-Alain Miller cited in Zupančič 2000, 26–27). This seems to confirm that in the case of every enjoyable conduct, the bourgeois fathoms the possibility of doing otherwise, a pressure of freedom that makes her responsible for what the realist modern fantasy defines as a 'natural necessity'. Very often this guilt is projected on the bourgeois' antagonistic other: within the modern fantasy, we imagine the colonised to be lazy by racial constitution and find her guilty of her lack of industriousness and efficiency; we imagine women to be innately comfort-seeking and nurturing and find them guilty of desiring domesticity and dependency; we imagine men to be sexually irrepressible by nature and find them guilty of being unfaithful, and we imagine gay sexuality as determined by genes and find gay people guilty of their perverted desires and of spreading their vice to our innocent children. This guilt for 'what we have not done but has been done to us' demonstrates precisely that, at some level, the bourgeois realises that the symbolic order, rather than being synonymous with natural order, has no guarantee of existence besides the contingency of its enunciation (ibid. 27–30) and our desire for its prohibitions. Defining bourgeois' submission to the law in terms of choice thus suggests that, as a result of the nature of her fundamental fantasy, the bourgeois has a notion, however vague, of the possibility of doing otherwise, even if she does not always have a notion of what this otherwise might be. Forgetting about this possibility follows the easy path of refusing to let go of her fantasies and enjoyment.

After her submission, the bourgeois remains afraid of being found guilty of transgression and losing the protection of the law, which would leave her unable to enjoy and equally afraid of being found guilty of obeying the law, which would violate the modern superego's command to enjoy transgression. Submission, while performed so as to alleviate anxiety, is itself anxiogenic. The bourgeois experiences her desire for being governed by an (arbitrary and lacking) authority as nothing less than obscene. Žižek (Butler et al. 2000, 314) maintains that the little legal disobediences that go unpunished as long as nobody talks about them, the law's 'open secret', provide the subject with the pleasures of transgression, which functions as the lubricant making the law run smoothly. This 'secret' is what Žižek calls the obscene underside of the law, or the obscene enjoyment at the core of the fantasy. The present analysis, however, assumes that obscenity is not an effect of going against any and all social norms, but an effect of going against those norms that constitute the bourgeois' conviction about what proper enjoyment is. Her conviction about the norms of proper enjoyment might be sincere, but is contradicted by her own enjoyment (confirming that the subject's truth is at the level of enjoyment, not conviction). Understanding obscenity simply as an effect of transgressing norms, as Žižek's argument suggests we should, makes no sense, since desire is always organised by prohibition without for this reason being perceived as obscene (e.g. drinking alcohol during prohibition is not experienced as obscene by the US middle-class partygoers of the time). But once understood as symptomatic of the subject's disavowed conflict with his own sincere beliefs about what is proper, obscenity explains why norms are cathected differentially by various bourgeois subjects: fantasies of incest are obscene only for one sincerely convinced that the relationship with the parents should be chaste; sexual fantasies are obscene only for one that truly believes impure thought is weakness and sinfulness; and fantasies of bourgeois prestige and consumption are obscene only for an authentic communist that believes the opposite should be her proper desire. Enjoying submission to the dominant ideological blueprints of being is obscene only for a subject defined by these very blueprints as an eminently independent being. In fact, channelling her anxiety into desire for authority is from the start a problematic solution to the bourgeois' problems, since it makes bourgeois desire the same with the desire that in the modern fantasy characterises her antagonists—the lower classes, the primitives, the colonised, and so on.

If Žižek (1991, 80) argues that the Kantian injunction to publicly 'obey the (absurd) law because it is the law' involves some form of lucidity about the nature of the Other and, therefore, secures a space of private dissidence and freedom of reflection, I would argue that in the case of the bourgeois, the contrary is true. The bourgeois fulfils the modern obligation to publicly defy the law through various faux-rebellious displays of enjoyment in order to better follow the law in private, in her most intimate fantasies. I will similarly twist Žižek's argument about the obscene underside of the law. From the perspective of the present work, it is more interesting to argue that the fake transgressions that the law permits do not work by providing the bourgeois with jouissance, but by camouflaging her true jouissance, which derives from obeying the law. This is why this fake transgression is never really kept hidden but rather flaunted in a covert manner, as if the subject secretly wants to be apprehended in the act: Ku Klux Klan's maniacal burning of massive crosses at night is, after all, a very obvious signal sent to the (big) Other.

We could reconfigure Freud's description of the ego-ideal in the light of this discussion. In *On Narcissism*, Freud (2001a, 73–105) argues that the ego-ideal binds the subject's narcissistic and homosexual libido to a variety of social ideals like the family, class, or nation; by doing so, it channels homosexual libido into social anxiety. In other words, bourgeois social anxiety results from the re-channelling of homosexual libido away from same-sex objects and towards the phallic objects authorised by the modern fantasy and liberal-capitalist dispositifs, namely towards a familist, heterosexual, patriotic, and class-specific identity. Trying to dismantle and re-assemble in a more interesting form the patriarchal logic that subtends Freud's passage, I would suggest that the generalised social anxiety of the bourgeois subject, rather than resulting from the sublimation of homosexuality, results from the sublimation of her desire for authority. More precisely, social anxiety results from the transformation of the libido attached to the abstract governing authorities that institute the subject into that subject's love for parents, family, father, boss, president, nation, for performing her gender/sex, and so on.

Faking Orgasm

There is an interesting twist in this story of anxiety, submission, and guilt: the most recent configurations of the modern fantasy became very able to disguise submission as rebellion. The contemporary ideological success of the realist fantasy resides in its allowance for a space of fake dissidence where obedience can masquerade as resistance. Paralleling Žižek's (2008) account,[5] Todd McGowan arrives at the same conclusion:

> Rather than being beset by disobedience and transgressive enjoyment, our society has become replete with obedience, with subjects who are wholly committed to sustaining their symbolic identity, their status within the prevailing social order. This obedience predominates precisely because it successfully disguises itself as its opposite—as rebellion, radicality, and difference. The most difficult obstacle to overcome today is the sense that one is radical or subversive, precisely because this sensibility is so pervasive, even among—or especially among—the most conservative subjects. In fact, convincing subjects that they are radical has become the primary function of ideology today. (McGowan 2004, 192)

In the 1930s and irrespective of the shortcomings of his 'vulgar' Freudian paradigm, Wilhelm Reich was already discussing the lower middle class' simultaneous rebellion against the father and desire for his authority: 'This ambivalence towards authority – rebellion against it coupled with acceptance and submission – is a basic feature of every middle-class structure from the age of puberty to full adulthood …' (Reich 1970, 71).

For the bourgeois, demonstrating to the Other that he enjoys transgressing is a more laborious task than hiding his enjoyment from authority or obeying the law and ends up in desperate and often aggressive displays of hedonism like Spring Break, 'Girls Gone Wild', Ibiza, summer festivals, or any contemporary music video dealing with 'partying'. The more enthusiastically the bourgeois obeys the imperative to enjoy, the more he feels he fails at it. This feeling of failing at enjoy-ing arises because the practices of jouissance that the bourgeois engages in are staged for the approving gaze of the same authority whose com-mands the bourgeois supposedly transgresses while enjoying. And if, as argued throughout, the truth of the subject, at least as far as the poten-tial for radical anti-capitalist transformation is concerned, is found in the domain of enjoyment, in the sense that what the bourgeois enjoys is, politically, the most representative element of her selfhood, then the deepest manner of binding one to authority is to have his enjoyment both produced and ratified by this authority: to enjoy what the domi-nant symbolic authority, whatever its incarnation (God, celebrities, one's parents, the media, advertising, a self-help manual, a personal trainer, or a public health campaign) signifies as enjoyable and to engage in these disciplined performances in order to appear desirable to the same authority that disciplines him.

The worrisome element is not that various dispositifs attempt to gov-ern enjoyment: this is their main function in contemporary capitalism. But that, despite the incoherent, haphazard, and frequently grotesque forms assumed by these dispositifs, they are surprisingly successful. What is worrisome, in other words, is that the bourgeois subject is so desirous to eliminate the gap between his experience and ideology that he extracts jouissance from being governed in this manner. This does not mean that his enjoyment is not self-conscious, contrived, unsatisfying, and some-what risky. It means that the bourgeois would rather content himself with this problematic jouissance than risk facing the Other's lack. One of the reasons for this placidity is that the disappointing nature of her jouissance creates the continuous need to refine and repeat these ritual practices, fill-ing up bourgeois life with the disciplined enjoyment of the drive.

The success of capitalism at winning the hearts of its subjects is enhanced by the fact that for a submissive creature like the bourgeois, who cannot imagine jouissance outside the master's gaze, the seductive voice of adver-tising sounds like the voice of the Other giving him direct advice on what he should be in order to be desirable. And by adopting the lexicon of advertising and media as the user's manual of enjoyment, the bourgeois succumbs to these dispositifs' centuries-long experience of erasing the distance between publicity image and self-experience and convincing the spectator that there is no difference between models posing enjoyment and these models' and the viewers' enjoyment (see McGowan 2004, 71). One can be as surprised as they want by the—seemingly absurd—corporate rebellion sold by Converse, Ray-Ban, Dr. Martens, blue jeans, beverage companies, or the music industry. The reason for the continuing popularity of mass-produced 'transgressive' enjoyment is the bourgeois' belief that these are the forms of enjoyment that the Other wants to see.

No doubt, the duty to enjoy rebelliously is more difficult to resist than prohibition since it cuts off all of the subject's escapes: turning against authority is already integrated in the capitalist governing apparatuses as one particularly enjoyable model of submission. After expanding their territory to hedonism, transgression, and illicit fun, these apparatuses seem at the moment to be controlling with an iron grip all imaginable forms of jouissance. But this is not so: jouissance appears to be fully colonised by capitalism only because most of us are happy to restrict our libidinal and ludic imagination to its familiar productions and scenarios and actively resist the possibility of disinvesting libidinally from them. Jouissance seems lost to the enemy only if we refuse experimenting with new modes of enjoying.

In the next section, I introduce the concept of the will-to-not-know as a tool for further explaining the functioning of bourgeois jouissance.

The Will-to-Not-Know

Let me sum up the concepts discussed so far and condense them in the concept of the will-to-not-know. The condition for the functioning of a law that in itself 'knows nothing' is the subject's passion for ignorance: his desire to know nothing of the law's lack, to follow the law 'blindly'. Under anxiogenic conditions of uncertainty, the bourgeois solves the contradictory modern injunction to enjoy obeying the law and to enjoy transgressing it by losing himself in a fantasmatic scenario in which the law is transcendental. This realist fantasy conjures a world of essences that the bourgeois can relish. In other words, while aware that there is no other justification for the law but the law itself, the bourgeois submits to its comforting authority and justifies this submission by creating an Other of the Other[6] that makes his submission seem inevitable and natural. However, since there is an element of choice involved in this submission and it disobeys the modern superego's injunction to 'permanently critique', the bourgeois represses[7] the memory of his choice. And since no complete repression is possible, the affect related to the repressed signifiers of submission returns, haunting bourgeois life with symptoms like guilt, resentment, anger, despair, meaninglessness, paranoia, narcissism, envy, and aggressiveness. Inspired by Salman Rushdie's (2008) literary explorations of such symptoms in the colonial other and their relationship to violence and self-violence, I group them under the name of 'shame'. Thus, shame insinuates itself in the space left open between the bourgeois and modern ideology. And the persistence of shame prompts compensatory mechanisms, which transmute its unpleasant affect into jouissance; I have condensed these mechanisms under the name 'will-to-not-know'.

To repeat, the role of the will-to-not-know is to channel the anxiety produced by the bourgeois' impossible relationship with the Other's lack into something enjoyable to do with the narcissistic demands of the ego. Because it is an attempt to bring together an array of bourgeois conduct in an efficient theoretical-political concept, the will-to-not-know condenses traits from several psychoanalytical categories—symptom, resistance, and disavowal. Let me explain them in turn.

Like the symptom, the will-to-not-know is a 'substitute representation': a compromise representation of the unacceptable memory of submission that the superego has censored (see Fink 1999, 4). And also like the symptom, the will-to-not-know is at the same time disturbing, apparently spoiling life, and the only thing that provides the subject with consistency and jouissance.[8] To the extent that it organises his relationship to jouissance, the will-to-not-know, like the symptom, defines bourgeois subjectivity: the bourgeois structures his life and enjoyment around the will-to-not-know, and without it, life would be even worse (see Žižek 1991, 78).

Like resistance, the will-to-not-know is an attempt to keep enjoying the symptom by refusing to engage in self-analysis. Resistance must be understood as an adjacent form of repression (see Freud 2001a, 246), as ego's attempt to keep at bay the encounter with the shameful source of its jouissance—submission in its relation to the Other's lack—whenever it faces direct pressures to get closer to it. The will-to-not-know is thus similar to Lacan's concept of the analysand's passionate refusal of knowledge, his drive *a ne rien vouloir savoir* (Fink 1999, 7), but applies to much more than the analytical setting, since it is a tool for elucidating some of the most pervasive and pernicious conducts of liberal-capitalist reality.

Finally, the will-to-not-know shares elements of the fetishist disavowal, which is a mechanism that denies the Other's lack by investing in the fantasy of an object—the fetish—that hides this lack (see Žižek 2008, 132). Through disavowal, the bourgeois both acknowledges and denies the same thought, on the lines of: 'I know that there is nothing transcendent in the law, that is has no grounding besides its own text; but I will behave as if obeying this law is a natural necessity'. Otherwise phrased, disavowal is the mechanism that allows the subject to ignore what he already knows: that the only thing maintaining the law is his desire for it. While Lacan considers disavowal to be specific of 'perversion', a clinical structure distinct from neurosis and psychosis, I find his insistence on a moral-normative category invented by bourgeois biosciences ('perversion') uninteresting. I am more inspired by the idea that perversion is an attempt to make the Other impose the law, that is, an attempt to give the law a more solid being than its linguistic essence grants: 'for the pervert, *the object of his desire is law itself* – the Law is the Ideal he is longing for, he wants to be fully acknowledged by the Law, integrated into its functioning' (Žižek 2008, 17). So defined, perversion becomes the basic structure of all bourgeois subjectivities.[9]

The mechanism of disavowal has already been used by Žižek (1991, 18) in his analysis of commodity fetishism, which shows the entire edifice of capitalist reality to rest on a form of non-knowledge on the part of the users of commodities: without the capitalist subject's 'I know the nature of commodity but I act as if I don't' stance, the capitalist system of exchange would not function (ibid. 21). Žižek's re-reading of Judith Butler's notion of passionate attachments can provide further assistance in understanding the operation of disavowal: Žižek (in Butler et al. 2000, 91) hypothesises that the subject's attachments to mechanisms of jouissance that contain her subjugation at their core (e.g. to gender dichotomy) represent inadmissible fixations (what I have been calling above 'obscene' fixations) which need to be disavowed. In other words, to cope with the obscenity of her libidinal conducts, the subject needs to disavow that she knows they are obscene whenever she aims to extract some jouissance from these conducts. Žižek (ibid.), being a passionate supporter of the idea that the gender/sex dichotomy is vital for the functioning of social order (see Chap. 4), considers these passionate attachments unavoidable and necessary. My analysis, based on the idea that interpellation is a two-step process, is more interested in the moment when the bourgeois subject could rescind her passionate attachments but refuses to. In other words, there is a moment in bourgeois life when she knows that continuing one's passionate attachments is no longer unavoidable or necessary. Otherwise, these attachments would not be obscene or, in Žižek's words, would not be inadmissible to the subject herself.

The rest of this chapter applies the concept of the will-to-not-know to a series of conducts that characterise the modern subject, further exploring the causes of liberal-capitalist structures' intractability.

The Will-to-Not-Know as Compulsion

To channel the negative affect of shame into enjoyment, the bourgeois starts by mobilising the familiar technique he uses to deal with all his conflicts and generally with the anxiety generated by the lack: chasing phallic objects. As Stavrakakis (2007, 246) observes, fantasy can function at one level as the foundation of the social order and at another as a symptom—the obsession with phallic objects that organises bourgeois reality returns, once re-triggered by shame, as symptom. Thus, after various loops, bourgeois jouissance returns to the same place: the comforting and often obscene enjoyment provided by liberal-capitalism. This return needs to be considered a political choice, even if it is a choice to reiterate the automatic cycles of a nonsensical machine[10] (Žižek 2007a, b, 36–37). The machine is composed of the various technologies that regulate bourgeois enjoyment in manners incomprehensible to her, in the same way in which the compulsive acts of capitalist production remain incomprehensible to the worker as long as she refuses to acknowledge their social nature and to take responsibility for them. It is therefore this subject's refusal to know anything about the ways in which her jouissance is governed that makes it irresistible and inalterable, running in cycles that are carefully programmed but experienced by the subject as an automatic reflex, in a word obsessive-compulsive.

One effect of the machinic nature of bourgeois jouissance is the ever-proliferating chain of addictions that fill up 'psy' science manuals—addiction to pornography, gambling, sex, gaming, Internet browsing, shopping, chocolate, work, and so on—and that map the transformation of modern enjoyment into the obsessive urges of the drive. The capitalist system both encourages the misinterpretation of these obsessions as following the subject's natural needs (for happiness, freedom, fulfilment, etc.) and keeps it dependent on its cycles of production/consumption. This is what Marcuse (2002, 6) calls 'euphoria in unhappiness', the subject's complete engrossment in ritual enjoyment that she mistakes for need satisfaction:

> … the overwhelming need for the production and consumption of waste; the need for stupefying work where it is no longer a real necessity; the need for modes of relaxation which soothe and prolong this stupefaction; the need for maintaining such deceptive liberties as free competition at administered prices, a free press which censors itself, free choice between brands and gadgets. (Marcuse 2002, 9)

The relationship between bourgeois shame, enjoyment, and the ritual pursuit of phallic objects is complex, involving various levels of fetishism and obsessive compulsion. The public exposure of the Other's lack, even if carefully plastered over by realist modernity, makes that, despite nurturing fantasies of inborn specialness, the bourgeois cannot directly or exclusively use these fantasies when presenting herself as desirable to the Other. The parallel fantasy of a reflexive, critical, self-made modern subject forces the bourgeois to prove her worth, which can be done only by a display of proper habitus.

Inspired by Bourdieu's use of the term, I call 'bourgeois habitus' the historically specific shape given by liberal-capitalist governing to this subject's pursuit of phallic objects (or of jouissance). The bourgeois, then, is a creature of habitus, meaning that her symbolic stability depends on learning and performing adequately various rituals of propriety that align her with her peers (while maintaining her individuality) and distinguish her from her abject others (the poor, the primitive, the colonised, the racialised, etc.). These habits span from social, and most emphatically financial, autonomy to hygiene, taste in art, or work ethic and remain the bourgeois' main instrument of ontic grounding. Sartre's self-hating bourgeois Mathieu senses the difficulty of this position:

> Perhaps it's inevitable; perhaps one has to choose between being nothing at all, or impersonating what one is. 'That would be terrible' he said to himself: 'it would mean that we were duped by nature'. (Sartre 1987, 173)

Habitus is a compulsive endeavour because it fails to achieve its aim, which is that of demonstrating to the Other that the bourgeois is worthy of love. The paradox being that the bourgeois aims to demonstrate the lovable nature of her being by displaying her collection of phallic objects, that is, a collection of objects artificially attached to the self. Habitus is also compulsive because if it stops, the bourgeois feels in danger of being exposed as a fraud: the more we hoard compulsions, the less of a chance there is that the Other will observe that we are not much more than a hoarding habit. Finally, these obsessive conducts are not simply efforts to obey the law but also to hold up its dead body with one's enjoyment. The accumulations supposed to insure the survival of the bourgeois' name in the symbolic (see Fink 1999, 129)—property, Facebook 'likes', travels, selfies, and so on—also desperately try to keep erect the effigy of the law which regulates them.

My bag from Whole Foods Market, a 'healthy and responsible' corporation, perfectly illustrates the bourgeois performance of being since, like most contemporary advertising, it does not even bother to articulate more than a heterogeneous group of signifiers, swirling around to form the shape of an apple and elusively pointing towards the (empty) core of bourgeois jouissance: 'food, organic, gourmet, fresh, natural, quality, satisfy, savour, delight, artisan, passionate, specialty, excellence, values, sustainable, supportive, conscientious, education, care, wellbeing, environment, community, farmers, respectful, health, local, partnerships'. Illustrative of the contemporary ideology's work of suture, a certain John Mackey, CEO of this shop for the bourgeois with a conscience, took it upon himself to pimp up the rather flaccid public image of capitalism and published a book that extols the virtues of the free market and hails corporate businessmen as 'modern heroes' without a trace of sarcasm. Here is the blurb:

> When you think about the word 'conscious,' what words come to mind? Aware? Mindful? Awake? What about 'capitalism?' Selfish? Greedy? Unethical? Unfortunately there are plenty of people out there who don't have a very positive perception of business in general. But what happens when you combine the concept of consciousness with capitalism? John Mackey, Whole Foods Market®'s co-founder and co-CEO, along with Raj Sisodia, a business professor at Bentley College, address that concept in their new book, 'Conscious Capitalism: Liberating the Heroic Spirit of Business'. (http://wholefoodsmarket.com/store/event/conscious-capitalism-book-release-store, 11 January 2013)

This pearl of 'neoliberalism with human face' wisdom shines on shelves of the grocery shop, among piles of organic fair trade bananas and 'natural' cosmetics products (not tested on animals). Here is a similar example: during the autumn of 2011, the private York School in Toronto, Canada, has put up on their website a promotional video meant to attract new enrolments (http://yorkschool.com/). The video incorporated prominently the school logo 'Be yourself. Be great.' and featured a series of 'multicultural' young people, supposedly exemplary of the school's progressive ethos, declaiming a list of 'what they are into'. The result is an incantation of today's bourgeois mantra of cool: student #1, boy: long boarding, sports cars, travelling (at which he pulls out a camera and starts taking photos), Tanzania, music ,and playing ultimate frisbee; student #2, girl: working with kids, speaking Spanish, dancing ballet, cool TV shows, and going to the best university; and student #3, girl: music, soccer, travel, zoology, reading, and 'helping out in an Indian orphanage was amazing!'

I will further illustrate the role compulsion plays in maintaining bourgeois reality with an example that, while not being strictly contemporary, exposes the genealogy of these bourgeois practices: the interwar *The New Book of Etiquette* (Eichler 1934). The space I give this book reflects not only the undisputable enjoyment that reading such a treasury of bourgeois fantasies provides me with but, more importantly, the treatise's ability to flesh out the modern subject's relation to authority. The book's initial argument is that modern etiquette, born in the wilderness of US pioneer life alongside another pinnacle of civilisational evolution, the 'typical American', represents not only a rupture with the sterile and stifling artifice of Old World tradition but also the only proper way to become bourgeois:

> The 'typical American' is honest and sincere, with a sense of the true values and a friendly, courteous attitude towards everyone. This is the heritage handed down to him by the early settlers who braved the ocean to make their home here ... The 'typical American' is, above all, courageous and unafraid, daring to do the thing he knows to be right, scorning all sham and artifice, recognizing no social forms that are not based upon instincts of genuine human kindliness ... Life [of the North American pioneers] was lived simply, even crudely, but there dwelt in the hearts and minds of these pioneers a philosophy rich in the traditions of America's first settlers – tolerance, justice, kindliness, sympathy. (Eichler 1934, 27–28)

It is indeed interesting that this book would attach such a fundamental importance to the concept of 'tolerance'. As Wendy Brown (2006) poignantly theorised, toleration is a key element of the current colonial order, differentiating the civilised white man from the barbarous pre-moderns he tolerates (or not); even the author of a book on etiquette does not fail to understand its ideological weight: 'Those who are truly cultured show respect for the customs, habits, and ways of people who are strange to them. They do not scoff at the things they do not understand. They are, above all, *tolerant*' (Eichler 1934, 362). After so magisterially having set the tone, Eichler proceeds to list the absolute dos and don'ts of the well-bred person. We are treated to a potentially infinite list of commands: etiquette for children (chapters include 'Correct Dress for Children', 'Children's Table Manners', and 'Certain Fundamentals of Child Training'); correct and incorrect ways of introduction and greeting; interminable lists of fine European wines and their appropriate glasses, temperatures, and accompanying meals; table manners, including a sub-chapter on 'The Simple Dinner Without Servants'; how to correctly lift your hat when saying hello ('profound and elaborate bows are not in good taste and not desirable ... The custom of touching the hat, instead of lifting it, is unmannerly and lazy ... The high hat or the derby is lifted by holding the brim directly in front, lifting it high enough to escape the head easily and bringing it forward a few inches. A soft hat may be taken by the crown instead of the brim, lifted slightly from the head and put on again. While lifting the hat the head should be inclined slightly' [47]); how to use one's voice in that delightfully clear, soft, well-modulated way (309); and how to shape speech ('... all authorities are agreed: the final test of a lady or a gentleman is the faultless pronunciation of words' [300]), and the obligatory 'Self-Improvement' chapter.

All throughout, the norms of bourgeois propriety circle around structural conflict: the typical American is tolerant, just and generous, except with 'primitives', prompting the author's valuable advice to foreigners to get rid of their repelling accents:[11] '... people who wish to identify themselves with American life and American activities must be able to speak the language intelligibly as well... Quite as great a handicap as not knowing the language is that of speaking it with a pronounced foreign accent...' (308). Poise is presented as the most desirable trait of etiquette (337), while the very existence of such a book on modern etiquette suggests a subject characterised by neurotic insecurity. Desiring money is deemed vulgar, while the bourgeois subject has since the birth of capitalism been defined through his earnings, profit, and consumption. And race and class-blindness are a must of bourgeois habitus, while modernity is the story of colonialism and of the birth of the great racial taxonomies. Anyway, 'The truly well-bred man or woman ... [judges] people not by their bank accounts or their ancestors, but by their own worth' (36).

However, the real value of this book for the present analysis resides in its attempt to eliminate the gap between being and habitus: Eichler's main thesis is that etiquette is properly performed only when it reflects and/or becomes who you are: 'Etiquette, however, is far more than a formal and superficial observance of social customs. It is something deep-rooted in the nature of a person' (v). The injunction is: 'become your true and unique self through submission to etiquette rituals'. Under 'Correct dress': '[the well-dressed woman] ... refuses to accept fashion as anything but a channel through which to express her own individual tastes and ideals in dress ... The thought that immediately occurs to you is not "what a beautiful gown!" but, "What a charming woman!" You are attracted not by the gown she wears but by the personality it expresses' (ibid. 339–341). While in the more densely theoretical chapter entitled 'The Meaning and Nature of Culture', we are informed that the well-bred bourgeois does not memorise great culture; she *is* that learned by rote ritual: 'True culture does not come from without, but from deep within oneself. It is no shining varnish to be applied at will, but an integral part of the personality' (360–361). Since 'cultural' materials are 'absorbed by the soul' (360), one is advised to exclusively pursue cultural interests that resonate with what one sincerely and naturally enjoys; after which, Eichler comically introduces us to the elements of true culture: 'The nine painters of undisputed glory, with whose work every person of culture should be at least familiar are: Leonardo da Vinci, Michelangelo, Titian, Rafael, Rubens, Rembrandt, Frans Hals, Velasquez, and Turner ... The three great sculptors with whose work every person of culture should be familiar are: Michelangelo, Rodin and Cellini ...' (369) and so on-and so on. And so, through obeying the nonsensical machine, a 'natural bourgeois' is born: 'Before long you will realize that you have developed an unconscious courtesy ... You will be courteous because courtesy has become your natural manner' (35). 'Let us, then, be truly and sincerely ourselves ... living the simple, generous philosophy that is America's heritage'[12] (39).

It is interesting to connect this interwar compendium of bourgeois sophistication with the contemporary tools for diagnosing obsessive-compulsive disorder, since it allows us to observe not just a continuity of habitus between the two but also the intensely contradictory nature of the current symbolic order, which pathologises bourgeois habitus whenever it judges it to have become excessive. The Y-BOCS diagnostic checklist (www.brainphysics.com), while no doubt the result of a naïve understanding of the workings of the psyche that often fuels fascist governing technologies, is interesting in that the obsessions and compulsions listed by these authoritative experts are an exact map of the conducts that give one being and enjoyment in the bourgeois order. In the 'Obsession Categories' column, this diagnostic tool lists: 'aggressive obsessions, contamination obsessions, sexual obsessions, hoarding/saving, religious obsessions, need for symmetry or exactness and somatic obsessions (hypochondria or body appearance)'. While in the 'Compulsion Categories' column it lists: 'cleaning/washing, checking, repeating rituals, counting, ordering/arranging and hoarding/collecting'.

Yet, despite the obstinate repetitions of these rituals, lived bourgeois identity remains insecure; this is not because the subject might take seriously the modern 'discovery' that there is a lack in the subject and the Other (the present work argues that the bourgeois never takes such assertions seriously), but because this very effort of ignoring the lack puts him in the position of being easily declassed and ridiculed by o/Others in his mundane experiences.[13] 'There's always someone, somewhere, with a big nose, that knows ...' as Morrissey astutely exposes the fraudulent poetic creativity of his love interest in The Smiths' song 'Cemetery Gates'. The most immediate illustration are the modernist discourses that equate the 'proper' bourgeois with the boring, obedient, ignorant, grotesque, or malevolent moppet of capitalism, and they are worth reiterating, since any bourgeois would rather forget about them. The examples are taken from literature and pop music precisely to demonstrate that it is not necessary for the bourgeois to read Marx, Nietzsche, or Sartre to be confronted with such derision. Since the turn of the twentieth century, anti-bourgeois messages are easily available in liberal-capitalist cultural products. They could have been equally well exemplified by (the already- mentioned) punk/rock music lyrics or, even, by advertisements that seduce the viewer into identifying with 'non-conformist', 'crazy', 'free', 'wild', or 'rebel' models, implicitly de-valorising the 'proper bourgeois' lifestyle. A well-known quote from Hermann Hesse sums up the disdain for bourgeois subjectivity that bourgeois society itself produces: 'The bourgeois prefers comfort to pleasure, convenience to liberty, and a pleasant temperature to the deathly inner consuming fire'. Using as starting point a 1930s ad for Bovex that reads 'Corner Table enjoys his meal with Bovex', Orwell's character Gordon Comstock, another exemplary self-hating bourgeois, expresses both sides of this modern dilemma:

> The idiotic grinning face, like the face of a self-satisfied rat, the slick black hair, the silly spectacles. Corner Table, heir of the ages; victor of Waterloo, Corner Table, Modern Man as his masters want him to be. A docile little porker, sitting in the money-sty, drinking Bovex. (Orwell 1975, 19)

And further on, about the same Bovex character:

> For can you not see, if you know how to look, that behind that slick self-satisfaction, that tittering fat-bellied triviality, there is nothing but a fright-

ful emptiness, a secret despair? The great death-wish of the modern world. (ibid. 21)

Joseph Roth's *Right and Left* offers a minutely observed derision of the bourgeois soul epitomised by the hero, Paul:

> His thirtieth birthday loomed on. Ambition tormented him like an incurable physical ailment ... As a miser counts up his unproductive treasures, Paul counted up his unproductive talents. He could paint, play music, write, be entertaining, he knew something of business, of human beings, of economics, of world affairs. He wasn't doing badly, he was making money. But not enough to be powerful, and too much to know the consolatory bitterness of poverty. There had to be another secret, the secret of success. In time he might come upon it. (Roth 2004, 75)

Or:

> Memories awakened in Lydia Markovna of a series of photographs called 'The Horsewoman', which happened in a 'leading' fashion journal, in shimmering blue-green on glossy paper, alongside another series called 'Mother and Child', and a third, 'Society Couples'. She saw the captions under the pictures: 'Frau Generaldirektor Blumenstein', or 'Countess of Hanau-Lichtenstern on horseback', or 'Morning Gallop' or 'Gentlemen-Riders'. And all the symbols of social distinction [...] now awoke in Lydia's mind, and made her socially ambitious. Show me the watchmaker's daughter from Kiev who wouldn't have yielded to such temptations. (Ibid. 206–207)

In the song 'Les Bourgeois', Jacques Brel follows three friends' endless repetitions of the bourgeois cycles of submission and fake rebellion. In the first strophe, the 20-year-old beer-guzzling rebels come out of the pub at midnight to show their arses and sing a little song to the notary public, a typical bourgeois bureaucrat, dining in the fancy hotel across the street. In the last strophe, the three friends, now themselves members of the notary public profession, report to the police that young punks come out at midnight from the pub across the street from the fancy hotel where they dine, showing their arses and singing the same little song: the bourgeois are like pigs; the older they get the stupider they get. The bourgeois are like pigs; the older they get, the more they turn into twats (my translation, from the LP 'Les Bourgeois', 1962).

To sum up, the bourgeois forms a sense of self through a repertoire of conducts learned by rote but under constant risk of being confronted by the superego's injunction to refuse tradition, habit, and authorities and to continually search for the New. As a result, his experiences are contradictory, trying to approximate a subject that is both submissive and rebellious; lacking substance and defined by substance (or embracing lack and denying lack); who gains worth and identity by correctly performing the rituals of bourgeois propriety *and* by refusing to obey them; and so on. The modern fantasy that orchestrates habitus performs an operation of suture, exposing the bourgeois' inadequacy only to promise a resolution that inserts him even more firmly into the realist modern discourses (see Silverman 1983, 231), namely further intensifying habitus. While comforting, this is not a fully satisfying solution, since it re-starts the same cycle. Compulsion needs therefore to be supplemented with parallel mechanisms that strengthen the will-to-not-know: disavowal and martyrdom.

The Will-to-Not-Know as Disavowal

If the will-to-not-know is to successfully channel shame into enjoyment, this process requires from the bourgeois to fiercely defend the realist fantasy, and thus liberal-capitalist order, against any attack. This defensive reaction is not directed against the threat of losing any particular enjoyment but against that of losing the entire fantasy frame that makes bourgeois enjoyment possible (Zupančič 2000, 9), that is, the modern fantasy of metaphysical substances: gender, race, truth, rationality, individuality, Nature, nation, God, order, progress, democracy, freedom, self-improvement, or beautiful shoes. Bourgeois enjoyment depends on living in a perpetual liberal-capitalist present defined by common sense, the self-evidently good, and obsessive repetition. Disavowal is one form in which the bourgeois protects his jouissance. And, as Morrissey convincingly argues, everything is hard to find if you will not open your eyes.

At the most general level, disavowal operates so that whenever confronted with discourses arguing that identity in its most natural and intimate aspects is manufactured by power/knowledge systems; that modernity is founded on colonialism, spoliation, and murder; or that liberal democracy is not equivalent to either civilisation, freedom, or political participation but rather perpetuates the disastrous effects of the modern order; the bourgeois refuses to consider the argument and starts the recitation of his protective mantras of metaphysical substances: 'we all know/It is an accepted fact that (women/they/things/people) are like this…'; or 'science has proven that …'; or 'but would you rather live in (mediaeval times, Iran, Africa, and so on)'; or 'maybe, but I personally believe that …'; or 'can't we just enjoy ourselves without thinking about this?' Such reactions are often phrased in the language of personal choice, reminding us of Žižek's (2008) definition of the fantasy as a narrative that both forces the subject's choice and maintains the illusion that the opposite choice was possible:

> Fantasy works both ways, it simultaneously *closes the actual span of choices* (fantasy renders and sustains the structure of the forced choice, it tells us how we are to choose if we are to maintain the freedom of choice – that is, it bridges the gap between the formal symbolic frame of choices and social reality by preventing the choice which, although formally allowed, would, if in fact made, ruin the system) and *maintains the false opening,* the idea that the excluded choice might have happened … (Žižek 2008, 39)

A little scene from the US TV series 'Glee' ironically displays the bourgeois enjoying his full immersion in the mundane: a woman starts work in the high school where her husband has been teaching for some time; he protests: 'You being here is bad for our marriage'. 'Us spending time together is bad for our marriage?' she retorts. 'Yes, we need separation; before we were sitting together in the evening and talking about our day. Now there is nothing to talk about'. The episode cuts to the couple eating dinner in silence. Her: 'There were loads of ants in the alleyway today …' In translation: to continue enjoying we must avoid talking about anything else but the most uncontroversial elements of bourgeois reality: what happened at work, what you did with your day, and so on. Otherwise we might accidentally stumble upon something that threatens our fantasy frame.

The following example, despite its trivialness, showcases the irresolvable but always exciting battle of jouissance between the mystical and the scientific factions of the realist modern fantasy (and to the extent that it promises the resolution of castration, religion is as much part of the realist modern fantasy as 'realist' science). The religion versus science debate, being a struggle between two realist fantasies, is enjoyable for bourgeois subjects on both sides of the conflict because it represents a minimal risk, keeping them at a safe distance from facing the Other's lack. Here is the comment of Christian pop star Brandon Flowers (of pop band The Killers) after a debate with evolutionary biologist Richard Dawkins:

> For him [Dawkins] he sees the beauty in science proving something and finding out origins of things. And that's enough for him. Nothing that science will ever find will disprove that God had a hand in it, for me. So it's a useless debate. And nothing that has been found has changed the gospel that I believe in. (From an interview with The Guardian, cited on the NME web page, http://www.nme.com/news/the-killers/66839, accessed 2.10.2012)

In this case, the bourgeois hears an argument that threatens his enjoyment and immediately discards it using various techniques that make his disavowal seem rational, justified, natural, or a private choice to be respected.

Here is another example of bourgeois disavowal, this time of a type that the Internet is filled with: on 25 April 2014, yahoo.ca featured an article by Amanda Bell (https://ca.movies.yahoo.com/blogs/movie-news/can-disney-s-new--jungle-book--overcome-the-story-s-racist-perceptions-211742065.html, accessed 28 April 2014) discussing Walt Disney Company's decision to remake their animation film from 1967, 'The Jungle Book'. Bell, quoting a media professor from Syracuse University and a communication professor from DePauw University, argues that Disney needs to clean up the film of Kipling's unapologetically imperial undertones as well as of Disney's own misogynist and racist overtones. The racism accusations against the initial film focused on the character of King Louie, a thinly veiled caricature of the African-American built from classical racist clichés: Louie is an orangutan of rudimentary linguistic skill who wants to become (like) a human and sings a little scat tune expressing this fundamental desire to learn to walk and talk like one and so on, in a voice imitating that of Louis Armstrong (the part was initially written for Armstrong but Disney, worried about accusations of racism, hired an Italo-American to imitate Armstrong's delivery instead). This is not very illuminating: Disney company's racism and right-wing leanings are not exactly news. Dorfman and Mattelart (1975) have already provided a reading of Disney as imperialist,[14] while Andreas Huyssen (2003, 85–86) drives direct parallels between Disney and Nazi ideology: 'Given their phobia about mice, the Nazis were unable to see how well Disney fit into their own ideological project: cleanliness, anti-urbanism, chauvinism, xenophobia combined with a privileging of grand spectacle and mass entertainment as it was organized by Goebbels' ministry of illusion'. Nor is it news to anyone interested in knowing that Kipling, author of *The White Man's Burden*, was a passionate supporter of the ideas that the imperial European forces were fulfilling the universal task of educating the primitives into 'becoming properly human', ideas also endorsed by John Stuart Mill, for example; or that bringing the colonised or slaves back to the animal sphere whenever they were becoming threateningly 'too human' is customary tactics of racism and colonialism—and we can recall a scene in Toni Morrison's *Beloved* when, as part of their educational process, their private teacher asks the plantation owner's offspring to make a two-column table listing Sethe's human versus her animal characteristics. What is rather interesting in this whole affair is the resolution with which the Canadian public fights for its right to enjoy the fantasy of a time when one could learn and display racism in the family, cinema, and kindergarten without having their pleasure spoiled and the association that some of the participants make between their right to get off on racism (or violence in general) and their Oedipal mommy-daddy fantasies. These quotes are a minute segment of the more than 5000 comments of more or less the same quality that followed Bell's feature:

> Why do people have such a problem with just simply watching a movie and enjoying it? Does everything in this world have to involve racism and politics? You can't change history. If that's the way it was then so be it. Stop being so thinskinned and insecure! Stop trying to read things into stuff and make things complicated. Most people watched the movie and didn't even

think of racism. You that did have a problem. Toughen up and get over it. Get on with your lives and stop lingering in the past! (Kathleen R)

I grew up with this movie. King Louie was my favorite character. Still is. I remember my father would pull his ears out and puff his cheeks and bang on my bed and pretend he was a Bander-Log until I was crying from laughter. Once we went to a really posh restaurant (I was five) and my father put a banana peel on his head and pretended *he* was the king of apes – I literally fell out of my kiddie seat laughing. This movie is a classic, and I have never, ever thought of it to be racist. Remaking it to be 'politically correct' is a crime. (Alex Rostov)

Let's get this racism in perspective. Amanda Bell has taken short pieces from two university professors to create a very slanted and biased article to push a racist agenda. (Room)

This movie is only racial when someone with nothing better to do wants to make it racial. I watched this as a young boy and never even had the slightest notion of it being racial in any way, shape or form. This movie was made for the entertainment of the young and old alike. Not as a catalyst for somebody's racial motives after the fact. (Shawn K)

I'm shocked!!! lol or just plain naive! I'm Black and this is one of my fav Disney cartoons … I never once in my life thought there was an issue with this scene. Its actually my fav scene of the movie. Just thought King Louie wanted to be human. (Daryl B)

That's alright they wanted to take Tom Sawyer and Huck Finn out of the library's once because the one character Jim was a slave and called Tom massa really this was written in the 1800's. I read both books and until some boob decided that was racist it never crossed my mind and to say they can change the story because it is a generation removed from Kipling is horrible what is next, what classic is going to be chopped up and spit out because someone decides it is not politically correct. (Tom H)

Are you serious right now?!?! This was my favorite movie when I was a kid – my best friend and I watched it 13 times in a row one day!!!! I would have had NO idea this was considered 'racist' if I hadn't of read this article. REALLY?! People need to stop creating problems where there aren't any. Of course the apes wouldn't talk like Mowgli – they are apes!!! (Melissa)

It seems that for the last 120 years or so, things have changed very little in the landscape of bourgeois disavowal: Franco Moretti (2014, 110) quotes an 1889 anonymous reviewer of Ibsen's *A Doll's House*: 'Ibsen discusses evils which we unfortunately know to exist but which it can serve no good purpose to drag into the light of the common day', before commenting himself: 'What is "unfortunate" here – the fact that certain evils exist or that we are made to *know* that they exist? Almost certainly the latter. Disavowal.'

Alternatively, if more logically inclined than in the above examples of disavowal, the bourgeois formally accepts the critique of her fantasy frame only to refuse to take seriously its relevance to her conducts or to 'real' power relations. In the second case, the bourgeois systematically forgets everything she knows the moment she is faced with her obsessive urges, often using the justification of the impossibility of alternatives: 'What are we supposed to do? There is nothing we can do! Nothing can change!' Or, even better, in the case of the left-leaning bourgeois: 'I will fight the system from inside! Just let me get in first...' These disavowal techniques of the thoughtful progressive bourgeois confirm Žižek/Sloterdijk's (Žižek 2007a, b, 29) description of the bourgeois cynic, for whom the enjoyment he has just critiqued becomes even more enjoyable. Here is a relevant quote from the 'alternative' magazine *Disappear Here* (winter 2008, issue 00): '66 things we love: welcome to the list that will change your life. No.42: Silky underwear in lurid colours. We've got lots of them. Literally millions of pairs of knickers. Where do they come from? Sweatshops full of children, of course, but you know what we mean, right?' This 'rebel bourgeois' provocation approximates McGowan's (2004, 6–7) description of the cynic embracing of ideology, where the subject's refusal to know is accomplished through a retreat in the realm of personal politics and a positing of the neoliberal order as inevitable that does not fail to make it inevitable. It now becomes more understandable why liberalism is so resilient to attacks and why it is so addictive for the modern subject: it is a symbolic/power regime that protects his compulsive investment into not knowing and constantly and insistently re-inscribes the will-to-not-know as enviable pleasure, worthy conduct, and the sign of an exceptional being.

The Passions of the Saints: Bourgeois Trauma as Jouissance

Disavowal and compulsion, however powerful, are not enough to protect the bourgeois from shame and anxiety. To gain the self-confidence he is supposed to embody, this modern hero has to show himself as more than just a stubborn accumulator: namely as a complex, tormented person that is persecuted by the law, rather than craving it. The mystique and drama craved by the bourgeois are provided by a couple of related tropes: the first one is reading the supremely banal events of bourgeois life—the typical stories of family, reproduction, sex, travelling, work, love, death, illness, bungee jumping, interior decoration, or marriage—as exceptional events, as proofs of a special soul and of an extra-ordinary life. The second, even more reliable and exciting trope—this reliability and excitement explaining its ubiquity—is to cultivate trauma, or martyrdom.

It is not surprising to notice that what Max Weber diagnosed as a disenchanted modern world quickly re-introduced through the back door all the fairy tales it could fit in. We, Western moderns, fervently believe in gods, aliens, reptilians, Atlantis, fairies, illuminati, horoscopes, divination, astrology, karma, fate, spirits, ghosts, and the mystical nature of the soul. This re-enchanted bourgeois world charges the dullest elements of bourgeois reality with magic valences: technology and science are 'miraculous'; art or creativity is 'incredible'; children, reproduction, and bourgeois family in general are 'a miracle' or a 'gift from heaven'; colonial tourism is 'incredible' and 'marvellous' too; nature, while being quite natural, is also 'miraculous'; and finally, Santa Claus is 'magic', and any critic of his ideological gifts is promptly lumped in with the enemies of wholesome fun, innocence, harmony, decency, the family, and finally world peace, freedom, and prosperity.

However attractive this re-enchantment is, though, a cursory look at the bourgeois strategies of self-preservation shows that mining his compulsions for traces of magic or rebellion is a less productive tactic than its reverse: presenting oneself as blessed not with supreme joy but with extra-ordinary suffering. As John Kucich (2007) reminds us, bourgeois martyrdom has a long genealogy: fantasies of suffering spurred, for example, British imperial desire even before Victorian evangelism attempted to Christianise all its recesses:

> Captain Cook in the South Pacific, General Wolfe in Canada, General Gordon in the Sudan; or else there was mass martyrdom (the Black Hole massacre in India) or crucifixion averted (the popular tale of Captain John Smith and Pocahontas in America) ... After Cook's death in 1779, poems by Helen Maria Williams, William Cowper, and Hannah More, along with a famous elegy by Anna Seward, all compared him to Christ and stressed his having been deified by the Hawaiians who killed him ... (Kucich 2007, 4–5)

These myths of martyrdom, many of them representing military defeats, effect a sanctification of the heroic agent of colonialism, suggesting that, as in the myth of Christ, this suffering is a beginning—an imperial resurrection—rather than an end (ibid.). While, of course, also representing the British colonisers as 'beneficent innocents', a technique copiously put to work today in the post-9/11 narratives of US imperial martyrdom (7). According to Kucich (10), these imperial fantasies of suffering trickle in capillary manner in the Victorian social tissue and, once appropriated by the middle classes as a sign of their moral upper ground, sustain their cultural hegemony. This middle-class moral crusade of redemption through suffering attracted the scorn of its contemporaries in terms uncannily paralleling the ones I use here: 'In *The English Constitution* (1867), Walter Bagehot excoriated middle-class culture for what he saw as its compulsive tendency to abase itself before authority' (ibid.). In one form or another, self-martyrdom is a central constituent of the emerging middle class[15] in Victorian Britain. The function of martyrdom in the colonial mythology is not too different from its contemporary one, where the representation of an event as a trauma, despite forcing most of the subject's subsequent enjoyment to orbit around this gravitational mass, is precisely for this reason perceived not as the end of the subject's history but as its beginning.

One is prompted to ask: 'what forms of recalling and interpreting an event, be it personal or collective, are foreclosed when we decide to represent that event as a trauma?' And when attempting to answer this question, we should probably keep in mind that, since the contemporary bourgeois order makes the narrativising and recounting of one's life into the obligatory condition for obtaining recognition (Butler 2005, 63–65), and since this narrative construction is governed by the rules of recognition of the liberal-capitalist dispositifs, it cannot fail to reproduce these dispositifs. At structural level, the invocation of trauma covers the anxiogenic lack with the familiar imaginary veil of a story of loss which, paradoxically, promises fullness. Trauma is manifested as the looping of a story of corruption of integrity, innocence, harmony, purity, bliss, the natural self, knowledge, power, and prestige or of (human) nature itself. Once an event is represented as trauma, these loops will obsessively return to it since, from now on, it signifies 'fall from fullness'. And through this looping, bourgeois shame is represented as the effect of a dramatic past experience, an accident rather than a constitutive feature. No wonder that trauma fits so perfectly with the bourgeois' obsessive-compulsive being: the traumatic symptom becomes as addictively enjoyable as pursuing phallic objects, a narcissistic exercise that feeds the myth of the coherent, unitary ego.

It is for his lost fullness that the traumatised demands recognition from authority—and we can list here the very literal process of demanding public apologies for past injuries from another State, as well as that of legal trials. For the traumatised, important in these processes is not the reparation obtained (or not), but the judging authority's recognition of the loss engendered by the perpetuator and thus of the victim's past fullness (which also points to the possibility of recovering this fullness in the future). That is, in the process of demanding reparation, the traumatised brings to the Other's attention that there was a moment of fullness that the traumatic event ruined; this recognition of the victim's potential to attain fullness becomes its own reward, yielding recognition for the subject's (past and, hypothetically, future) fullness each time it is reiterated and hiding the scarier possibility of acknowledging that lack is structural.

But the transformation of the event into a trauma also generates additional shame, since it indicates the subject's submission to the authority that decides what constitutes castration or not, or, more precisely, that decides what the traumatised subject is or not: a sovereign subject, State, human, citizen, body, man, woman, and so on. Otherwise phrased, the bourgeois' active mobilisation of trauma confirms her libidinal investment in the law that makes possible the representation of the event as traumatic; or, confirms her libidinal investment in the authority that governs the rules of recognition and that safeguards said law. Thus, the representation of an event as trauma depends on identifying with the authority that grants recognition or, more generally, on the victim's libidinal investment in authority and its rules of recognition. No wonder that one is often shamed and aggressive when demanding recognition from this authority, as if, for example, the case when asking the patriarchal and heterosexist bourgeois regime to recognise one's gender trauma in the name of her 'woman's rights' (see Brown 2002).

Wendy Brown deconstructs the mechanism of the fantasy of punishment by authority in her reading of *A Child Is Being Beaten*, a reading that encourages us to regard Freud's customary staging of psychic drama within the bourgeois family amorous triangle as a metaphor for more general processes of identity-formation in relation to phallic authority. In Freud's account of this fantasy of correction, the little girls' desire for punishment at the hand of authority (the father) is the form taken by her guilty incestuous desire and gratifies and perpetuates this desire (Brown 2001, 49–50). Ritual correction, that is, a fantasy of suffering, turns shame into enjoyment. As a result, the sufferer's enjoyment depends on recalling the traumatic moment and, with each repetition, her allegiance to the symbolic order that made it possible (desire for the father). Once channelled into such fantasies of suffering at the hands of authority, the subject's systematic and satisfying paranoia directed towards phallic authority figures does not fuel resistance to such figures but, on the contrary, the enjoyment of being their victim (ibid. 58). This mechanism is further confirmed by Žižek's analysis of the inauthentic political act, which he illustrates with the example of the False Memory Syndrome. Žižek argues that in such syndromes, the problem lies not with the fabricated nature of the memory of molestation; in fact, it is less relevant if the memory is fabricated under the guidance of the therapist or if the person was molested as a child. What is crucial is that the act of recalling the trauma of molestation allows 'the subject to assume a neutral position of a passive victim of external injurious circumstances, obliterating the crucial question of his or her *own libidinal investment* in what happened to him or her' (Butler et al. 2000, 135, note 55).

At the mundane level of bourgeois performance, trauma fuels a panoply of forms of jouissance. One's publicly displayed suffering at the hands of 'fate/authority'—the State, world, parents, job, traffic, communist regime, and so on—that Kucich (2007, 8) calls 'histrionic martyrdom' transforms a bourgeois that, in the light of his acts, might have been considered a narcissistic slave of ritual, into something of a hero: a Promethean champion pitted against the mighty gods. Thus, whenever the bourgeois subject experiences a libidinal conflict that threatens his enjoyment, the invocation of personal trauma allows him to evade the critical analysis of this enjoyment that the conflict urges. This display delegates responsibility for one's (libidinal) choices to the Other ('They forced me...' or 'I had to...' or 'It was the only way ...'), allowing the bourgeois to demand compensation for her lost jouissance/fullness (see Fink 1999, 70 and 242, note 43). Additionally, once seen through the lens of the trauma, the mediocre experiences that the bourgeois tries to re-enchant—alienation, isolation, boredom, cowardice, petty humiliation, family drama, or everyday compulsions—start resembling events of historical-revolutionary importance. Trauma allows the bourgeois to hide his submission shame, defuse his anxiety, exhibit his unique self, and command the recognition—the care, attention, empathy, sympathy, and so on—of whoever recognises this trauma.

This enhanced form of bourgeois narcissism legitimises the reduction of the whole spectrum of social relations to a complete obsession with the 'I': from the moment when his trauma is recognised on, the bourgeois commands the position of a quasi-saint and submits social reality to a form of imperial control with himself as the centre. Indeed, in a relationship ruled by the demands and desires of the martyr, any interlocutor has the obligation to deplore the martyr's loss, recognise his specialness, and share his aggressiveness: to the extent that one has a duty of sympathy and support towards the traumatised, she also has an obligation to share his enmities, enemies, phobias, and so on. Traumatic narcissism aims to obliterate the other and replace it with oneself.

Let us also recall that in Freud's story, the masochistic element of the correction fantasy is easily transformed into the more acceptable but not less enjoyable sadistic fantasy of watching others being punished by the father (Brown 2001, 58). The ease of this transformation from punished into sadistic witness of someone else's punishment is explained by the trauma's ability to project the shame of the martyrised self on others with unflinching resolve. Judith Butler (2005, 100) makes a similar argument: the feeling of victimhood related to one's formation through an unwilled exposure to the Other's desire, once it is successfully represented as a violence that the subject endures at the hands of the o/Other (which is a fairly systematic construal in bourgeois culture), is most often used by the subject as a permission to enact atrocities against others in the name of self-defence. All throughout this aggressive process, the martyr preserves his aura of innocence.

The very banal event of road rage suggests, to my mind, how martyrdom and aggression constantly mutate into each other in the bourgeois psyche: becoming enraged while driving is fully irrational since we all know, at least from personal experience, that the rigorously disciplined life of a liberal-capitalist metropolis inevitably causes traffic jams. But as the film 'Falling Down', Wim Wenders' traffic jam scene in 'Wings of Desire', or R.E.M.'s video 'Everybody Hurts' illustrate, the rage of a driver is not really aimed at the stagnating traffic or the incompetence of other drivers but rather at one's own debasing condition as a subject: such moments of being 'trapped in traffic' seem to have the uncanny effect of confronting one, in the form of intense anxiety and alienation, with the shame of everyday submission to authority as a worker, parent, driver, consumer, and generally desiring being. Immediately, road rage steps in to mask this moment of reflection and transform it into the doubled jouissance of being the righteous martyr tormented by an unjust world (here, traffic) and of aggressing, barricaded in the privacy of one's vehicle, the others.

A not strictly contemporary but undoubtedly fine example of bourgeois martyrdom comes from Barthes' analysis of Marguerite's love for Armand (*La Dame aux Camélias*)[16]:

It is a very particular type of myth, defined by a semi-awareness, or to be more precise a parasitic awareness. Marguerite *is aware* of her alienation, that is to say she sees reality as alienation. But she follows this awareness by a purely servile behaviour: either she plays the part which the masters expect from her, or she tries to reach a *value* which is in fact part of this same world of the masters. In either case, Marguerite is never anything more than an alienated awareness: she sees that she suffers, but imagines no remedy which is not parasitic to her own suffering; she knows herself to be an object but cannot think of any destination for herself other than that of ornament in the museum of the masters. (Barthes 1972, 105)

In this semi-aware form, Marguerite's 'noble' sacrifice is even more pernicious than if it was a result of her unawareness, sending the petty-bourgeois spectator of the sacrificial drama straight into the slumber of bourgeois pleasure and empathy (ibid.). And here we also understand why the present bourgeois order never tires of sentimentalism, giving lie to the modern pretences of dry rationality and irony. As a trope, sentimentalism asks the viewer to 'feel' rather than think, in other words, to directly identify with symbolic codes displayed, often in hidden form, by the melodramatic image or narrative, without ever inquiring into their processes of production. And identification with a sentimental scene always reiterates the machinic enjoyment learned early and by now deeply familiar, thus reiterating dominant ideology: one is emotionally affected by stories related to the suffering of the family (the heartbreaking struggles of mommy and/or daddy, of the lost or abandoned child, of the vulnerable, persecuted poor or single woman), or by tales of noble bourgeois sacrifice (struggle for the survival of the liberal 'community', rags to riches success, expressing one's talent or resolve against systematic duress, self-denying protestant ethics, vanquishing exclusion and adversity because of one's uniqueness or difference from the norm, and so on), without contesting the fundamental premises of the bourgeois order. Even the rare cases of poignantly constructed sentimental social critiques allow a performance of the will-to-not-know in which the suffering of the bourgeois spectator alongside the protagonist exonerates the former of responsibility for his subsequent enjoyment. Empathy assuages bourgeois guilt without any further need for a change of desire or conduct, without responsibility: making a show of it in front of the Other is enough.

If understanding bourgeois trauma as based on identification with authority, on narcissism and on the annexation of the other as an instrument of this narcissism, we move closer to understanding the irresistible appeal of memory and trauma in the contemporary capitalist landscape:

> The desire for narratives of the past, for re-creations, re-readings, re-productions seems boundless at every level of our culture. History in a certain canonical form may be delegitimized as far as its core pedagogical and philosophical mission is concerned, but the seduction of the archive and its trove of histories of human achievement and suffering has never been greater. (Huyssen 2003, 5)

The contemporary appeal of trauma does not stem from its genealogical potential to display the lack, that is, from its potential to bring to light the knowledge that the fundamental 'part of us' that trauma supposedly took away was already missing, and that the wholeness that the trauma either destroyed or prevented us from attaining was unattainable to start with. In other words, trauma is not appealing to the bourgeois order because it makes visible the constitutive vulnerability, the impossible to close wound of being, but because it promises to anchor both the subject and the social in something real, palpable, indisputable: in the unmediated joy and pain of being. Similarly, trauma is no longer an underside that can expose the failure of modernity, the nation, or capitalism, but, on the contrary, is the obscene supplement that fuels neoliberalism up with the promise of fullness and, indeed, of enjoyment provided as reparation for one's loss by the very same authority that made possible the trauma.

From this perspective, the recalling of trauma is part of the mechanism of the will-to-not-know, especially so if we consider the commercialisation of trauma in contemporary neoliberalism. This commercialisation pushes bourgeois narcissism into new artistic formats, as is, for example, the currently flourishing trauma literature, an exacerbated version of the 'public display of intimacy' already discussed by Lauren Berlant (1997, 11–25) or of the 'wounded attachments' discussed by Wendy Brown (1996, 52–77). The invocation of trauma also performs the mythical function of pointing beyond that traumatic event and towards progress, reconciliation, cohesion, truth, justice, and in a word towards neoliberal fullness. Huyssen (2003, 8) identifies a string of such exemplary cultivations of trauma in the pleasure we take listening to witness and survivor testimonies correlated with discourses about AIDS, slavery, family violence, child abuse, recovered memory syndrome, and so on, and mostly in the universalist valence gained by the Holocaust as stumbling block of the fantasy of European Enlightenment, a universalisation that could serve 'as a screen memory or simply [to] block insight into specific local histories' (14). After all, the mechanisms that generated these modern traumas are not different from the mechanisms that presently generate bourgeois reality, suggesting that the ritual invoking of trauma functions to dissimulate our reiteration of what made the horror possible, while our fear of forgetting the trauma is the fear of losing the memory screen and being faced with our obscene fantasy. This reading also suggests that, in the current bourgeois order, the function of the public monument is to mask the libidinal continuities between past and present[17] rather than to expose the connections between trauma, enjoyment, violence, and the will-to-not-know.

Notes

1. Adorno and Horkheimer (quoted in Jameson 2012, 157), for example, phrase modernist invention as being not so much a positive achievement but a process of placing taboos on the old positivities, including on old forms of subjectivity: '… each supposed advance in knowledge and science is grasped as a kind of defamiliarization which relegates the previous moment of rationality to the status of superstition … Each subsequent generation, beginning, if you like, with the Romantics, feels the unsatisfactory inherited linguistic schema of subjectivity to be an artificial convention, which it is challenged to replace with some new representational substitute'.
2. I am puzzled by the stubborn appeal of this 'late capitalism' term, which exhibits the belief that whatever epoch we consider ourselves to be living in represents some sort of culmination, maturity, or end of history. There is no manner of knowing if we live in early, mid, or late capitalism and should maybe wait until capitalism is finally dead and buried before referring to it in this way.
3. Lacan's example remains misogyny-flavoured to my taste: the praying mantis recalls the M/other, the devouring, dangerous, lethal desires of the feminine subject who, once again, is axiomatically posited as the major threat to social

order and the subject's viability. Fink's (1999) introduction to clinical Lacanian practice displays similarly disparaging representations of the feminine: as castrated man ('In Freudian terms, women never stop resenting their mothers for having deprived them of a penis' [Fink 1999, 69]); as object of men's desire (phallus); or as some sort of animalistic, primordial, incompletely symbolised being. Without agreeing with all of Irigaray's (1985) ideas, I think she is most perceptive when arguing that, in psychoanalytical theory, the feminine designates an empty space whose function is to harbour masculine desire.

4. McGowan (2013, 146–147) discusses a similar two-step process when referring to the subject's entry into the social bond.

5. Building himself on Sloterdijk, Žižek (2008, 29) describes as cynicism the form taken in contemporary capitalism by this acting to preserve the ideological mystification; the cynic acknowledges the mechanisms of ideology but refuses to change the way she enjoys them, so that they continue acting as fetishes. For example, while affirming that she knows perfectly that money is an expression of social relations, the cynic continues acting as if money represents an embodiment of wealth as such and somehow manages to misrecognise this fetishism (Žižek 2008, 31–32). The cynic overlooks the fact that they are acting as if they do not know how the mechanisms of ideology operate, for example, that the Nation is a nationalist fabrication rather than a natural community of being, or that capitalist consumption fuels immiseration.

6. One must, nevertheless, remember that Lacan insists on the existence of an Other of the Other, the transcendent signifier that is the Name-of-the-Father, until late in his career (see e.g. Chiesa, 2007). It is only after he renounces these remnants of metaphysical thought that the phallus and the Name-of-the-Father become same, the Real becomes intrinsic to the symbolic, and we can really think the Other and the subject as lacking any extra-linguistic support.

7. In Lacanian terms, a knowledge that we refuse to know we know, or an ignorance that is not equivalent with lack of knowledge but with the active refusal of knowledge (Jones 2003, 7).

8. Following what seems to be a systematic (symptomatic) tendency to condense and compress Lacanian concepts, I would discard Lacan's distinction between a pleasurable jouissance offered by the fantasy of fullness and a displeasurable jouissance offered by the symptom (Jacques-Alain Miller in Stavrakakis 2007, 78). The displeasure of the symptom is a form of intense anxiety, often expressed somatically, but its mechanism of providing the sufferer with enjoyment is to mobilise fantasies of self-coherence and

uniqueness. In other words, the symptom acts like superglue, binding together the fragments of the ego and making possible autoerotic investment in the ego. And it cannot do so without mixing the pleasures of the fantasy of fullness into its displeasurable display. In fact, the pleasure or displeasure factor is quite irrelevant when discussing jouissance, since jouissance represents an intensity of affect that makes the distinction between pleasure and displeasure rather difficult to make. What the bourgeois subject looks for through all her actions is attaining this intensity.

9. An idea suggested by the latter Lacan (cited in Fink 1999, 166) when he argues that *objet a* has something fetishistic about it. Or that perversion represents a hegemonic structure best illustrated by capitalist discourse and that the neurotic resolution of the Oedipus is itself a perversion (père-version) aiming to mask the lack in the Other (Chiesa 2007, 7).

10. Žižek (1991, 37) merges the idea of machinic enjoyment that shapes conviction derived from Pascal with Lacan's definition of the unconscious as the automaton, the senseless letter that unknowingly leads the mind.

11. At the moment of writing, a Toronto, Canada private company is offering specialised 'de-accenting classes' to immigrants.

12. The author quotes a presumably kindred book, *Social forces in American History* by A.M. Simons, which posits that the North American frontier, nothing less than an evolutionary philosopher's stone, took the European and in a lifetime transmogrified him (sic) into the product of a hundred generations of racial evolution to create that epitomal twentieth-century man: 'the typical American' (Eichler 1934, 27).

13. Ridiculing the bourgeoisie has been a most efficient instrument during the early modern class wars in Europe, as evidenced by the theatre of Moliere or Goldoni (also see Moretti 2014, 162).

14. In pop culture, the problematisation of Disney ideology has been initiated by comics such as Mad, which in a number from 1955 published a Harvey Kurtzman and Will Elder parody of Disney called 'Mickey Rodent'.

15. Here 'class' should be understood as rhetoric of community that constitutes social stratification, rather than being its result (Kucich 2007, 14). Also see the discussion of the relationship between the continental term 'bourgeois' and the Victorian one 'middle class' in Chap. 1.

16. In Freudian terms, this example would suggest that bourgeois repression happens through displacement rather than through amnesia.

17. See Huyssen's (2003, 32) discussion of the proposed monument to the Holocaust, to be erected in Berlin on the precise site of a very similarly conceived monument to the glory of the *Third Reich* by Albert Speer.

References

Althusser, L. (2008). Ideology and ideological state apparatuses. In A. Louis (Ed.), *On ideology* (pp. 1–61). London/New York: Verso.

Badiou, A. (2003). Lack and destruction. *UMBR(a): Ignorance of the Law.*

Barthes, R. (1972). *Mythologies*. New York: Hill and Wang.

Berlant, L. (1997). *The queen of America goes to Washington city: Essays on sex and citizenship*. Durham/London: Duke University Press.

Boteels, B. (2014). *The actuality of communism*. London/New York: Verso.

Bourdieu, P. (2003). *Language and symbolic power*. Cambridge: Harvard University Press.

Brown, W. (1996). *States of injury*. Princeton: Princeton University Press.

Brown, W. (2001). *Politics out of history*. Princeton/Oxford: Princeton University Press.

Brown, W. (2002). Suffering the paradoxes of rights. In B. Wendy & H. Janet (Eds.), *Left legalism/left critique* (pp. 420–434). Durham: Duke University Press.

Brown, W. (2006). *Regulating aversion: Tolerance in the age of identity and empire*. Princeton/Oxford: Princeton University Press.

Butler, J. (1997). *The psychic life of power: Theories in subjection*. Stanford: Stanford University Press.

Butler, J. (2005). *Giving an account of oneself*. New York: Fordham University Press.

Butler, J., Laclau, E., & Žižek, S. (2000). *Contingency, hegemony, universality: Contemporary dialogues on the left*. London/New York: Verso.

Chiesa, L. (2007). *Subjectivity and otherness: A philosophical reading of Lacan*. Cambridge: The MIT Press.

Driscoll, M. (2004). Reverse postcoloniality. *Social Text 78, 22*(1), 59–84.

Dorfman, A., & Mattelart, A. (1975). *How to read Donald Duck: Imperialist ideology in the Disney comic*. New York: International General.

Driscoll, Mark. 2004. 'Reverse Postcoloniality'. Social Text 78, Vol. 22, No. 1, Spring. Eichler, L. (1934). *The new book of etiquette*. Garden City: Nelson Doubleday, Inc.

Fink, B. (1999). *A clinical introduction to Lacanian psychoanalysis: Theory and technique*. Cambridge: Harvard University Press.

Foucault, M. (1982). The subject and power. *Critical Inquiry, 8*(4), 777–795.

Foucault, M. (1984). What is enlightenment? In P. Rabinow (Ed.), *The Foucault reader* (pp. 32–50). New York: Pantheon Books.

Freud, S. (2001a). *The standard edition of the complete psychological works of Sigmund Freud* (Vol. XIV). London: Vintage.

Freud, S. (2001b). *The standard edition of the complete psychological works of Sigmund Freud* (Vol. XVIII). London: Vintage.

Huyssen, A. (2003). *Present pasts: Urban palimpsests and the politics of memory.* Stanford/California: Stanford University Press.

Irigaray, L. (1985). *This sex which is not one.* New York: Cornell University Press.

Jones, A. L. (2003). Editorial: Ignorance of the law…. *Umbr(a): Ignorance of the Law, 1,* 131–5, 4–9.

Joseph, R. (2004). *Right and left.* Woodstock/New York: The Overlook Press.

Kucich, J. (2007). *Imperial masochism: British fiction, fantasy and social class.* Princeton/Woodstock: Princeton University Press.

Lacan, J. (1998). *The four fundamental concepts of psychoanalysis: The seminar of Jacques Lacan Book XI.* London/New York: W.W. Norton and Co.

Lacan, J. (2004). *Anxiety. The seminar of Jacques Lacan Book X.* Cambridge/Malden: Polity Press.

Marcuse, H. (2002). *One-dimensional man: Studies in the ideology of advanced industrial society.* London/New York: Routlege.

McGowan, T. (2004). *The end of dissatisfaction? Jacques Lacan and the emerging society of enjoyment.* Albany: State University of New York Press.

McGowan, T. (2013). *Enjoying what we don't have: The political project of psychoanalysis.* Lincoln/London: University of Nebraska Press.

Moretti, F. (2014). *The bourgeois: Between history and literature.* London/New York: Verso.

Orwell, G. (1975). *Keep the aspidistra flying.* Harmondsworth: Penguin Books.

Reich, W. (1970). *The mass psychology of fascism.* London: Penguin.

Rushdie, S. (2008). *Shame.* New York: Random House Trade Paperbacks.

Sartre, J.-P. (1987). *The age of reason.* London: Penguin.

Silverman, K. (1983). *The subject of semiotics.* New York: Oxford University Press.

Stavrakakis, Y. (2007). *The Lacanian left: Psychoanalysis, theory.* Politics: Edinburgh University Press.

Žižek, S. (1991). *The sublime object of ideology.* London/New York: Verso.

Žižek, S. (1994). *The metastases of enjoyment: Six essays on women and causality.* London/New York: Verso.

Žižek, S. (2007a). *The plague of fantasies.* London/New York: Verso.

Žižek, S. (2007b). Trotsky's "terrorism and communism", or, despair and utopia in the turbulent year of 1920. In T. Leon (Ed.), *Terrorism and communism.* London/New York: Verso.

Žižek, S. (2008). *In defense of lost causes.* London/New York: Verso.

Zupančič, A. (2000). *Ethics of the real: Kant, Lacan.* London/New York: Verso.

3

The Nonmodern Bourgeois

This chapter discusses the mechanism of the will-to-not-know in the case of a subject who is defined by the modern fantasy as the opposite of the proper: the primitive or nonmodern subject. More precisely, it engages with the psychic economy of a subject that, while classified as 'racially improper' through various colonial technologies, continues to rely on the modern fantasy in order to 'learn how to enjoy and desire'. The discussion starts from the premise that racialisation plays a fundamental role in the formation of the modern psyche, a role that the genital obsessions of traditional psychoanalysis willingly obscure. Within the modern fantasy, it is impossible to understand a subject's sexualisation without analysing her simultaneous racialisation. When adopting the modern fantasy as a template for desiring, one also adopts their assigned 'race' as that 'who they really are' and subsequently struggles to attain a stage of non-castration both racially and sexually. It is not by accident that the modern technologies deployed in the colonies and metropolis govern sexuality as a class- and race-specific conduct[1] (see e.g. Stoler 1995; Valverde 1996).

In order to define the proper, modern, or civilised subject, the modern fantasy conjures the antagonistic specular image of the primitive

© The Author(s) 2016
M. Panu, *Enjoyment and Submission in Modern Fantasy*,
DOI 10.1057/978-1-137-51321-2_3

or nonmodern: the primitive/nonmodern is the fantasmatic figure whose obsessively catalogued and yet shifting racial attributes supposedly represent everything the proper bourgeois is not.[2] And in order to unveil the 'open secret' of the modern fantasy's intractability and of the enduring success of Europe's colonial technologies, I suggest that we need to understand the nonmodern subject's affective investment in the founding myths of modernity. One might then have the (fake) surprise of finding out that global colonial dispositifs extract their vitality from the enjoyment they provide for some of the very subjects they designate as inferior. The subaltern whose enjoyment and identifications are shaped by the modern-colonial fantasy is the 'nonmodern bourgeois' that gives this chapter its title, and the conducts of this 'racially inferior bourgeois' support the weighty edifice of colonial modernity.

The definition of the 'nonmodern bourgeois' I propose is not very precise by classical sociological or, even, cultural theory standards and does not aim to be. While a reader that takes pleasure in the taxonomic drives of these disciplines (and we all do, to some extent) might argue that the term 'nonmodern bourgeois' describes a multiplicity of subjects so diverse 'socio-culturally' that it becomes meaningless, I consider that making this definition more precise would reiterate the modern hierarchies of difference—anthropological, sociological, national, ethnic, religious, civilisational, developmental, and so on—and the will to truth that this analysis confronts. Diana Fuss (1995, 144) takes to task the notion of the imaginary *other* on these terms: 'To invoke "the Other" as an ontological or existentialist category paradoxically risks eliding the very range of cultural differences that the designation is intended to represent'. For Fuss (ibid.), relying upon the category of *other* risks to flatten difference and to exclude the subjects that are left outside the binary self/other by the colonial discourse. As this chapter tries to point out, I am more concerned about the colonial authority's interpellation of the nonmodern subject than by this subject's exclusion from the modern fantasy, and more interested in the processes that construct our—also fantasmatic—modern notions of difference, rather than in the risk of erasing difference. Constructing the *other* as fundamentally different from the metropolitan bourgeois remains a central technology in colonial governing even if, like any governing attempt, it is never fully successful. And while the heterogeneity of the subjects to which it refers would, in theory, make meaningless the modern 'difference' between the civilised and the primitive, such colonial taxonomies never became meaningless for either coloniser or colonised, maybe on the contrary. Attention to the specific details of colonial dispositifs is crucial in the local struggles to dismantle them, but when discussing these dispositifs at a general strategic level, I find the term 'nonmodern bourgeois' adequate because of its very 'imprecision'. This lack of taxonomic exactness points with particular insistence towards the ability of diffuse, heterogeneous, and diversely located colonial technologies to produce patterns of desire that share a similar relation with Europe and the 'white man' as phallic signifiers.

By nonmodern bourgeois, I do not mean a subject whose psychic structures are fundamentally different from those of a mythical proper bourgeois, the white Western European. As argued in the previous chapters, any bourgeois subject is an *other* of herself: our subjectivity's creation in language and the tensions inherent in the modern fantasy make access to the position of 'proper bourgeois' (and more generally self-coincidence) impossible. The term nonmodern bourgeois, then, describes the tensions of a libidinal economy that is both bourgeois *and* constructed by a hostile modern environment that categorises it as racially inferior.

I was arguing in the first chapter that we should understand modernity as a fantasy rather than as a specific set of events. Despite its staging of liberal-capitalism as synonymous with constant growth, change, or progress, this fantasy locks desire in obsessive loops governed by the master signifiers 'Europe' and its metaphorical equivalent, 'white man'. More precisely, the promise of fullness encapsulated by the words progress, civilisation, democracy, career, prosperity, and freedom in their connection to 'Europe' traps the nonmodern bourgeois in a passionate and racially forbidden relationship of identification with the fantasmatic figure of the 'proper (white) bourgeois'. It is from this tension between his desire for authority and that authority's rejection that stem the specific conducts of the nonmodern bourgeois' will-to-not-know.

Modern Identifications

I give identification—or the field that Lacan calls the 'imaginary'—a prominent function in the libidinal economy of the nonmodern bourgeois and assume that the ego is brought into being by the subject's identification with a series of external images (Chiesa 2007, 15). Identification is the 'detour through the *other* that defines a self' (Fuss 1995, 2, my italics). This means that the ego represents the symbolically mediated[3] internalisation of how we imagine that the Other sees us, and identifications are shaped by what the fantasy tells us that the Other would find desirable when looking at us. The external images that, once internalised, form the ego thus depend on a symbolic scheme, on a regulated system of desirability. Our imagining of a desirable image is governed in relation to figures having particular ontological weight or desirability in our symbolic order, be they fictional characters, celebrities, politicians, parents, teachers, peers, and so on: '*Imagos* are images which are already assumed in the symbolic order and are consequently capable of "symbolic efficacy"' (Lacan cited in Chiesa 2007, 28). And because they involve an ideal perceived as external to the self, these identifications are simultaneously self-defining and self-alienating; thus, according to psychoanalytical theory, they engender aggressive impulses: in the imaginary field, the subject tries either to subsume the threatening image of the *other* to the self or to destroy it. How do these elements play out in the field of the nonmodern subject's identification with an image as alluring and alienating as that of the 'proper' (white) bourgeois?

To further adapt the Lacanian vocabulary of identification for my purposes, I will argue that the nonmodern bourgeois' self-apprehension as well as her perception of the Western 'proper' bourgeois are governed by the relationship between herself, the gaze, and the screen. We can explain the screen[4] as a system of desirable images organised by the modern fantasy in terms of, for example, race, class, sex/gender, sexuality, habitus, and so on and from which the subject is invited to select the ego-ideal she wishes to identify with. The gaze[5] represents the subject's hypothesis of how she is seen by the Other. And the alignment between the ego and the image projected on the screen is possible only if ratified by the gaze (Silverman 1996, 18). That is, the successful internalisation of the ego-ideal displayed on the screen depends on this identification being approved as legitimate and desirable by the Other's gaze. After all, the ego-ideal represents the way in which we would like to be seen by the Other, the image of ourselves that we imagine the Other will find lovable.

In the case of the nonmodern bourgeois, this system of identification yields interesting effects, since his identifications are with an image, the 'white', forbidden by the racial classifications of the modern fantasy and take place under a gaze which polices these classifications, leading to a situation in which the nonmodern bourgeois engages in various libidinal tactics that try to escape this lock without giving up the modern fantasy as his main desiring framework. These tactics, as we shall see, make the nonmodern bourgeois malleable to colonial governing techniques, something Judith Butler hints at in the more general context of identificatory processes:

> Identification is unstable: it can be an unconscious effort to approximate an ideal which one consciously loathes, or to repudiate on an unconscious level an identification which one explicitly champions … It can become even more complicated, however, when the very political flag that one waves compels an identification and investment that lead one into a situation of being exploited or domesticated through regulation. (Judith Butler in Butler et al. 2000, 150)

In our case, the complication is created by the fact that the colonial system of desirability is ratified by the nonmodern subject's desire for it; that is, by the fact that within the colonial fantasy, Europe's phallic position becomes indispensable to the subaltern's enjoyment. Thus, in order to continue self-defining, desiring, and enjoying according to the framework of the modern fantasy, which frames the European master as beyond castration (i.e. without lack), the nonmodern bourgeois feels compelled to take upon himself the master's lack by accepting the racial inferiority this fantasy ascribes to him. Or, the other way around, once the nonmodern bourgeois accepts as true the modern taxonomies that posit him as racially inferior in relation to the 'proper' European bourgeois, his enjoyment depends on systematically covering up Europe's lack. This moves his anxiety from the symbolic field, where it is related to the Other's lack, to the imaginary field, where it is related to the racial classifications of modernity. Paradoxically, the pleasure that Lacan insists is associated with the gaze (see Krips 2010, 93) can be understood as the nonmodern subject's exhibitionistic pleasure of being scrutinised by the master's eye which classifies him as racially inferior: in this field of colonial identifications, the nonmodern bourgeois develops a set of conducts that make the discomfort of the master's gaze enjoyable.

In this colonised form, the enjoyment of the nonmodern bourgeois conforms to the model of managed risk I have been commenting upon in the first chapter. By covering up the Other's lack through his acceptance of the verdict of racial inferiority, the nonmodern bourgeois does face the risk that his jouissance might expose his own lack imaginarised as racial deficiency, that is, expose his impossibility to ever become his 'white' ego-ideal. But this risk is defused by the fact that his identifications reinforce the colonial dispositifs and taxonomies of being on which his subjectivity depends, perpetuating the cycles of affinity/discomposure that shape his drive.

Everywhere in the 'peripheral' territories—and with acute intensity in the Romanian spaces I discuss in this chapter—the phallicising of Europe transforms it into a tool for re-signifying structural lack as an imaginary deficiency, the racialised 'primitivism', or 'backwardness' that the nonmodern bourgeois can extract jouissance from. This colonisation of enjoyment happens to such an extent that, no matter what experience of the West the nonmodern bourgeois has and no matter what critique of the West he hears, he will not discard Europe as the phallus. Acknowledging the castration of Europe would amount to nothing less than losing his framework of jouissance. This is the nonmodern bourgeois' will-to-not-know, and the pleasures it offers are as aggressive as those of the metropolitan bourgeois. Before detailing these conducts, though, I will further analyse the mechanisms through which the nonmodern bourgeois effects this 'imaginarisation' of the Other's lack.

His Master's Gaze

While no particular human look can approximate the gaze—in the same way in which no subject can ever 'be' the image she identifies with—the specificity of the nonmodern bourgeois position is that it conflates the gaze with the look of the 'white' bourgeois. The modern fantasy is the screen, the mediating agency of cultural representation that makes possible this conflation (Silverman 1996, 28). And, to repeat, this conflation replaces the (symbolic) anxiety produced by the knowledge of the Other's lack with the (imaginary) guilt of being classified as inferior by the white man's gaze.

Otherwise phrased: the nonmodern bourgeois' identifications, while contingent, reversible, and contradictory, are anchored by a particular element: his most significant *other* is the 'white' Western European, a figure that, as already mentioned, is metonymically connected with the phallic signifier 'Europe' and deforms with its gravity the libidinal strings, the nonmodern bourgeois' psychic cosmos. In Lacanian language, this means confusing the *other's* image with *objet a*, a confusion that ties one's fantasies of self-knowledge, mastery, unity, and completeness to her desire for (the desire of) the *other* (Rose 2005, 74–76; also see Silverman 1996, 74–75); in our case, these fantasies are tied to the 'white man'. And according to Lacan (quoted in Silverman 1996, 73), when the subject confers upon another the ideality of the ego-ideal, this approximates the master-slave relationship.[6]

Now we can understand the nonmodern bourgeois' experience of the white Western European as the one that casts on the world his dissecting eyes, those eyes that cut to the truth of their object with sharp microtomes, 'the only valid eyes' (Fanon 2008, 95). In the modern fantasy as lived by the nonmodern subject, the 'proper (Western) bourgeois' is ascribed the fictional characteristics of the discourse-producing machine: 'omnipotent and coercive gaze, ability to generate narrative, castrating authority of the law' (Silverman 1983, 232). So, the 'white' is endowed with the powers of the mythical master, unaffected by the world but creating it with demiurgic powers, harnessing it to its will, using it to its desire, and in a word having absolute control over nature, truth, destiny, self, and others. This fantasy introduces in the nonmodern bourgeois' psyche the fiction that the white European's desire is unaffected by that of the subaltern: the white man is the one whose desire curates, recognises, assesses, and possesses Others and not the other way around.[7] 'Whiteness', 'the North', and the coloniser thus become associated with the stupendous ability of transcending castration. From then on his desire ('What am I for it?'), jouissance ('It has all the jouissance!') and demand ('What does it ask from me?') (see Salecl 2004, 62) are tethered to obtaining the master's recognition.

As already mentioned, according to the classical psychoanalytical account, the realisation of the distance between one's ego (nonmodern bourgeois) and the ideal image he tries to be ('white') leads either to attempts at assimilating the *other* to the self or to a murderous rivalry that aims to annihilate the *other* (see e.g. Silverman 1996, 42; Chiesa 2007, 20 and 25). However, this description of aggressiveness as a primary element of selfhood, that is, as a universal trait of subjectivity, misses what makes specific modern aggressiveness: it overlaps precisely and systematically with the ontological hierarchies of modernity. For the nonmodern bourgeois who adopts wholesale the modern fantasy, subsuming or destroying the ideal image is not a serious alternative, since he labours to maintain the aura of the master, rather than challenging it. His energies therefore focus on displacing various *others*—the poor, disabled, homosexuals, ethnic minorities, immigrants, leftists, and so on—the conflicts that result from submitting to an authority that openly debases him (more on which below).

A discussion of Alexander Kiossev's (2006) analysis of gaze[8] and recognition can help the present discussion. Starting from the classic example of being put 'in the same bag' with people from other Balkanic countries by a German student—he was mistaken for a Romanian after having already identified himself as Bulgarian —Kiossev wonders why such misrecognition is so offensive to the subaltern. According to him, what offends the Balkanic is the Westerner's refusal to recognise his 'difference' and thus to discern between the various subaltern ethnic identities. Her refusal to differentiate him from other 'similar types' means that she does not see him as a distinct, specific, recognisable ethnic unit; in other words, she does not recognise him as a sovereign, European, modern subject defined by national identity. Thus, Kiossev argues that the Balkanic is offended by being refused a basic form of 'civility' or politeness that, it is implied, consists in respecting the modern taxonomies of identity. This explanation does not exhaust the entire analytical horizon of his observation; I would argue that the offence results from the nonmodern bourgeois' relationship with the master's gaze (in this case embodied in the figure of the German student) and more precisely from the master's refusal to ratify his identification with the 'white' ego-ideal (in this case represented by national identity). More plainly: the offence stems from the distance between the ways in which the gaze ratifies the difference between, say, French and German but not that between Bulgarian and Romanian, which in the nonmodern bourgeois' fantasy measures the distance placed by the gaze between himself and the 'white' ideal. It is not coincidental that, in Kiossev's examples, the offence is perpetuated either by a German (white) misrecognising a Bulgarian (nonmodern), or by a Bulgarian (almost white) misrecognising Africans (nonmodern).

This is therefore not about the difference or lack thereof between subalterns or about some 'basic' civility, but about the difference between subalterns and the proper European. The racial offence stems from one's embodied scheme of selfhood being relegated to that displeasing set of figures that the modern screen uses to define what the white is not. Thus, the offence of being made undistinguishable from one's geographical neighbours is the symmetrical equivalent of the offence Fanon (2008) experiences when he is 'spontaneously' classified by the master's gaze as fundamentally different (from the 'white'), or of the offence that Kiossev himself experiences when he is told by yet another German student that he has a Balkanic habitus (a recognition of difference, but still as distance from the 'white'). The subaltern is equally offended by the master's lack of differentiation among subalterns and by her implication that there is a fundamental difference between the subaltern and the master. Being amalgamated with the generic group of others or being distinguished as culturally/racially *other* equally undermines his effort of identification. In Kiossev's case, this forced identification as 'non-white' is particular hurtful since he asks to be recognised as a typically modern identity: the ethnic/national identity of Bulgarian, Romanian, and so on. The nonmodern bourgeois is thus refused access to identification with the ego-ideal despite passionately embracing the modern framework that promised him recognition as a proper (European) subject. To insist: here, the master refuses to recognise the ethnic identity (Bulgarian) given the Balkanic as a reward for submitting to the regulation of the white authority, that is, for recognising himself as a sovereign subject according to the ethnic system of differences constructed by the modern fantasy. Kiossev himself notices that the form of identity that the Balkanic is asking recognition for is a nineteenth-century construction of nationality and ethnicity intimately tied in with the Balkanic nation and subject's personal strive towards sovereignty and emancipation. Unlike the Western bourgeois, who gets a modicum of protection from the modern authority he submits to, the Balkanic bourgeois is further chastised for this submission by being treated as if his (modern) identity is either not differentiated enough or too different.

Tactically, at least according to the politics espoused by this analysis, the problem lies with the nonmodern bourgeois, not with the master: the (modern ethnic) identity he claims recognition for is precisely the identity he should renounce; and the gaze he submits to results from confusing the white look with the gaze that is to say, of the European with the master, a confusion he should rectify. However, none of these events brings the nonmodern bourgeois closer to acknowledging 'white' lack. Indeed, that Kiossev himself used his racial offence as the starting point of an article rendering homage to the work of Axel Honneth illustrates how the nonmodern bourgeois is able to extract some analytic jouissance from such painful misrecognitions *and* fuel the phallic aura of Europe.

It is worth restating that the 'white gaze' is a fantasy of omnipotence impossible to realise in the symbolic/imaginary reality: any subject looks at the world from a position internal to the field of vision, that is, no one is ever a spectator without also being a spectacle for the gaze (Silverman 1996, 60 and 132–133). However, it is not just the nonmodern bourgeois that enjoys this fantasy of 'white' omnipotence; encouraged by his idealised image projected on the screen of the modern fantasy and by the transferential recognition he gets from the nonmodern bourgeois, the 'white' bourgeois shares the same fantasy. His effort of approximating the camera position[9] involves attempts to make a spectacle out of the nonmodern subject while pretending that he is not, in turn, gazed at. Despite these attempts, the 'proper Western bourgeois' experiences as acutely as his nonmodern counterpart the anxiety of being watched continuously, an anxiety that does not allow him to fully forget about the distance between his own look and the gaze. And the proper bourgeois' greatest fear is that the subaltern might notice his castration, notice that he desires the subaltern's desire and fears the Father's gaze. This is not an imminent danger as far as the nonmodern bourgeois is concerned, since his will-to-not-know makes sure that Europe's castration will always be disavowed, no matter how blatantly it is exposed. But not all nonmodern subjects are bourgeois, and there is no guarantee that one will remain bourgeois forever. Hence, the metropolitan deployment of a variety of tactics meant to hide castration. World-famous (i.e. Western) contemporary museums or art scenes, for example, are part of the imperial screen that aestheticises and mythicises the fiction that the West does not need the Other's desire since it represents the 'one' which confers value, truth, and pleasure, transforming this myth into self-evident, common sense reality.[10] While the Western obsession with travelling abroad and especially to 'exotic' places is in great part spurred by the desire to parade as the machine gaze, registering and cataloguing the nonmodern subject, and enrols techniques ranging from the literal use of cameras to record the nonmodern subject's strange enjoyment to the tourists' pretence that they are unaffected by the look and desire of this nonmodern subject.

Otherness and Effeminacy

Diana Fuss (1995, 48) analyses Freud's framing of identification as a supremely masculine process, a moulding of one's ego in the image of the Father/phallus. The Freudian representation of identification as a 'stiffening of the ego', as an attempt to approximate the erect phallic position, which Lacan also proposes, results in psychoanalysis' glorification of the phallus and of the masculine and in the homosocial rigidity and lifelessness of its concepts (ibid.). Fuss is right, and the effects of the implicit connection between phallus and penis that psychoanalysis makes need to be continuously interrogated critically. When analysing how the nonmodern bourgeois' fantasy of becoming like the white master conflates with his fantasy of superseding castration, the rigidity of the Freudian model cannot account for the technologies through which this subject counteracts the constant failure of his identifications. However, it must also be recognised that, since the nonmodern bourgeois' homosocial identification with the master is governed by the masculinising modern fantasy, what the nonmodern bourgeois desires to obtain from this identification is precisely a virile hardening of his ego.

Despite his great ability to tear apart the libidinal technologies of the modern fantasy, Fanon himself fails to entirely escape its circuits, most visibly in his attempts to avoid the label of 'feminine' this fantasy casts on the nonmodern man. Fanon's discussions of both femininity and homosexuality are symptomatic of his impossibility to fully turn his back on this master-fantasy, to ignore its aggressive and constant interpellation that calls to order one of the most intimate elements of the nonmodern bourgeois' subjectivity, his masculinity. One example is Fanon's conflation of the Algerian woman with both 'natural mimicry' and the Algerian nation (for a critical summary of these discussions, see Fuss 1995, 149–152), which makes her into a figure meant primarily to sustain the Algerian man's sense of a strong ego and whose boundaries are policed by men, be they the French colonists or the Algerian anti-colonial fighters. Another is his discussion of women in 'Black Skin … ', either of the black woman who fully identifies with the white ideal and on whom Fanon (2008, 120–185) refuses to volunteer any other detail, or of the white woman whose defining psychopathology is the fantasy of being raped by a black man. As Fuss (156) also acknowledges—while trying to some extent to justify it—Fanon does not propose any serious critique of how the masculinising character of the imperial fantasy, that is, this fantasy's production of an unflinching masculinity, is central to colonial domination. This blind spot is extended to Fanon's (2008) description of homosexuality as a white man's perversion that does not affect the black man, and to his highly problematic association of white racism, or Negrophobia, with perversion, more precisely with homosexuality. Fanon identifies both homosexuality and racism as regressive (or primitive) pathologies of castration and dis-identifies from homosexuality in order to refuse the colonial label of primitivism. Reading Fanon's hypermasculine objectification of femininity and homosexuality I am left wondering: if for him racism is a specific offshoot of homosexuality, then what pathology would Fanon associate with homophobia or misogyny?

These examples suggest that, in the colonial disposition of looks, gaze, and screen, the jouissance of the nonmodern bourgeois is shaped by another disturbing element: the modern fantasy's framing of being gazed at as effemination. The modern fantasy associates woman with spectacle, with the object of the look and gaze on one hand, and man with the camera or machine gaze on the other (Silverman 1996, 126). Thus, being observed by the white gaze, as the nonmodern bourgeois fantasies he is, means to lose masculinity, that is, to have to imagine one's body according to a scheme that is not only racialised but also feminised. The colonial screen's representation of the racialised *other* as feminised[11] is systematic, as exemplified by the maps of sexual perversion fantasised by Richard Burton or Havelock Ellis where each inferior race is described in (homo) sexual terms[12] (Fuss 1995, 159–160). And while this screen also inscribes the black man as the penis which might, to some extent, threaten the white man's corporeal scheme (see Fanon 2008, Silverman 1996, 30–31), this virile image is neutralised by the association of the nonmodern subject with spectacle or with the object of study and of the phallus with European valences (knowledge, culture, civilisation, wealth, technology, and so on).

The association between the object of the colonial gaze and effeminacy is what David L. Eng (2001, 150–151) calls 'racial castration': the white man's castration of the Asian male places him in a position of lesser masculinity and secures the former's position of greater masculinity. In other words, the purpose of castrating the non-white man is denying the castration of the white man. Although Eng's work focuses on Asian Americans within the USA, his analysis can to some extent be extrapolated to other colonial encounters. The first step in this extrapolation, as mentioned, is the contestation of the psychoanalytical focus on sexualisation as the primordial factor structuring modern psychic lives. While traditional psychoanalysis subsumes all other markers of difference—race, ethnicity, class, language, nationality, and so on—to sex difference, making these differences ahistorical, a more nuanced perspective must acknowledge that racial and sexual boundaries are always mutually produced (Eng, 5). Castration is always racial. When contemporary psychoanalysis refuses to acknowledge that the correlations between (deviant) sexuality and racialisation as embodied by the figure of the savage, primitive, and so on, or that the connections between race, ontogeny, and phylogeny illustrate the fundamental logic of the Freudian oeuvre, it chooses to indiscriminately reiterate the modern racist-colonial and misogynist fantasies and dispositifs (8–14). The consolidation of the (bourgeois) symbolic order depends on the invisibility of the norms of heterosexuality and whiteness that structure this order, and it is through their invisibility that whiteness and heterosexuality maintain their structuring role (142). Psychoanalysis' erasure from its theories of the trope of racial difference they implicitly invoke secures this invisibility.

There are poignant similarities between the analyses of wounded masculinity performed by scholars of Asian-American studies and the one performed here: in 1971, Derald and Stanley Sue publish a study identifying the 'Marginal Man' as an Asian American male that acutely aspires to identify with mainstream American society, a process that demands him to deny the structural racism of his ideal and to demonstrate a:

> faithful allegiance to the universal norms of abstract equality and collective national membership at the same time as he displays an uncomfortable understanding of his utter disenfranchisement from these democratic ideals. (cited in Eng 2001, 22)

This fetishistic disavowal can be psychologically accommodated only through a fantasy of seamless equivalence between bourgeois subjects, which conditions the marginal man's identifications on his acceptance of the liberal fictions of universalism and harmony (23). More precisely, the nonmodern bourgeois' identification with the white ideal both presupposes and reiterates the ideological operations of the modern fantasy.

In the early 2000s, when the USA sent to Bucharest an openly gay ambassador, many young Romanians I have conversed with experienced this as an attempt to 'humiliate us as a nation', making homophobia, heterosexism, and implicitly, a form of Christian orthodox moral rectitude the essence of Romanian-ness, much in the same way as Fanon denied the existence of 'true' homosexuality among the men of Martinique. At the time of writing, the homophobia (homosexuality has been made illegal in Russia) and misogyny (especially understood as the desire to keep women 'in their place') of the public discourse in many Eastern European countries are acute. In the same breath, Romania, Bulgaria, Hungary, and Croatia's response to the circuits of immigration coming from war-torn Syria through fascist discourses, armed citizens' militia patrolling the borders, police and army violence, and the building of walls around their borders seems to confirm Wendy Brown's (2010, 107–133) insight that the desire for walls encompasses the desire for recuperating one's masculinity or sovereignty threatened by the penetration and the weakening of the protective State, and is further complicated by the tactic of countries like Canada, Germany, or Sweden to accept asylum seek-ers, in limited numbers and sometimes hand-picked.[13]

I can offer some more mundane examples of the nonmodern bour-geois' relation with effeminacy. In a conversation I had in 2010 with a rich Romanian entrepreneur in his mid-40s, he volunteered insights about his European travels that outline the shape of the modern racial-sexual fan-tasy in the psyche of the nonmodern bourgeois: during a one-week busi-ness trip to Sweden, he managed to discover deep secrets: 'Sweden had no delinquency to speak of before they brought over Arab and Turkish men to invigorate the degenerating stock of the Nation; these have brought in crime now'. This fantasy of racial degeneracy—of the placid, overfed, asexual Northern men and of the virile, over-breeding, criminal brown men—not only sutures reality for my interlocutor but also allows him to gain some dignity in his rocky relationship with the phallic white master.

In what follows, I will analyse the elements of the psychic economy I call the nonmodern bourgeois using a variety of data: academic and media discourses as well as 'anecdotal' data collected directly through informal discussions. This anecdotal information, as its official appel-lative indicates, is a type of data that those branches of social analysis mired in the fantasy of accuracy, objectivity, and generally scientism dis-card as vulgar and apocryphal, void of the prestige and epistemological value guaranteed by rigorous research methods. This scorn is to my mind misplaced: this is the 'purest' type of data one can collect, since elicited by everyday games of desire and identification and, as such, mobilising well-rehearsed, habitual mechanisms of self-presentation and jouissance. Informal conversations often bring to the fore tactics of the self used when one's image and position in the racial-erotic classifications of modernity are challenged much more poignantly than the highly formalised envi-ronments of sociological interviews or focus groups.

Ethnic Jouissance

The examples I use to exemplify the jouissance of the nonmodern bour-geois are drawn from Romania, a periphery that only very problemati-cally occupies the position of 'white' or 'European' in the modern fantasy.

Eastern Europe, in its various guises, has been for centuries a Western fantasy, a pseudo-Orient that represents everything reviled and secretly desired: lasciviousness, perversion, barbarism, despotism, cruelty, primitivism, irrationality, backwardness, animalism, and so on. This liminal position of this Eastern European space, inside/outside Europe, makes it a most interesting for a discussion of the nonmodern bourgeois' identifications and jouissance.

Alexander Kiossev (2008) has already been touching on the issue of the relationship between the Eastern European ego and the European gaze. His essay points out some of the elements of the Eastern European nonmodern bourgeois' will-to-not-know that the present analysis also considers central: the phallic position assumed by Europe in the nonmodern bourgeois' fantasies and the traumatic aspect of his eager identification with the master. Since it is employing Charles Taylor's concept of 'social imagination', which refers to a body of vaguely defined 'intuitive knowledge' or 'pre-theoretical shared perceptions', Kiossev's essay cannot account for the mechanisms that turn such 'pre-theoretical perceptions' into ego-boosting mechanisms, that is, for the mechanisms that invest these perceptions with libidinal valences. But it initiates a discussion of how colonial apparatuses manage to create a 'public stage' on which the colonial subject imagines himself standing, assessed by the colonial gaze, and that prompts him to adopt a language of backwardness or underdevelopment in order to self-describe. I would once more insist on the strict correlation between the confinement of the subaltern's conducts to the colonial public stage and his adoption of the modern fantasy as an overarching narrative frame: no subject can be fantasmatically placed under the European gaze unless he desires Europe. For the nonmodern subjects that reject the modern fantasy, the only colonial governmental solutions are the surveillance of the concentration or work camp or extermination. Therefore, driving a sharp divide between the psychology of the subjects colonised de facto (e.g. India) and that of those colonised only hegemonically (e.g. Romania), as Kiossev does in order to define the process of 'self-colonising' as specifically Balkanic, seems misplaced. Any successful colonisation, be it in India or in Romania, involves a process of 'self-colonisation', that is, the subaltern's adoption of the hegemonic dispositifs of modernity as the sources of his desire and enjoyment. Thus, the lack of anti-colonial radicalness in Eastern European subjects, which Kiossev compares negatively with Fanon's anti-colonialism, cannot be explained simply by the absence of direct military or administrative control from Western powers. They must be analysed in relation to these various subjects' fraught processes of identification with the 'white' master within the framework of the modern fantasy: there is radical resistance in Romania and 'self-colonisation' in Algeria, India, or Martinique.

Fanon (2008, 101), in his own study of the 'self-colonisation' of the Antillean, argues that the positioning of the colonised under the white gaze creates a feeling of impotence and shame, leading to specific forms of neurosis:

> The black man (sic) stops behaving as an *actional* person. His actions are destined for 'the Other' (in the guise of the white man), since only 'the Other' can enhance his status and give him self-esteem. (Fanon 2008, 132)

His account, while gesturing significantly towards the obsessive loops of recognition between coloniser and colonised, remains mired in Sartre's hyper-isolationist ontology where the *other* is always an intrusion upon the self. However, this self-referential loneliness is not an absolute ontological condition of subjectivity; it is an effect of modern governing technologies, which create the possibility of imagining absolute difference by erasing the structuring presence of the *other* from the self. In which case, the actions of *any* subject are destined for the O/other, the only guarantees of selfhood. The particularity of the colonial relation rather consists in manufacturing an ontological antagonism between the coloniser and the colonised, and in the nonmodern bourgeois' mistaking of the white man for the source of the gaze. The source of the impotence and shame experienced by the nonmodern bourgeois is that of any bourgeois shame: his submission to the pleasures promised by the modern fantasy. However, within this relation, the nonmodern bourgeois is shamed not only because of having submitted to the law but also because this law is that of the colonial master. As a result, the nonmodern bourgeois develops a fetishistic attachment to Europe as a transcendent object of desire,[14] combined with a masochistic enjoyment of one's racial trauma and symptomatically expressed as a pronounced tendency towards self-debasement.

We should remember Wendy Brown's (2001, 46) analysis of masochistic political desire already discussed in the previous chapter, where one's shameful desire for the law mutates into the desire to be punished for one's otherness, to keep restaging one's scene of subjection and violation. The pleasurable repetition of this moment of injury at the master's hands becomes a compulsive need of the othered subject, since it is through this recognition that doubles as a punishment that he is reassured of the solidity of his identity and of the wholeness of the entire modern fantasy on which this identity depends (Brown, 56). Each repetition of the injurious recognition re-confirms the status of the master as the phallic entity that can grant recognition and, thus, being. The nonmodern bourgeois constructs specific forms of enjoyable injury: 'the white master punishes my kind and we well deserve it, since we failed to become civilized', which often pass through interesting contortions of the type 'I am not of my own kind'.

I will describe below a set of symptoms connected to the fantasy of nation and ethnicity, a most delicate matter for a subject ethnically relegated to the status of nonmodern. Before that, though, I will reiterate in the context of nationalism a point already made, namely my distrust of any postulation of pre-social and pre-linguistic origins of subjectivity. The modern subject's libidinal investments in the I/*other* constructions staged by the modern fantasy go a long way towards explaining the quasi-religious passion that the nation, or ethnicity, elicits in the subject (Stavrakakis 2007, 193–194). It is, however, more perilous to suggest, as Stavrakakis (ibid.) does, that this attachment happens through the post-hoc investment of nationalist discourses with affect deriving from a pre-symbolic libidinal reservoir. Freud famously hypothesises that such an inborn reservoir exists, as if affect is produced and stored in some sort of endocrine gland. Moreover, he suggests that this stock of libido has natural, pre-dug psychic paths: the pleasure drive and the death drive. But the fascist discourses and power relations that Stavrakakis and I equally attack can very easily appropriate such nineteenth-century bioscientific explanations of nationalism. After all, today's fascist discourses are all about 'ethnicity/culture' and more precisely about a given (Euro-Christian) people's impossibility to accommodate the libidinal charges elicited by their forced cohabitation with a 'different' (immigrant, Muslim, and so on) people. Fascists are thus able to capitalise on the idea that any of their notions of 'Us' (nation, culture, the people, race, religion, and so on) is—even if post-hoc—invested by pre-linguistic, irrepressible drives and thus to re-consolidate racism into a quasi-biological entity. The liberal solution to this conundrum would be to educate the fascists into accepting 'difference'. This facile solution leaves unquestioned the most crucial technologies of modern governing: the dispositifs that construct difference; the fundamental connections between racism and liberal governing (see Foucault 2003, 239–265); and related, the mechanisms through which modern subjects extract jouissance from racism. I would, in turn, suggest that certain authoritative constructions that shape subjectivity—for example, gender, race, ethnicity, culture, or nationality—also shape the subject's libidinal economy: her demands for love/recognition, her desire, and her enjoyment are from the beginning gendered, racialised, ethnicised, or nationalist. Identity and the affect invested in it emerge and transform simultaneously, not through post-hoc libidinal investments; indeed, it is absurd to try to separate a subject's specific jouissance from the technologies of subjectivation that shaped her. It is not education that the fascist needs, then, but to escape the modern technology of the self that reduces his jouissance to the destruction of the *other*; since it is the liberal-capitalist dispositifs themselves that regulate this jouissance, they will continue to breed fascism.

The symbiosis of identity and affect can help us understand the ambiguity of national identifications in a Euro-periphery like Romania, where the nonmodern bourgeois' attempt to boost up his personal prestige using a nationalist discourse is undermined by his investment in the modern fantasy that catalogues his nation as deficient. Hence, a tension between his yearning for nationalist jouissance and the definition of 'proper' national jouissance by the colonial dispositifs, which tether peripheral nationalist discourses and affect to the 'catching up with the West' scenario. Various historical events complicate this equation. For example, after mid-nineteenth century, the Wallachian, Transylvanian, and Moldavian progressive bourgeoisie trained in the European centres promoted autochthonism and nationalism as a form of gaining sovereignty from the Turkish and Austro-Hungarian empires and of joining the group of 'civilised' liberal nations of Europe (see e.g. Cornis-Pope 2007, 17–18). However, after the World War II, aggressive nationalism became the fief of a socialist regime that was attacking everything the local bourgeoisie held dear and thus started being perceived by the latter as a form of distancing Romania from Western Europe. Hence the nonmodern bourgeois' fraught relationship with Romanian nationalism, associated in his psyche with the jouissance of despots[15] and of the lowly masses. Since the nonmodern bourgeois feels that he cannot enjoy the nationalist myth as fully as those white masters living in civilised and successful nations, he procures some alternative enjoyment by projecting his ethnic shame on the internal *other*, the 'vulgum' that enjoys in obscene and unself-conscious manners, 'dragging us down' in the international polls of propriety and desirability. After 1990, the collective rituals of the 'uneducated masses', from barbequing in the public spaces to the enjoyment of traditional Romanian music, remained in the eyes of the nonmodern bourgeois primitive forms of enjoyment, not only revulsive to witness but also offending the eyes of the master, 'making us look bad'. The nonmodern bourgeois' gut-felt hatred of the oriental-pop music style 'manele', whose popularity is possibly the most significant musical phenomenon in Romania after 1990, brings even more to the fore the racist foundations of this entire projection, since 'manele' was predominantly created and performed by the Rroma community.

Nationalist fantasies of fall from grace and the 'golden age' no doubt persist in the nonmodern bourgeois' libidinal panoply, but they usually represent one's castration at the hand of an even more reviled nonmodern: the Turks, the Mongols, the Russians, the communists, and so on. Studying the Oriental fantasies of writers North and South of the Danube, Cornis-Pope (2007, 14) notices that on the proto-Romanian shore, the Ottoman empire was represented as 'evil', dysfunctional, and yet enslaving, non-Christian, irrational and mystical. An 1853 text by the mayor of Timișoara, a Transylvanian city, displays all the core elements of the modern fantasy's framing of 'difference' between the civilised West and the primitive East: the mayor calls his city 'the furthermost bastion of contemporary civilization towards the Orient … where the brilliant spirit of modern civilization [exemplified by the flourishing cities of Germany and Austria] is still struggling to take root' (Cornis-Pope, ibid.). When looking towards the West, this resolutely modern mayor sees fantasy itself, the place where the 'spiritual formations of an entire section of the World are reflected in a converging mirror' (ibid. 14–15). Today, Romanian nonmodern bourgeois born in Transylvania, which was colonised up to 1918 by the severe Austro-Hungarian Empire, can still show their disgust at the lazy, dirty, dishonest, and cunning Balkanised Southerners that until 1877 used to be part of the lax Ottoman empire. The effect of these obsessions is not always comical: often they are transposed into fascist fantasies of social order, racial degeneracy, and racial cleansing that parallel those of the Euro-masters.

As a result of this fraught relationship with nationalism and ethnicity, forms of self-racism that equate 'Romanian' and 'primitive' became historically a common discursive tactic of the local bourgeoisie and survive today in various forms. The Romanian nonmodern bourgeois delights in expressions like 'Ca la noi la nimeni', roughly 'nowhere in the world is as bad as here'; or 'Suntem un neam necivilizat'— 'we are an uncivilized people'. Disappointed by the vulgarity (again, in its original sense as conducts of the *vulgum*, people), mediocrity, and backwardness of his compatriots, the nonmodern bourgeois enjoys this very disappointment that, he knows, makes him more like the master. Thus, he equates Romanians with savagery, animalism, barbarity, orientalism, balkanisation, slovenliness, corruption, and so on, the very same traits ascribed them by the modern fantasy (and more recently applied by the liberal discourses of degeneracy to the internal other, the 'part of no part'; see Agamben 1998; Foucault 2003).

Since the master's gaze is permanently present in the nonmodern bourgeois' psyche, it results in such interesting productions as 'Romania in the UK', broadcasted by the most 'Americanised' private TV channel in Romania, ProTV. Through interviews with émigrés that 'made it' into respectable professional positions in London, this exposé tries to dispel the British myth that all Romanians are primitives, criminals, or prostitutes. That is an attempt to compel the master's gaze to make the same class distinctions that the nonmodern bourgeois does, between the jouissance of the primitive Romanian masses and the proper jouissance of the Romanian bourgeois who desires to become like the master and/or take his position. I have recently witnessed a conversation in the Carturesti bookshop in Bucharest which exemplifies this conduct fairly well: an expat lady was browsing with evident glee through books on world conspiracy and the socialist secret police while describing to a friend the Germans she now lives among: 'Pai ce calitate, ce educatie au oamenii aia!' 'Oh, but what quality, what education these people have!' She didn't mean that Germans are better trained in understanding Heidegger, say, but that their habitus is that of proper, civilised, 'white' people. And, in a modified form of exchange-value fetishism, she equated 'quality' with an essence of the object, that is, with a racial trait of the Germans that the Romanians can never accede to. Her symptom offered this nonmodern bourgeois the double thrill of enjoying the Romanians' punishment by the severe German father and of momentarily enjoying the position of the gaze. This sliding between habitus, 'quality', and race/ethnicity explains why the nonmodern bourgeois' difficult relationship with the nation fuels her obsession with propriety.

The Colonial Habitus Wars and 'Switched at Birth'

If any bourgeois subject is a creature of habitus whose sense of self is predicated on performing properly, repeatedly, and under risk of disqualification from socio-ontological status ritual acts of symbolic belonging—eating, hygiene, grooming, dressing, speech and vocabulary, and so on; then the nonmodern bourgeois is particularly obsessed with such proper performance. Indeed, the socialist bourgeoisie's desire to 'return to civilisation' (or, in its more normative version, to 'return to normality') was fuelled by their notion that this civilisation/normality—that is, liberal-capitalism— nurtures the 'natural' differences between social groups, more precisely between the elites and the vulgum. Their discontent was provoked by the socialist regime's (partial) levelling of income and consumption that allowed no distinction between their civilised status and the primitivism of the working classes, who were driving the same cars, eating the same food; living in the same houses; going to the same schools, theatres, and opera houses; and holidaying in the same places.

After 1990, the nonmodern bourgeois started engaging in a desperate race to discover the philosopher's stone that will transmute him into a proper, European bourgeois. Aurelia Marinescu's (2015) best-selling *The code of good manners today*, for example, a book on etiquette, went through four editions at the time of writing. Not at all relegated to the status of interbellum quirk, the nonmodern bourgeois' hunger for 'proper manners' is as burning as ever:

> Following the extraordinary success of the book with the public … [the author] has been invited to talk on radio and television, to give interviews, to write about civilised behaviour in wide distribution magazines, to teach courses on proper manners at the University of Bucharest's Faculty of Communication and Public Relations. (Marinescu 2015, inner sleeve publicity blurb)

The 1995 edition of the book features a back cover endorsement by a 'Romanian student' who argues: 'this book should be read by twenty-two million people', that is, by the entire population of Romania at the time. Here, the population is enlisted en masse under the signifier 'uncivilised' or 'lacking quality' and needs active re-education into proper habitus in order to join the Western family of great nations. In the preface to the 2015 edition, Marinescu, now 83 years old, allegedly after conversations with some of her young followers, notices a change in social norms towards a more 'natural, spontaneous and relaxed' manner, a striking similarity with Eichler's (1934; see the discussion in the second chapter) assessment of American manners. And, like Eichler before her, Marinescu wants the rules of civilised behaviour prescribed by her book to become a 'second nature'. Bourgeois habitus seems to permanently (but asymptotically) strive towards naturalness and spontaneity, towards becoming the invisible substance of 'normal life' that one does not need to learn, and seems to permanently be in need of having its naturalness bolstered by new editions of etiquette books or whatever their current equivalent is. 'Become what you are!' the already-mentioned performative act that becomes the subject's *fatum* (Bourdieu 2003, 122) is in the case of the bourgeois in need of constant reiteration. Such setbacks are irrelevant to Marinescu (2015, 6), who remains a staunch believer in the natural, universal, transcendent, even, essence of bourgeois propriety: 'Without abdicating from the basic principles of good manners, which I consider to be eternal, I have however "sweetened" some norms of conduct'. And further, 'good manners are not, and will never become, useless, because they are what makes the human respect herself in the first place' (19), or 'etiquette has not been added arbitrarily to social structures. They have roots in a deep human feeling, which aspires towards harmony between behaviour and ethics, between the human's beauty of character and her morality' (20). And in a moment of theoretical lucidity that comes close to Althusser's (2008) theory of interpellation, Marinescu (ibid.) exposes the integration of bourgeois habitus with the law: as any normal (sic) person lives with the fear of the policeman that might appear at any moment and catch them in the illegal act, they should equally be afraid of breaking the laws of etiquette.

Marinescu's chapters are almost identical in focus with those of Eichler's book, sporting titles like 'How a mannered person looks and behaves' (with subchapters like 'Less perfume, more soap...' or 'How to move, how to sit down, how to walk, how to behave'); 'How to say hello'; 'How to introduce oneself'; 'The art of conversation' (among the subchapters: 'Compliments'; 'What needs to be excluded from conversation'; 'How to keep up and how to finish a conversation'); 'Table manners – the cornerstone of education' (Marinescu teaches her readers how to match their wines with their fish or hors d'oeuvres and what aperitifs or digestifs are proper; 'The ladies will be served liqueur and the gents cognac, in special glasses'); 'How to behave in public and professional life' (stand-out subchapters: 'In front of authorities and the court'; 'How to treat the serving personnel'), and so on. Deference to authority remains a central element of 'natural bourgeois propriety', since social hierarchy is itself a defining element of a civilised society. Marinescu informs us at some point that, while it is forbidden to use one's surname while greeting them (e.g. 'Hello, Mr Popescu!'), the director of a big factory or an officer might do so with their subalterns, and it should be considered as a compliment paid to the subaltern that the authority knows their name. The initiation of the greeting, we are also taught, should be done by the person of 'superior social rank'.

At a first glance, the bourgeois habitus prescribed in Marinescu's book seems imported wholesale from equivalent texts written by Westerners. However, if one is attentive, the positional difference between the metropolitan bourgeois and the nonmodern bourgeois remains visible. All throughout this manual, there is an insinuation, never clearly stated but ever-present: the ideal that Romanians should strive to become and the gaze that scrutinises the adequacy of Romanian propriety is the Westerner. 'In certain countries, where people are careful about their health, like in Germany, people do not smoke inside the house' (124). 'Clothes for going out in the city do not include hoodies, down jackets, boots or après-ski. In our country, due to poverty, cold and the misery of the past decades, to go to work in such outfits (proper for mountaineering) became a habit. No matter how non-conformist the people in the West might be, such "equipment" will cause a sensation in any of the great Western-European capitals' (133). The contrast between Romanian 'misery' and the necessity to match your fish with specific types of white wine does not strike Marinescu—after all, it is not for these misery-stricken people that she is writing. 'For a citizen coming from a *civilised* country, the disorder that characterises traffic in our country is inconceivable. I have seen people in Sweden waiting patiently at the red light, although it was past midnight and the streets were deserted' (147, my emphasis); finally, '[Gifting money to the doctor or nurse abroad is out of the question] because every citizen of a *civilised* country is insured medically' (158; I'm afraid that, without realising, Marinescu disqualified from the status of 'civilised' the USA she so admires as a civilisational model).

In the early 1990s, this bourgeois obsession with Western propriety resulted in the wholesale adoption of Western advertising messages, often understood as the Western ego-ideal's confidential advice, to the extent that within a few years the eating habits of an entire embourgeoisement-starved social group in Romania changed. One example is the rapid move from vulgar, cholesterol-heavy butter to the sophisticated Westerners' choice of healthy, modern margarine, an event that is even funnier if one reads Barthes' (1972) essay 'Operation margarine'. These ridiculously overpriced tubs of bourgeois propriety, imported from Germany or the Netherlands, reigned on the tables of all nonmodern bourgeois families until margarine was exposed as a mass-production ploy by the new 'natural' food fashion of the West, determining them to return to butter. Today, the quest is for the most sophisticated Western European butter—I have heard the distinguished-sounding French label 'President' mentioned by homemakers in the know. Some might also remember the much-ridiculed hours-long queues for gaining entry to the first Eastern bloc McDonald's in the early 1990s, which were accurately interpreted by Westerners as the true symptom of their symbolic victory over 'communism'. Around the same time, Romanian men had eagerly joined the international masculinity-pursuing regiments and proudly displayed their new, sophisticated manhood in the form of loyalty to Western beer brands, one of the most vital fluids of masculinity. In the early 2000s, I have often been met with the question 'what brand of beer do you like?' and I suspect the answer readily positions one in the local hierarchies of civilisation and homosociality (see Sedgwick 1990). When one is connected with his brand in such a profound manner, it is most comforting to gain from it the confirmation that one's penis is the phallus. So much so that Tuborg Romania proudly displays on the label of its flagship product: 'brewed under the supervision of Tuborg, Denmark', a seal of European quality that also rubs on the consumer and, one assumes, his privates. If the examples in this paragraph seem unimportant, one should recall the profound restructuring of power and social relations engendered in Eastern Europe by the colonial economic strategies of the European Union, a restructuring similar to what had happened in the European de jure colonies and whose effects become more and more evident in the latest crisis of capitalism.

Hygiene is another crucial signifier of this bourgeois universe, one that distinguishes proper subjects from the dirty nonmodern; and in the orders of modernity, the category nonmodern coincides most of the time with the category 'dirty'. Here, the English 'proper' returns to its semantic roots: 'propre' means 'personal ', 'property', 'proper', and 'clean' in French. Thus, 'cleanliness' can decide a bourgeois' judgement of a person, household, restaurant, plaza, city, country, continent, or entire population: 'I liked it, it was very clean … very civilized'. When I have asked a middle-class Romanian what she had found to be the most unbearable aspect of living in socialism, she answered promptly: 'lacking freedom'. She subsequently disaggregated this lack into five bourgeois obsessions: lack of career opportunities; lack of electoral competition and liberal pluralism in general; obligation to exalt publicly the party line; inability to travel abroad; and 'the lack of crucial products: toilet paper, detergent, soap, deodorant, tampons'. The socialist project was brought to its knees, in part, by its lack of consideration for bourgeois hygiene rituals. As expected, the Romanian nonmodern bourgeois is usually repulsed by the perceived dirtiness or disorder of their own city and country and fantasises the spotlessness, asepsis, and order of the West. And wherever this champion of hygiene goes, his eyes are firmly cast on the ground and in the ditches, gutters, toilets, and rubbish bins; he critically assesses the state of layers of paint, asphalt, public benches, bathroom utilities, cutlery, crockery, and bed linen, towels, hems, shirt collars, and fingernails. A Romanian bourgeois confessed he was appalled to notice that there are weeds growing on the side of the M40 motorway between London and Oxford—that overgrowth spoiled his fantasy of the perfectly groomed West.

Classifying Romanians as primitive, however, requires a concomitant strategy that absolves the Romanian bourgeois from this categorisation. This is the nonmodern bourgeois' fantasy of having being abandoned at birth by the white family of nations—a version of the poor person's fantasy of having being abandoned at birth by an aristocratic family. Born 'different' from his stock, a swan among ducks, the nonmodern bourgeois can fantasise that he is a superior being *and* preserve belief in the racial taxonomies of modernity that classify his peers as deficient. This fantasy of difference at times results in the bourgeois' literal accusation that she was abandoned by an unloving parent in the middle of a hostile, primitive social space. Observe blurts like: 'I was cursed to be born here!' (a Romanian acquaintance) or: 'Nu ne-am nascut la locul potrivit' ('We were born in the wrong place') (song by the Romanian hip-hop band Guess Who about the necessity of the 1970s cohorts to flee West). Or more generally, the ritual litany of the bourgeois under socialist regimes: 'They (the Westerners/USA/civilized or free world) have abandoned us (in the hands of evil stepmother Russia)!' The enthusiasm of the majority of Romanians for the opening of USA military bases on the national territory is the offshoot of this fantasy of abandonment ('They finally came!!') and of its other side, the paranoid fantasy that Russia will invade.

The Master's Correction and Virile Violence

This volatile mix of shame and love spurs on the nonmodern bourgeois' fantasies of being punished by the white authority ('we – or more often "they" – deserve to be punished since they are such a disappointment'). At times, this fantasy takes the form of an overt longing for the authoritarian leader who would forcefully educate the degenerate masses and rid the nation of nepotism, corruption, moral laxity, inefficiency, and any enjoyment or social relations not governed by liberal contractualism. A variety of fantasmatic figures—king, emperor, president, pope, God, fascist dictators, the Americans, or the Germans (again!)—take turns in occupying this position. The previously mentioned émigré that praised the superior education of the Germans uttered in the same breath: 'Numai cu frica ii poti educa pe astia!' ('The only way to educate those [that is, Romanians] is through fear!'). The international celebrity and historical villain extraordinaire Vlad Tepes is a particularly popular historical hero in Romania not because of his associations with vampirism but because, since the nineteenth century, bourgeois nationalist narratives represent him as a king whose sadistic exercise of sovereign power made his kingdom the 'safest' in the area, a story much liked by the nonmodern bourgeois. In the summer of 2010, citizens commemorating 20 years from the 1990 anti-communist protests in the Piata Universitatii, protests which seamlessly merged neoliberal and ultra-orthodox fascist fantasies, had banners reading: 'Vino Tepes Doamne si ridicateapa in Bucurestisa ne scapi de communism, hotiesicoruptie!'/'Come, O Lord Tepes, and raise the stake in Bucharest to rid us of communism, thievery and corruption!' There is only one step between his fantasy of a fifteenth-century despot coming back to civilise the country and the nonmodern bourgeois' allegiance to the most ruthless neoliberal leaders, for example, Margaret Thatcher or Ronald Reagan; to authoritarian modernising leaders like Peter the Great, Ataturk, or, in the Romanian case, the king Alexandru Ioan Cuza[16]; or to fascist leaders like Orban in Hungary. Indeed, just a bit South of Romania, neo-Islamists like Recep Tayyip Erdoğan—at the moment of writing, Turkish prime minister, moderniser, and resolute fascist leader—reverse the suspicions of Western liberals: they do not use the message of liberal modernisation and progress to dissimulate their true Islamic agenda; on the contrary, they complement their sincere and ruthless neoliberalism, including in its recurrent ethnic cleansing impulses, with the spiritual cover of Islam. To realise this sincerity and also the permanent fantasmatic correlation between 'neoliberalism' and 'Europe-as-phallus' in Erdoğan's public declarations, it suffices to watch the few speech extracts displayed by the documentary on Istanbul gentrification, 'Ecumenopolis': at one point Erdoğan squarely states that 'Istanbul will become the financial centre of the world!' What is this blunt but the fantasmatic re-centring of the peripheral object of spectacle (Turkey) as the point from which the capitalist light/gaze emerges?

Thus, the nonmodern bourgeois' allegiance to neoliberalism, conservatism, or downright fascism is not a whim but a coherent tactic in his arsenal of transmutation conducts.[17] Such an ultra-aggressive, unforgiving, and uncompromisingly modern stance cannot fail to demonstrate to the Other that he is a true bourgeois: hard working; law-abiding; desirous of comfort, order, and hierarchy; and individualist, competitive, able to secure, and protect his property and family. Worlds apart from the nonmodern subjects who are feeble, lazy, traditionalist, extended-family oriented bent on bargaining and negotiating, depending on mutual help and informal exchange relations and so on. The fascist fantasy is for the nonmodern bourgeois a last chance to appear to the master's gaze as the member of a strong and pure nation, with glorious historical roots. To appear as intolerant of degenerate *others* (poor, disabled, homosexuals, ethnic minorities, immigrants, communists and more generally the left,[18] etc.) as the master himself at his most virile.

I have proposed a tentative list of *others* on which the nonmodern bourgeois displaces the aggressiveness he cannot direct at the figure of the white master. This list suggests that the nonmodern bourgeois actively searches for the spectacle of feminised objects, attempting to re-assume the phallic position associated with the gaze. On the other hand, whenever such violence against 'minorities' occurs in the periphery, the Western Europeans jump at the opportunity to repress their own castration anxiety by reprimanding these barbaric *others* for their intolerance and by reaffirming themselves as the example to follow when dealing with 'difference'. This admonishing turns aggressiveness, the very conduct that in the nonmodern bourgeois' fantasy makes him more like the master, back into a spectacle, further debasing him. And reiterates the fantasy of the European's look as gaze and of his masculinity as beyond castration: 'they' are man enough to tolerate the threatening effeminate/racialised *other* without fearing the loss of their penis/phallus. The result is a hysterical escalation of the nonmodern subject's aggressiveness: further castrated by the master's scolding, his customary way out is to defy this surplus-castration and intensify the aggressive conducts the master disapproves of, since both the master's prohibition and the violence against the racialised/effeminate *other* yield masculinising jouissance.[19] This becomes one of the cycles of the nonmodern subject's drive: every time he indulges in those enjoyable acts of violence, he is further castrated by the scolding gaze, which determines a further escalation of humiliation and thus a further escalation of aggressiveness. Only so we can explain the apparently irrational fury of the Eastern Europeans against the *other*: it is not a result of ignorance, backwardness, communist brainwashing, cultural isolation, or other such liberal scapegoats, but of the same castration anxiety that generates fascism in the West. Both in the metropolis and the periphery, the modern fantasy teases out the paranoia related to the *other* as an instrument for bolstering the subject's belief in the stability of social authority and of his identity. But while the mechanism of fascism presented above is not different in the core and periphery, it does explain why the periphery exhibits such intriguing subjective forms as the 'racially inferior fascist'.

The next two sections on 'Colonial administrators' are a discussion of the nonmodern bourgeois' psychic loops as represented in 'intellectual'[20] discourses. My focus is a conscious tactic of exposing the colonial elites' and administrators' consuming desire for the white master, since these elites are constantly being groomed by their Western counterparts as the true and only voices of Eastern Europe. This was the case before World War II, when the financial-intellectual elites were the only ones invited to an audience in the master's palace. This was the case during the Cold War, when the strident cries of the anti-communist dissidents constituted a central element of Western propaganda and were given a great deal of attention, while any local endorsement of socialism was discarded as a symptom of ideological brainwashing. And it continues being the case after 1990, when these elites' aggressive desire for strict governing by Western authorities, for modernisation, and for Europeanisation made them into the colonial administrators of the 'transition towards normality'. That being said, the diffusion of the modern fantasy cannot be reduced to a top-down model but, as always the case in modern governing, is a capillary process—I will discuss the implications of this capillarity in the 'Ideology and the Masses' section, below.

The Colonial Administrators: 'Why We Love Americans'

The paranoid but highly enjoyable discourse of inadequacy in relation to the white ideal being a trait of Romanian bourgeois discourse since its inception, it was only natural that it became the loudest voice in the public discourse after 1990, when socialist-nationalist checks on the public expression of the 'intellectuals' passionate desire for the Western master were removed. A torrent of such 'intellectual' productions condemning the savagery and underdevelopment of Romania in contrast with the great nations of Europe flooded the public spaces and became the chic line of argument for anyone aspiring to the position of sophisticated, Westernised thinker. 'Grupul de Dialog Social' (The Group for Social Dialogue), 'Dilema' (The Dilemma), and 'Romania Curata' (Clean Romania) are some of the platforms that hosted these tirades. The following two sections discuss the work of two such 'intellectuals', and I will confess that I have stumbled upon their work half randomly. In fact, the particulars of these 'intellectuals' and their work are largely irrelevant to the argument; my comments are not personal attacks but attacks on a psychic economy. Thus, despite the space I am dedicating to discussing them, there is nothing particular about these examples either than being part of a fairly constant flow of similar productions on the 'Romanian situation'. I could have easily picked other 'intellectual' names and production with very similar results.

In this section, I will focus on the superbly titled 'Clean Romania' (in Romanian 'curata', 'clean' is used as an adjective, not a verb) whose catchphrase is 'Cu ochii pe voi!' ('We've got our eyes on you!'). The website hosts commentaries on the theme of corruption, starting from the classical premise that liberal-capitalism is the supreme form of social organisation, and therefore, its lack of proper functioning in backwards nations like Romania is due to their primitivism: their lack of rationality, democratic experience, honesty, personal initiative and autonomy, respect of the law, and so on. In a word: to their corruption. The articles are usually written in a vernacular but self-righteous tone, exhibiting the arrogance of the colonial lackey feeling protected in the shadow of the master. What unites most of the authors publishing on this platform is the already-mentioned desire for an authoritarian leader or form of governing, and neoliberalism embodies for them this virile strength. I will comment on a series of texts published on this formidable platform by one of its most committed master-adoring and primitive-flagellating 'intellectuals', Alina Mungiu-Pippidi.

Mungiu-Pippidi is both an arduous political commentator in Romania and a zealous colonial administrator,[21] acting as an intermediary between the white master's interests, his gaze, and the nonmodern. It is relevant that this passionate admirer of the West is an expert in State building, democracy, and anti-corruption, some of the central discursive tools of contemporary colonialism. And indeed, her relationship with the Western ego-ideal is nothing less than unbridled adoration: the first text I will engage with is entitled 'Why We Love Americans' (http://www.romania-curata.ro/de-ce-iubim-americanii/), an erotically charged ode to the hyper-masculine ideal of the Trans-Atlantic white man. This love sonnet starts dramatically: a parallel is drawn between the 9/11 United Airlines flight 93 incident and the Amsterdam-Paris Thalys train incident in 2015. The similarity Mungiu-Pippidi draws out is that, in both cases, courageous passengers attacked their attackers. In the first case, the brave plane passengers were mostly Americans; in the second, the three men that first attacked the person armed with a machine gun that was menacing the train passengers were also Americans. You can feel the author's libidinal flows swirling around these almost divine effigies of virile martial bravery: '*Miraculously* in the train there were three Americans, one from the Air Force (off duty), one from the National Guard (taking a holiday from Afghanistan in tranquil Europe) and a third a Californian, their friend' (my emphasis). I will continue with a quote which compensates for its length by displaying a very rich tapestry of nonmodern bourgeois identifications: the contrast between the bravery and gallantry of the white men and the cowardice and lack of civility of the Romanian locals; the continuity between the demi-godly qualities of these virile men and Western liberal democracy, freedom, wealth, and so on; the idealisation of the Western society as a space of perfect harmony and homogenous (white, masculinist, neoliberal, and settler colonial) values, a space which creates the superior qualities of these American men effortlessly, almost naturally; the author's identification with the great men of Western civilisation (in this case Thomas Jefferson); and her persistent attempts—which characterise the entire body of work she publishes in 'Clean Romania'—to place herself on the side of the white gaze, dissociate herself from the abject Eastern European subjects and make herself not only similar but also desirable to the master. On top of which, the text oozes a delightfully infatuated tone, full of invocations of impregnation, and ethereal discharges:

And actually, you can only ask yourself what kind of culture is this Anglo-Saxon one, which creates such men, while in our countries if a thief aggresses an old lady on the bus, people don't know how to look the other way faster? And it's not by chance. A few years ago, I was on my way to see Thomas Jefferson's house, one of the fathers of the American Constitution I very much admire, in Monticello, Virginia. [follows a story of one of the tires on her old car exploding and her being rescued by yet another macho gallant figure, a US Marine she describes as 'a boy of around 30 years old'] ... [the Marine] had never been to Monticello and didn't plan to. He knew Jefferson from the photo in his primary school textbooks. Blessed these cultures that have internalised such values: courage, solidarity, integrity, dignity, initiative, transmitted by the sports coach, the parents and the community without any need for special moral, religious or civic education classes or museum visits (although the latter are worth it). Which [values] impregnate one from the people around him and then exude towards anyone happening to pass through these lands, a highway companion for example [that is, herself].

The text is followed by a string of comments from the readers, which suggest that the love for the white master and the (self-)hatred of the subaltern extend beyond the confines of the rarefied environment of the 'intellectuals':

Paun: It's fine to admire them, but it would be even better to learn how to take on their educational model in family and society. The model that determines them to behave in this manner. Decided, rationally judging the situation and acting subsequently. If you're going to die, at least you should try something.

Emil: As a psychiatrist [the contributor misspells 'psychiatrist' in Romanian; in fact Mungiu-Pippidi graduated from the Faculty of Psychology of the Bucharest University] you understand better than lay people the 'reward system' [in English in original] and 'reinforcement mechanisms' [in English in original] and how they contribute to morality ('moral brain' [in English in original])—I have used the English terms for precision, I am not a professional and I don't possess the jargon, in fact I suspect that it doesn't really exist in Romanian, in a society which, through its leaders, looked for pretexts like Transcendental Meditation in order to take psychology off the list of sciences. This is where the difference lies. Romanian society, built by communists and by Illich's 'social democrats', looks more like the footage of the experiment that went viral on YouTube, about a group of monkeys that perform the same activity but some receive as reward grapes and others slices of cucumber. ['Illich' is the nickname given to the social-democrat politician Ion Iliescu, former Romanian president, by the liberal centre-right]

Parintele: I, as a priest, realise that the Americans are our true Orthodox and Catholic, meaning universal, Christians, at the same time. May God give them health and prosperity! [this intervention is rather awkwardly phrased, I tried to preserve some of this clumsiness while also making it intelligible].

Radu Radoslav: Too bad nothing is done in order to understand individualistic cultures, so that we can ourselves change our behaviour.

Spânu: In what regards cowardice (let's not shy away from the truth), Mrs Pippidi argued a statistical point, it doesn't mean there aren't exceptions, but they confirm the rule: how many times, in the street or in the public transport, have we seen 20–30 'citizens' witnessing like sheep, their eyes turned away (if they could they would also turn away their ears) the aggression of a thief or a drunk (when there are 2–3 of them we cannot count on any reaction), the dirty words or spitting? Actually, I believe, this explains the lack of civic spirit and of any reaction concerning the gross thefts from public funds (meaning our funds). When, with the crassest lack of propriety, the officials raised their wages a few times, not even one hundred crazy people went out in the public spaces to protest ... it happened during the holidays, ha ha!

I will not extend much longer this discussion of Pippidi's texts—suffice to say that all her arguments display the same blend of eroticised investment in the figure of the white master and strong belief in the infallibility, truthfulness, and goodness of neoliberal governing. The entry called 'how a successful country looks like and why we [Romania] are not one of them', using data from her book on governance and corruption published by Cambridge University Press, displays her other passion: the quantification and measurement of social development according to the classical liberal-capitalist criteria of GDP growth, income/capita, Global Competitiveness Scores, corruption, and so on, and showcases her profound aversion against any form of deviation from the model of individualism exhibited by the USA. Such deviation is treated as a symptom of weakness, feminisation, and primitivism (about a Romanian government that used 40 % of its budget on public spending she says 'some liberal government we had, they spent more than the socialists!'). This obsessive measuring and comparing of countries using indexes of good administrative innovation, governance, and competitiveness devised by the liberal Western experts allows Mungiu-Pippidi to jubilantly prove, again and again, the deficiency of her nation. Romania seems to constantly rank last in Europe in her classifications. These national rankings, of course, are a thinly veiled substitute for the colonial civilisational or developmental hierarchies in which one's position is assessed according to how much they resemble the Western model as described by the Western experts themselves. I will give one, last, quote of how these rankings are displayed and how imbricated they are with fantasies in which desirability and success are equated with one nation's identification with another, 'whiter' nation:

> The top of countries that received international anti-corruption assistance is one of failure—Ukraine, Nigeria, Egypt, Vietnam, Western Balkans (sic), Bulgaria, and so on. What really functions are passionate locals that aspire by themselves to become like others—Estonians like the Finns, Koreans like the Japanese, Slovenians like Austrians—and adopt reforms by themselves, which is also why they put them in practice.

The Colonial Administrators: Primitivism and Mass Trauma

I discuss next (Popescu-Sandu 2010) an academic paper written by a Romanian émigré working in a US university and published in an English-language edited book on post-communist nostalgia: a text addressed directly to the white man. For the first decade after 1990, most studies on the 'post-communist situation' have been performed by Western 'experts', considered the only ones in control of the master knowledge that would allow dis-entangling this messy affair of the East. In the same vein, since 1990, the 'know-how' about social organisation—democratisation, 'free-market' economics, social policy, the non-governmental sector, culture, urbanisation, entertainment and even resistance, and social movements—has been provided by Western European companies and experts, of course at prices adequate for such a crucial service. The white gaze has been, for more than a century now, materialised as 'expertise' and lucratively exported around the world.

Popescu-Sandu's text is a study of the 'Eastern European psyche' and mobilises all the sapiential authority conferred by the white master's formal endorsement. Its underlying theme reiterates the standard conservative political science construction of the 'communist man': brainwashed by decades of totalitarian regime, this poor soul has lost all ability to resist authority and is reduced to a passive and complete identification with State propaganda, unable to make choices, to find his own path, to think for himself, or to engage in the dynamic, innovative, and risk-taking activities specific to a proper (Western) subject. The over-determined figure of the 'communist man' used by various liberals to explain the East's inability to ever 'catch up' with its Western ego-ideal is an adaptation of the colonial description of the 'primitive', the wretched creature forever stuck at an embryonic stage of development from which her circular socio-psychological processes are unable to extricate her. That the nonmodern bourgeois enjoys repeating this discourse is symptomatic of the mesmeric effect the modern fantasy has on her libidinal economy. The impossible to bridge gap between the primitive and the master that all these 'intellectuals' obsessively invoke is a projection of their own racial castration anxiety, of the impossible to bridge gap between themselves and the white ego-ideal.

Popescu-Sandu's (114) question is: 'why is it that some post-Communist subjects are not equipped for and cannot sustain their own transition through the present?' I will remind the reader that throughout the shock therapy decades imposed by the International Monetary Fund, these 'unequipped' subjects had to deal with the effects of a violent phase of capitalist primitive accumulation: abrupt and disastrous immiseration, wildly escalating prices and inflation, rampant unemployment due to the closure or privatisation of most of Romania's industrial production units and national services (water, telephone, electricity, and so on), and aggressive efforts to re-engineer desire and enjoyment that affected both self-understandings and social networks, at times bringing certain social spaces in Romania on the brink of civil war. I would hypothesise that, despite Popescu-Sandu's positing of their chronic lack of proper equipment for dealing with change, the Romanian 'subjects' managed to survive a fast succession of degrading radical social transformations. Oblivious to these transformations, the author resolutely continues her line of argument: the 'communist person' is stuck in a position of total passivity, unable to 'contribute' to the capitalist present and equally unable to nostalgically mobilise the socialist past as a resource (115). Comically failing to understand Žižek's (see, for example, his intervention in Butler et al. 2000, 121–4) discussion of 'choosing the impossible' and of the false choice involved by the socialism-to-capitalism transition,[22] she somehow thinks it refers to the pathology of the communist person: 'This wave of [capitalist] choices comes to a group of people who are not accustomed to choose a path for themselves, especially in political and social terms … ' (115). Plainly put, Romanians simply do not have what it takes to become a modern (capitalist) subject: ' … few post-Communist citizens had the knowledge, the energy, and the courage to adapt to capitalism and succeed' (115). She repeats this conviction further on in a classical neoliberal argument that equates any form of resistance to capitalism with primitivism or 'fear of change':

> Besides, the post-Communist present is not the static life of Communist present, which some people have described as frozen in time. The Golden

Age of Capitalism will not materialize itself ... for both internal and external reasons. Among the internal reasons, one of the strongest is fear of change. This particular fear is even stronger in Romania where the transformations of the thaw and of perestroika did not have any effect. (116)

While Popescu-Sandu (2010, 115) quotes Svetlana Boym's argument according to which communist teleology was an intoxicating ideology that the post-communist masses have difficulties replacing, the present work makes the opposite argument. It is the metropolitan bourgeoisie—including the émigrés—that is most intoxicated by liberal-capitalist ideology and most passionately in love with the authorities governing them. In Romania under socialism, as in any regime that governs predominantly through sovereign power, the population's distance from and distrust of authority and official ideology is comparatively greater. This distrust of (autochthonous) governing authorities became even more acute recently. Unfortunately, the carefully engineered absence of fantasmatic alternatives to capitalism, an absence to which Popescu-Sanda's text is a minor contributor, makes these subjects an easy prey for the modern fantasy, and the 2016 anti-governmental protests in Romania were performed under the typical nonmodern bourgeois banners of 'anti-corruption' and demands for a 'technocratic government'. While hating local authorities, the young protesters seemed to be in love with the white master.

What, then, accounts for the persistence of this chronic inability Romanians have in becoming proper capitalist subjects? Paradoxically, a lack of trauma. And more specifically, a lack of national trauma written and performed in narcissistic key, that is, as martyrdom at the hands of socialism. The memory of the nation, that is, the traumatic memory of socialism, survived 'in the marginal circles of intellectuals, but the common person is completely confused' (Tismăneanu quoted in Popescu-Sandu 2010, 118). There is no consensus about the necessity to represent this past as traumatic in the collective memory—survivors' testimonies and the secret police's archives are being ignored, and 'their existence has not been widely known and has not been inscribed into the discourse of the public sphere' (ibid.). And, for the author and her kind, the problem is that any properly modern subject would register the socialist past as traumatic, since it represents a violent deviation from the developmental path prescribed by the modern fantasy, the antithesis of the modern West, a historical abomination. Only a subject that does not idealise the West and its achievements would fail to register socialism as abominable. And of course, only a barbarian fails to idealise the West. To cope with this rejection of the West, Popescu-Sandu reads as pathology the Romanian population's refusal to represent socialism as a trauma: a desire to regress to an infantile stage of ontogenesis and phylogenesis, the very same position she ascribes to this subject from the start. This population is not only primitive but also desiring to stay so.

I have already argued (see Chap. 2) that bourgeois trauma and its symptoms do not stimulate the subject's critical engagement with the mechanisms through which a particular event is represented as a trauma. Instead, bourgeois trauma hides the subject's castration and his libidinal investment in what happened (his enjoyment of authoritative regulation) behind imaginary curtains. It is the bourgeois' necessity to cover up his shameful libidinal traces that transforms events into traumas. And once represented, mnemonically, discursively, or otherwise, as a trauma, an experience not only becomes the gravitational centre around which all psychic processes circle, but also manages to produce, at each loop, symptoms that are enjoyable enough to blind the sufferer to any structural context, social relation, experience, or communication that does not refer back to the subject's suffering. The bourgeois mobilisation of trauma then, even when unconscious, is an instrument for demanding unconditional recognition, including from one's masters, in the name of one's suffering.

This is the specific trauma of the Romanian 'intellectual': witness, as an example of 'proper' cultivation of martyrdom, Herta Müller's obsessive campaign against Romanian communism, a fantasmatic evil that continues to galvanise her. Not only her acceptance speech for the Noble Prize recounted, yet again, her suffering at the hands of the Romanian secret police. But in 2010, she warned the European Union that its lack of including a clause about investigating communist crimes among the conditions for the accession of new countries, including Romania, has been naïve. This compulsive staging of trauma for the benefit of the white gaze blames Müller's lack, past and present, on the persecutions of 'communism', the nemesis of Western civilisation, and uses the trauma of the 'dissidents' under the socialist regime to enact her rapprochement to the structural position of the white gaze. Her staging of heroic martyrdom, on the other hand, displays Müller's unconditional submission to the liberal-capitalist ideology of freedom and progress.

So, Popescu-Sandu's secret fear symptomatically expressed as panic at the Romanians' lack of trauma is that Romanians fail to idealise the white master. And the symptom provides the cure: the only way out of this conundrum is constructing a homogenous representation of the socialist past as trauma according to the narratives produced by the 'intellectuals'. This, like its Western model, would be a society of 'survivors' where history is established by State bureaucrats and bourgeois 'intellectuals' ('historians', 'official archives', etc.). The aim is ambitious: nothing less than to stop the slide of signification: the 2006 Tismaneanu Report on the 'Communism and its abuses' (121) is, according to her, 'meant to give added intellectual, moral, and official weight to historical events and to stop the sliding of memory' (ibid.).

Popescu-Sandu's decrying of a lack of public discussion of socialism is imagined: in Romania, there have already been produced a sleuth of memoirs, articles, books, films, and documentaries on the 'crimes of communism'; her fear is, as already suggested, engendered by something else than the absence of such materials, namely by the refusal of the great part of the population to make this interpretation of the past into the determining factor of their present life. A tendency that, of course, is amplified in the younger generations, filling these middle-aged 'intellectuals' with the panic that they are losing the battle over who can define 'what holds everyone together', to use Bruno Latour's term.[23] In fact, the only ones addicted to stagnation are these 'intellectuals' that want to preserve their colonial fantasy in the formaldehyde of trauma. Unable to perceive anything about Romania that does not fit the modern narrative of inferiority, they will probably continue to ask the same tired questions for quite a long time.

Ideology and the 'Masses'

Adapting a point already made in studies of nationalism (see e.g. Benedict Anderson 2006, 37–83), Alexander Kiossev (2008) argues that the diffusion of the modern fantasy and its transformation into a fundamental libidinal framework in Eastern Europe were performed by the bourgeois elites educated abroad. Once returning to their 'backwards' homelands, these missionaries of modernity pushed the notions of sovereign nation and invented local historical traditions, managing to enact a top-down colonisation of desire. Kiossev suggests that, in Eastern Europe, as a result of this top-down imposition of the colonial fantasy, there is a rift between the 'official' or 'public' discourses and those 'private' discourses encountered in everyday life, which remain replete with resistance and vitality, mocking the efforts of the 'West-mongers' and setting up different paths of Europeanisation. Kiossev describes this resistance to modern ideology in terms not different from the post-colonial definitions of mimicry (see Bhabha 1994, 109–128), a set of willed travesties and transformations that has the ability to subvert the colonial discourse. My scepticism towards top-down models of power and towards the axiomatic positing of strict divisions between a private and a public space, especially in matters as subtle as the shaping of collective fantasies; as well as my reservations regarding the possibility of subverting colonial discourse through mimicry make me rather cautious in relation to this hypothesis, no matter how attractive politically it is. We should not forget that the private/public boundary in nothing but an effect of liberal governing: it is specifically the

> … tactics of government which make possible the continual definition and redefinition of what is within the competence of the state and what is not, the public versus the private, and so on. (Foucault 1991, 103)

Since liberal-capitalist governing relies heavily on the ideology of the public/private divide and of bourgeois privacy as the space of subversion and freedom, prudence is advised when arguing that certain spaces breed resistance simply because they are 'private', 'proletarian', or 'poor'. No space within the bourgeois ecosystem, be it 'private' or 'public', or the psyche of the 'proletarian' or that of 'women', can claim resistance as its intrinsic characteristic or as a spontaneous result of its 'objective location'. Resistance must be understood as the subject's active processes of dis-identifying from the 'natural' characteristics of bourgeois spaces and subjects, as her processes of dissociation from the common sense or 'spontaneous' perception shaped by the modern fantasy.

To what extent does 'informal' popular culture in Romania and more generally in the European periphery resist and subvert the modern narrative framework remains uncertain for now; it is clear that the colonial fantasy does not affect exclusively the professionals, 'intellectuals', or politicians. On the contrary, this fantasy has dominion over great part of the spaces classically defined by liberal theory as 'private' and extends much beyond what Marxist theory defines as 'class' formations. At this moment in the anti-colonial struggle, I would therefore avoid counterposing the resisting 'masses' to the subservient elites and suggest that the modern fantasy circulates in capillary manners, from the psyche of the working class or peasant child to that of the bourgeois elites. A crucial scene in Radu Jude's 2015 film 'Aferim!'—which, despite exhibiting familiar forms of liberal-masochism as discussed by Wendy Brown (2001, 45–62), is probably the first serious cinematographic discussion of the genealogy of racism in Romania—has a nineteenth-century Roma slave, the ultimate racial other, reminisce about the trips he took to Paris and Vienna with one of his masters in terms that constantly compare the wonders of the West to 'whatever we have here' and make the latter seem insignificant, ridiculous, or provincial. This is the process through which the West assumes its fantasmatic position in the subaltern's psyche as the only place where unbridled jouissance is possible. It is mostly the 'masses' that constitute the estimated 4 million Romanian immigrants and, no matter how much these immigrants might mock their Western destinations or subvert their systems of signification, which many do, they also simultaneously idealise them. For any emigrant, the country of destination and its inhabitants have the valences of an ego-ideal and hold the promise of full jouissance even when cynically critiqued or, maybe, especially then. In other words, while the embracing of the modern fantasy by the colonised elites is quite certain, the extent to which the 'masses' resist and subvert this fantasy is less so.

That being said, resistance to and subversion of the modern fantasy are main sources of anti-colonial politics and must be continuously nurtured. And uncompromising anti-colonial resistances exist in Romania, both in popular culture and in 'elitist', 'public', or 'official' format. They connect the anti-colonial and anti-capitalist texts published on the Left East and Critic Atac platforms to the 'Idea' magazine and the decolonial work of the sociology department at Cluj University, to work published in the Gazeta de Arta Politica (the Gazette of Political Art), to the Platforma de Teatru Politic (the Platform for Political Theatre), and to grass roots initiatives like the now defunct anti-racist, anti-gentrification, and anti-colonial Centrul Social La Bomba (The Bomb Social Centre) or the Centrul de Lecturi Feministe (Centre for Feminist Readings). They are timidly present in the ambivalent online comment that Nicolae Dorobantu left to Mungiu-Pippidi's above-mentioned article 'What a successful country looks like...' and that, while not being free of issues (including its embracing of the modern developmental paradigm), is at least a resistance to the willed ignorance of this 'intellectual':

> P.S. Egypt and Nigeria are not countries that received [international] anti-corruption assistance, what we are talking about here are two colonies subdued through brutal military methods and for different purposes, one because of its position and control of a canal of colossal importance, the other for natural resources. The democratisation and progress of these colonies are absolutely NOT desired by the West!

As Raluca Parvu's (2005) interview-based work shows, such resistance to the modern fantasy was more widespread during the early 2000s struggles over who defines the nature of the truth and the good in Romania, struggles which in the public and academic discourses remained buried under the overarching teleological paradigm of 'catching up to the West', 'return to normality', and the retrieval of the 'natural' liberal-capitalist subjectivity. I will give a lengthy quote since it matches the present argument perfectly:

> The post-socialist subject, supposedly damaged by years of unnatural practices, was expected to return to its natural state of competitive individual-

ism and acquisitive consumption under the spur of economic shock therapies. In the eyes of the overseers (Western experts, policy-makers, entire political science departments) it did so painfully, disappointingly, often relapsing. However, throughout the interviews, these recalcitrant patients showed themselves able to contest categories that are considered fundamental to the extent that they are never questioned by the therapeutic theories and policies – the meaning of the good society, sociality, the individual, freedom, democracy, capitalism, market – showing a reflexivity obscured by the majority of the studies that focus on their deficient character and that shore up a version of 'transition' legitimising the naturalness and desirability of liberal capitalism and its attendant forms of subjectivisation ... Lastly, ideas of social justice kept on surfacing in interviews, including a fairly wide rejection of the legitimacy of blatant social inequality, of a society divided between winners and losers, and of capitalism-engendered poverty ... (Parvu 2005, 242)

Turning Our Backs?

In this 'Europe' from which civilisation supposedly springs forth, the Western bourgeoisie's relationship to the nonmodern *other* oscillates schizophrenically between imperial 'noblesse oblige' and crude fascism, and its attitude towards capitalism cycles blindly between toothless rants against the corruption of the liberal political class and prayers that the rulers will solve the economic crisis so that we can resume consuming like it's 2001. It is the task of the eternally deficient and improper peripheries to transform their impropriety and deficiency into the blade that will sever the libidinal ties with this 'white' bourgeoisie and 'civilisation' that some can already see in all their ugly nakedness.

This, however, is not an easy task. Even when the declared purpose of the nonmodern bourgeois is to contest the phallic position of Europe, her efforts will backfire unless she contests not just Europe's phallic position but the entire modern fantasy that endows it with this aura. It is difficult to find demands for freedom and emancipation, or anti-colonial critiques of the West coming from the periphery that are not framed in terms subsumed to 'Europe' and its historical coding and governing of 'freedom'. Most such resistances are formulated in the language of (human) rights, (parliamentary) democracy, (juridically governed) social justice, (liberal) freedom, progress, modernisation, development, and autochthonism (its reverse); or as attacks against (third world) authoritarianism and corruption that implicitly counter-pose this despotism to the true democracy of the West. To this, we can add resistances phrased in the language of traditional liberal economics, sociology, political science, or law. From this perspective, Wallerstein's (1997, 101) observation that many of the critiques levelled against Eurocentrism hide at their core an admiration and desire for Europe is perceptive:

> What is clear, however, is that for many the idea of progress has become labelled as a European idea, and hence has come under the attack on grounds of its Eurocentrism. This attack is often however rendered quite contradictory by the efforts of other non-Westerners to appropriate progress for part or all of the non-Western world, pushing Europe out of the picture, but not progress. (Wallerstein 1997, 101)

Wallerstein (ibid. 107) identifies the subaltern's desire for Europe in the critiques of Eurocentrism phrased either in terms of the lack of exceptionalism of Europe ('whatever Europe did, others were also in the process of doing it'), or in terms of Europe's history being a continuation of processes that were happening elsewhere for a long time. Fanon (2004, 5) has already argued that one of the results of colonialism is the production of fantasies of taking the master's place. This fantasy founds any anti-Eurocentric argument maintaining that Europe has appropriated from the nonmodern whatever it is supposed to have achieved (science, capitalism, technology, democracy, wealth, and so on), which simply reverses the master/slave position, reinforcing the idea that these achievements are something remarkable and enviable 'that modernity—or capitalism—is miraculous, and wonderful' (Wallerstein, 107). By using all those forms of fake anti-Eurocentric resistance as points of support and relay (see Foucault 1982), liberal-capitalist modernity increases its credibility, its 'naturalness', and its hold on the colonies and reconfirms Europe as the 'locomotive of history' pulling towards progress everyone else like carriages filled with 'ethnic specificity'.

Modern ideology's most subtle function, then, is not that of making one believe that, in order to achieve authentic democracy, she needs to emulate the European parliamentary arrangements, which are thus elevated from particular geohistorical arrangements to an objective stage of history. On the contrary, its most insidious function is to 'particularise' everyone's desire so that it always points towards Europe, no matter how abstract or universal its declared object is. The problem is not that 'Europe' was ideologically made to stand in for 'democracy', but that 'democracy' was ideologically made to stand in for 'Europe', so that when the nonmodern bourgeois utters: 'We need democracy! We want freedom! We want well-being!' what he truly wants is to be like or, even better, in Europe. The real ideological operation of the modern fantasy, then, is to connect every object of desire—and especially the most equivocal ones like civilisation, democracy freedom, happiness, success, love, or dignity—to Europe, so that Europe in its positivity, contingency, and particularity becomes the transcendent object of the subaltern's desire. Like an invisible cat, the desire for Europe manages to hide behind every universalist smile of modernity. This desire is a crucial ideological element to sustain, as Baudrillard (2008, 7) has already noticed:

> The superiority of the Western culture is sustained only by the desire of the rest of the world to join it. When there is the least sign of refusal, the slightest ebbing of that desire, the West loses its seductive appeal in its own eyes.

This desire to 'become Europe', rather than the abstract desire 'for democracy', dominated the Ukrainian Maidan movement, which framed its anti-governmental struggle in the language of 'Europeanisation'. Unsurprisingly, Maidan ended up incorporating right-wing discourses and groups. A bit more surprising was the support given in 2014 to this movement by a group of Western academics that—somewhat presumptuously—introduce themselves as 'we, representatives of the international academic community' and that include among others Zygmunt Bauman, Ulrich Beck, Seyla Benhabib, Charles Taylor, Bryan S. Turner, and Slavoj Žižek. The (fake) surprise is that these luminaries, some of which are vocal proponents of anti-capitalist revolution and critics of modernity, were so deeply mesmerised by the colonial fantasy as to ignore Europe's (and European Union's) imperial valences and to end up reinforcing its metaphorical connection with 'civilisation, progress, democracy', and so on, helping it maintain its phallic erection. These leading intellectuals churned out a typical 'progressive' bourgeois discourse, seasoned with Eurocentrism, the liberal praising of non-violence, and the promise of harmony within the political-institutional framework of Western modernity:

> In contrast to the government, Ukrainian society has displayed admirable civic maturity. Its determination to keep its protest within the realm of legality and its unwavering rejection of violence are a model for the defence of civil rights. Today, the Ukrainian Maidan represents Europe at its best – what many thinkers in the past and present assume to be fundamental European values. (http://www.theguardian.com/world/2014/jan/03/support-ukrainians-build-fairer-europe)

Since the Ukrainian fascist party Svoboda (formerly, 'Social-National Party of Ukraine'), with strong connections with the French Front National and other Euro-fascist organisations, was in the autumn of 2013 one of the organisers of the Maidan Movement (Budraitskis 2014), I am fully agreeing with the self-appointed representatives of the international academic community assertion that Maidan's discourse represents 'Europe at its best'. Not the Europe draped in the starry blue sugar-coating of harmony, peacefulness, democracy, progress, tolerance, integration, or civilisation that these signatories got so excited over, but in its neoliberal, imperialist, and fascist everyday clothing, the Europe experienced by many of those unlucky enough to find themselves outside the 'international academic community'. That thinkers proclaiming themselves anti-capitalist and anti-colonial can fall into the trap of mistaking Maidan for the 'event' is further proof that the revolutionary discourse emitted by the academic elites is a cover-up for bourgeois pleasures (on which more in the fifth chapter). Or, in the words of Ilya Budraitskis:

> It is important that this voice in support of the 'European choice' came from the political left, which in the critical moment discovered in itself no less passion for familiar, simple schemes for interpreting events than the Cold [War] Warriors of the political right ... (Budraitskis 2014)

In the preface to Fanon's 'Wretched of the Earth', originally written in 1961, Sartre[24] (2014) presents his belief that the violent process of decolonisation under way at the time will result in nothing less but the radical restructuring of the global order. The agent of this global change will be the new man (the agent of history is still a man, as much for Sartre as for Fanon himself) represented by the anti-colonial fighter, and his ascendance on the world stage will leave no imperialist or capitalist stone unturned. Europe, on its path to self-destruction, will have to learn from this agent how to decolonise itself if it is to survive this event at all.

Leaving aside the much-discussed and certainly problematic nature of using anti-colonial struggles as the negativity of world history in Sartre's Hegelian dialectic schema, all his otherwise uncompromising statements about radical transformation have been proven wrong. The serious governmental transformations undertaken by colonialism after the 1960s resulted not in a global anti-colonial socialist revolution, as Sartre predicts, but in its opposite: the hegemonic instauration of the modern fantasy as the fundamental structure of global desire. It is maybe time for decolonial movements, however, to fantasmatically return to that moment when the anti-colonial struggle was approached as an impending global conflict, with all the violence, fear, and uncertainty this involves, and to re-capture some of the militant urgency and tactical dilemmas of those texts.

The element in Sartre's short text that I find most useful as a first step in decolonising the European peripheries is the injunction to dissociate from the gaze of the master and from the colonial screen as founding elements of our subjectivity. For Sartre, this detachment has already happened in Europe's colonies; again, he is wrong. Instead of creating radical collectives of revolutionary anti-colonial fighters, the governmental techniques of global capitalism proliferated the nonmodern bourgeois and native colonial administrators and inflamed even further their desire for Europe. Sartre's belief is that the time when the most cherished objects of desire were, for the colonised, the master's prizes are over: 'Gone are the black Goncourts and the yellow Nobels: the days of the colonized prizewinners are over' (xlvi). Once again, he is wrong: prize winners from the colonies are an everyday figure in contemporary liberal-capitalist global governing, be they politicians; NGO workers; pro-liberal and pro-West dissidents; heads of Western banks, media, or IT multinationals; or indeed, the various 'exotic' artists and intellectuals hand-picked by the Western curators and displayed on their metropolitan stages. Sartre (ibid.) also believes that the colonised do not waste time condemning the crimes of colonialism: both these events and the Europeans themselves are reduced to objects of study in the process of developing anti-colonial strategies and tactics. Wrong again: there never was such a flaming desire to transform the colonial experience into a trauma and to use it so as to obtain the recognition of the coloniser. And yet, all these 'wrongs' do not in the least invalidate Sartre's text: we simply need to take it as a political-libidinal objective.

Sartre's original metaphor is here the opposite of the Freudian one and, in my opinion, much more relevant politically: far from plotting to murder the omnipotent Father and devour him, thus internalising his law in manners so profound that the first 'father-free' action of the parricide sons is to institute the father's law as the cornerstone of their community, Sartre's brotherhood/sisterhood learns to remain indifferent to the Father's gaze, even while planning how to destroy his governing dispositifs. As the European approaches the fire around which the strangers discuss the fate of his trading posts and armies of mercenaries, his presence fails to interpellate them:

> They might see you, but they will go on talking among themselves without even lowering their voices. Their indifference strikes home: their fathers, creatures living in the shadows, your creatures, were dead souls; you afforded them light, you were their sole interlocutor, you did not take the trouble to answer the zombies. The sons ignore you. The fire that warms and enlightens them is not yours. You, standing at a respectful distance, you now feel eclipsed, nocturnal, and numbed. It's your turn now. In the darkness that will dawn into another day, you have turned into the zombie.[25] (xlviii)

And when the metropolitan left—which considers itself the spiritual parent of any anti-colonial or anti-capitalist movement and therefore feels in its right to curate any revolt, to recommend what actions are suitable and which are 'undemocratic', and to judge guerrilla by the rules of liberal chivalry—threatens to withdraw their (moral) support to the violent anti-colonial struggle, Sartre does not mince his words:

They don't care a shit for [the Western Left's] support; it can shove it up its ass for what it's worth. As soon as the war began, they realized the harsh truth: we are all equally as good as each other. We have all taken advantage of them, they have nothing to prove, they won't give anyone preferential treatment. A single duty, a single objective: drive out colonialism by *every* means. (liv–lv)

Talking about the Antillean black man's neurosis, Fanon suggests that his combination of inferiority complexes and desire to become white will be surpassed through eliciting in him an increasing awareness of the structural conditions of colonialism: '… I must help my patient "conscious-nessize" his unconscious, to no longer be tempted by a hallucinatory lactification, but also to act along the lines of a change in social structure' (Fanon 2008, 80). What is necessary is attacking the deep recesses where the fantasy of modernity connects with the pleasures of the nonmodern subject. But for the nonmodern bourgeois, who has a fetishistic and masochistic attachment to the fantasy of modernity, being placed by the great catalogues of modernity in the 'inferior' category is both painful and pleasurable. This being the case, the nonmodern bourgeois' attachment to Europe is beyond the rational, and it is certainly misled to hope that simply exposing the truth about the historical processes that shaped the current colonial order will do. We need to experiment with new manners of severing the connection Europe = jouissance; to turn our backs on the master, ignore his gaze and talk among ourselves. Only thus we can bring to light the master's castration that was always there but that we didn't see while blinded by his phallic glow. De-occupying the symbolic/geographic spaces for so long invaded by the modern fantasy's differentiation between centre and periphery and inventing new modes of enjoying are the most important challenges a radically decolonial movement faces today.

I will confess that writing this chapter has made me uncomfortable: here I am, using my native knowledge in order to present yet another case study of the subaltern for the perusal pleasure of the Western audiences. My excuse for having engaged in this bourgeois-colonial conduct is that I imagined it as tactically useful for the Southern and Eastern European decolonial struggle, to the extent that it might assist one, and first of all myself, in taking the first steps towards identifying her (hopefully residual) attachments to the modern fantasy. And to the extent that it helps recognising what will be a most serious enemy for any the collective engaged in this struggle: the nonmodern bourgeois.

Notes

1. In the European colonies, the racialised and sexualised taxonomies of inferiority are systematically applied to the colonisers of European stock, not only to women but also to the sensuous, self-control-lacking working classes (see Stoler 1995).

2. In Lacanian parlance, this is the definition of the 'imaginary other', the external image in relation to which the subject constructs the image of herself. This image can be specific, like one's reflection in the mirror, one's mother, or a movie star or can be abstract, like 'the Jew', 'the Muslim', or 'the Black'. In order to avoid confusions with the symbolic Other who plays such a central function in the present analysis, I will denote this imaginary other using italics: the *other*.

3. Assuming the imaginary to be a pre-discursive realm, as some Lacanians do, is a fallacy since no image, and especially not one of unity or wholeness, can be structured without a symbolic scaffolding, that is, without a simultaneous perception of structural incompleteness (see Silverman 1996, 46). Indeed, it makes no sense to speak of a mirror stage unless we understand it as a bringing into being of an imaginary order that is structured by the symbolic (Fink 1999, 88). It is more fruitful to understand the images of fullness that the subject conjures and identifies with as a protection against the void introduced by language or the Other's desire. Also see Jameson (1977, 360).

4. 'The screen represents the site at which the gaze is defined for a particular society and is consequently responsible both for the way in which the inhabitants of that society experience the gaze's effects, and for much of the seeming particularity of that society's visual regime' (Silverman 1996, 135). If the modern subject imagines the Other's gaze as machinic, as the gaze of the camera, then the screen, like in the cinema, is the site where the gaze projects its symbolically governed images. It is only as an image on the screen that the subject can ever apprehend the gaze visually.

5. 'The gaze is the 'unapprehensible' agency through which we are socially ratified or negated as a spectacle' (Silverman 1996, 132).

6. This process gives lie to Freud's painstaking effort of dissociating desire and identification as mutually exclusive psychic processes, an effort that Diana Fuss (1995) perceptively deconstructs: in the case of the nonmodern bourgeois, the Westerner is at the same time the imaginarised *objet a*, the fundamental object of desire; and the ideal image projected on the modern fantasy's screen with which he identifies.

7. Thus, while within the colonial fantasy the black man is defined in relation to the white, the reverse is not true, since the white man occupies a position of self-referentiality that absolves him from defining himself in relation to the Other: the white is never a 'non-black' but a signifier that refers only back to himself (Fuss 1995, 142–143). In Fuss's (144–145) formulation, 'white' operates as its own Other, freed from any dependency upon the sign 'black' for its constitution'. 'Black' on the other hand, exists exclusively as a comparison, the negative term to be incorporated under the self-same logic of 'white' (ibid.). In other words, the subaltern exists exclusively under the injunction to perform the master's fantasy of absolute difference (146). Her only possible alternative within this fantasy, then, is to become a spectacle that supports this fantasy's imperial logic.

8. Even if Kiossev (2006) does not distinguish in his work the gaze from the look.

9. Defining the fantasy of the camera gaze as 'modern' is supported by the argument that between the optical apparatuses of the European Renaissance and the photographic camera, there is no rupture, but rather a refining of the techniques through which the gaze is dissociated from the look (Silverman 140–143).

10. According to Mosquera (cited in Slater 1998, 651), the centres of the global circuits of power construct the 'universal values', send their art to the periphery, and select what art from the periphery comes to the centre thus dividing the world into 'curating cultures and curated cultures'.

11. See, for example, Eng (2001) and Nandy (2009). Also, see Fausto-Sterling (1995) for an example of how modern science specularises and eroticises femininity and racial difference simultaneously.

12. For Burton, Turks are born pederasts, the Chinese defined by debauchery, North American 'Indians' are cannibals and sodomites, and Algeria is the most dangerous area of contagion for homosexuality (quoted in Fuss 1995, 160).

13. Without having the space to expand on this issue, I will notice that this 'generosity' of the Western European nations to accept Syrian refugees is a wily liberal tactic of replacing sovereign rejection with biopolitical tolerance that, as Brown (2006) demonstrates, allows the master not only to present

itself to the gaze of the Other as a morally and ontologically superior being, but also to gain legitimacy for refusing subsequent waves of immigration: 'We have done our duty, after all our tolerance has a limit'.

14. Transcendent because, in the modern fantasy, its value is detached from its processes of social production; fetishistic because it preserves its appeal even when the subject is confronted with the nagging evidence that he is chasing an object empty of intrinsic value, as in Žižek's (1991, 23–27) take on Marx's descriptions of fetishism.

15. The European fantasy of the oriental despot analysed by Grosrichard (1998), with its mix of emasculation and hyper-virility, ridicule, and hyperbolic jouissance, applies perfectly to the Romanian bourgeoisie's collective fantasy of socialist leaders like Nicolae Ceausescu. Mladen Dolar's introduction to the Verso edition is also relevant to this point.

16. In a 1999 survey, Romanian respondents chose Cuza as 'the most important historical personality' of the nation (Lucian Boia quoted in Popescu Sanda 2010, 123).

17. I will recall that 'nonmodern bourgeois' is not equivalent to 'middle class'; to the extent that members of what is traditionally considered the 'working class' exhibit fascist elements, they have adopted elements of the 'nonmodern bourgeois' fantasy frame.

18. The association of the left with effeminacy and homosexuality is constant in the liberal-fascist fantasy, as evident, for example, in the Cold War liberal discourses in the USA (see Eng 2001, 148), or in right-wing discourses and the generalisation of torture camps in Chile during the military dictatorship (see Palacios 2011).

19. Eng (2001, 20–21) identifies a similar tendency in the Asian-American context. The editors of *Aiiieeeee! An Anthology of Asian-American Writers* engage in a cultural critique perceptive enough to identify the state of 'self-contempt, self-rejection and disintegration' to which Asian Americans are reduced by racism, only to further on express their intense anger at the 'feminization, emasculation and homosexualization of the Asian-American male'. The editors propose to redress this wounded masculinity through a martial Asian nationalism that, Eng (ibid.) notices, only works to reinforce the heterosexist and racist structures that determine this male's self-hatred.

20. I use the term intellectual in inverted commas to describe this kind of nonmodern bourgeois because this was their class appellative in the pseudo-Marxist discourses of the socialist regime. The term is still used, especially by the literary and academic nonmodern bourgeois, to self-describe. The inverted commas reflect my own distrust of such class taxonomies ('work-

ers', 'intellectuals', and so on) and of the 'thinking/unthinking classes' dichotomy in general, as well as my opinion that the 'intellectuals' described in this chapter lack the most elementary critical reflexivity skills in relation to how they are governed by the modern fantasy and its tributary dispositifs.

21. Mungiu-Pippidi's CV, published on the website of the European Research Centre for Anti-Corruption and State Building (http://anticorrp.eu/author/alina-mungiu-pippidi/), informs us that she is teaching Democratisation and Policy Studies at the Hertie School of Governance in Germany; directs the European Research Centre for Anti-Corruption and State Building (www.againstcorruption.eu); and is Chair of Policy Pillar and of WP12 for the EU FP7 ANTICORRP project. She also serves as an advisor on issues of anti-corruption to the European Commission DG Home, after having consulted in the past for UNDP, Freedom House, NORAD, DFID, and the World Bank, among others.

22. I suspect that the author also fails to understand the ironic nuances of the main discourse she analyses, the lyrics of a pop song by Romanian band Taxi, taking at face value what is a mockery of the population's total abdication of responsibility to the Western authorities.

23. Another neoliberal extraordinaire, Daniel Daianu (2006), former Romanian finance minister, voices the same fears over loss of the traumatic memory of socialism in the Romanian youth.

24. I discuss Sartre rather than Fanon because the former presents himself as a member of the European colonial elite, a symbolic position that I find suited tactically for the Eastern and Southern European decolonial struggles.

25. Thanks to Robbie Shilliam for making me as obsessed with this quote as he was some years ago.

References

Agamben, G. (1998). *Homo sacer: Sovereign power and bare life*. Stanford: Stanford University Press.

Althusser, L. (2008). Ideology and ideological state apparatuses. In A. Louis (Ed.), *On ideology* (pp. 1–61). London/New York: Verso.

Anderson, B. (2006). *Imagined communities: Reflections on the origin and spread of nationalism*. New York/London: Verso.

Barthes, R. (1972). *Mythologies*. New York: Hill and Wang.

Baudrillard, J. (2008). The pyres of autumn. *New Left Review, 37,* 5–7.

Bhabha, H.,. K. (1994). *The location of culture*. London: Routlege.

Bourdieu, P. (2003). *Language and symbolic power*. Cambridge: Harvard University Press.

Brown, W. (2001). *Politics out of history*. Princeton/Oxford: Princeton University Press.

Brown, W. (2006). *Regulating aversion: Tolerance in the age of identity and empire*. Princeton/Oxford: Princeton University Press.

Brown, W. (2010). *Walled states, waning sovereignty*. New York: Zone Books.

Budraitskis, I. (2014). Intellectuals and the "The New Cold War": from the tragedy to the farce of choice. LeftEast, http://www.criticatac.ro/lefteast/intellectuals-and-the-new-cold-war/. Accessed 8 June 2015.

Butler, J., Laclau, E., & Žižek, S. (2000). *Contingency, hegemony, universality: Contemporary dialogues on the left*. London/New York: Verso.

Chiesa, L. (2007). *Subjectivity and otherness: A philosophical reading of Lacan*. Cambridge: The MIT Press.

Cornis-Pope, M. (2007). Danubian bridges and divides: Balkan multiculturality north and south of the Danube. In T. Aleksić (Ed.), *Mythistory and narratives of the nation in the Balkans* (pp. 12–22). Newcastle: Cambridge Scholars Publishing.

Daianu, D. (2006). Why fast economic growth isn't enough. *Southeast European Times*. http://www.setimes.com. Accessed 3 Oct 2010.

Eichler, L. (1934). *The new book of etiquette*. Garden City: Nelson Doubleday, Inc.

Eng, D. L. (2001). *Racial castration: Managing masculinity in Asian America*. Durham/London: Duke University Press.

Fanon, F. (2004). *The wretched of the earth*. New York: Grove.

Fanon, F. (2008). *Black skin, white masks*. New York: Grove Press.

Fausto-Sterling, A. (1995). Gender, race and nation: The comparative anatomy of the "Hottentot" women in Europe, 1815–1817. In J. Terry & J. Urla (Eds.), *Deviant bodies* (pp. 19–49). Bloomington/Indianapolis: Indiana University Press.

Fink, B. (1999). *A clinical introduction to Lacanian psychoanalysis: Theory and technique*. Cambridge: Harvard University Press.

Foucault, M. (1982). The subject and power. *Critical Inquiry, 8*(4), 777–795.

Foucault, M. (1991). Governmentality. In G. Burchell, C. Gordon, & P. Miller (Eds.), *The Foucault effect: Studies in governmentality* (pp. 87–105). Brighton: Harvester Wheatsheaf.

Foucault, M. (2003). *Society must be defended*. London: Penguin Books.

Fuss, D. (1995). *Identification papers*. London/New York: Routlege.

Grosrichard, A. (1998). *The Sultan's court: European fantasies of the West*. London/ New York: Verso.

Jameson, F. (1977). Imaginary and symbolic in Lacan: Marxism, psychoanalytic criticism and the problem of the subject. *Yale French Studies* No. 55/56, Literature and Psychoanalysis. The Question of Reading: Otherwise, 338–395.

Kiossev, A. (2006). Gaze and acknowledgement. http://www.eurozine.com/ articles/2006-12-12-kiossev-en.html. Accessed 1 Oct 2015.

Kiossev, A. (2008). The self-colonizing metaphor. http://monumenttotransformation.org/atlas-of-transformation/html/s/self-colonization/the-self-colonizing-metaphor-alexander-kiossev.html. Accessed 1 Oct 2015.

Krips, H. (2010). The politics of the gaze: Foucault, Lacan and Žižek. *Culture Unbound, 2*, 91–102.

Marinescu, A. (2015). *Codul Bunelor Maniere Astazi*. Bucuresti: Humanitas.

Nandy, A. (2009). *The intimate enemy: Loss and recovery of self under colonialism*. Oxford: Oxford University Press.

Palacios, M. (2011). A psychosocial interpretation of political violence: Chile 1970–1973. *Psychoanalysis, Culture and Society, 16*(3), 244–260.

Parvu, R. (2005). *Space of representation, places of identity. The case of post-communist Romania*. Unpublished PhD thesis, Department of Sociology, University of Surrey, UK.

Popescu-Sandu, O. (2010). "Let's all freeze up until 2100 or so": Nostalgic direction in post-communist Romania. In M. Todorova & Z. Gille (Eds.), *Post-communist nostalgia*. New York/Oxford: Berghahn Books.

Rose, J. (2005). *Sexuality in the field of vision*. London/New York: Verso.

Salecl, R. (2004). *On anxiety*. London/New York: Routlege.

Sedgwick, E. K. (1990). *Epistemology of the closet*. Berkeley: California University Press.

Silverman, K. (1983). *The subject of semiotics*. New York: Oxford University Press.

Silverman, K. (1996). *The threshold of the visible world*. New York/London: Routlege.

Slater, D. (1998). 'Post-colonial questions for global times'. *Review of International Political Economy* 5:4 Winter, 647–678.

Stavrakakis, Y. (2007). *The Lacanian left: Psychoanalysis, theory*. Politics: Edinburgh University Press.

Stoler, A. L. (1995). *Race and the education of desire: Foucault's "history of sexuality" and the colonial order of things*. Durham/London: Duke University Press.

Valverde, M. (1996). "Despotism" and ethical liberal governance. *Economy and Society, 25*(3), 357–372.

Wallerstein, I. (1997). Eurocentrism and its avatars: The dilemmas of social science. *New Left Review, 226*(November–December), 93–107.

4

Bourgeois Sex Fantasy

Re-opening the question of the bourgeois family and reproduction is a difficult endeavour from at least three perspectives: first, because the critical analysis of the nuclear family has been virtually abandoned by the left. About 35 years ago, Jacques Donzelot (1980, 53) was noticing that, while the critique of the bourgeois family used to be a central element of the French socialists' opposition to capitalism, it has been gradually mollified and finally disappeared, replaced with standard bourgeois demands for improving the life conditions of 'disadvantaged' families. The left thus retreats into a conservative position where the nuclear family is the answer to neoliberalisation rather than one of its pillars, allowing familism, the bourgeois ideology of the family, to occupy the very ground of the 'natural order of society'. This leaves the left in the rather strange position of imagining a radically different society built on the foundational stone of the bourgeois one: the mommy-daddy-offspring nucleus. We are thus in a situation in which the family and intra-familial reproduction function as the point of departure of any socio-political project, the sacred institutions equally defended by the State, medical profession, psychologists, psychoanalysts, socialists and fascists, patriarchs and feminists, deconstructionists, and positivists.

© The Author(s) 2016
M. Panu, *Enjoyment and Submission in Modern Fantasy*,
DOI 10.1057/978-1-137-51321-2_4

Second, because the maternalist brand of feminism embraces the nuclear family, with clear mommy and daddy roles, in order to think women's emancipation from patriarchy and thus considers any critiques of motherhood—or of 'feminine jouissance/desire'—to be patriarchal. And third, because one cannot engage in a critique of the family without engaging in a critique of sex difference, entering the by now slightly sterile debate between the supporters of the psychoanalytical theory of sexualisation and their foes, the infamous 'post-modernists' or 'post-structuralists' that are blamed for 'censoring' the most radical elements in Freud and Lacan. Despite these difficulties, the critical analysis of parenting as a governing technique is worth re-engaging with, if only because it contributes to the elucidation of the relationship between reproduction, the bourgeois ego, and the will-to-not-know.

The realist bourgeois fantasy stages the body as the site of intimacy and individuality, a bio-entity whose characteristics are natural, thus at the same time uniquely individual and spontaneous, true, or authentic. Evidently, in the wake of feminism and post-structuralism, we are a bit less naïve about the relationship between bodies and power and, at least some of us, approach the contemporary experience of the body as the result of minute, exhaustive, and relentless disciplinary operations. In other words, the body is a privileged instrument of the liberal-capitalist dispositifs. To the extent that the modern political anatomy acts on the body in order to install an ideological framework that will guide the subject's most private conducts, the soul is indeed the prison of the body (Foucault 1977). Phrased in a different vocabulary, since the ego depends on identification and on a corporeal scheme, our most intimate bodily experiences are organised from the start by symbolic/imaginary governing technologies. Any mobilisation of the body as a political tool needs therefore to be critically interrogated, since such a thoroughly disciplined element of selfhood, especially in a moment of crisis of subjectivity, risks to fall back on tropes implemented by the modern dispositifs as the subject's 'true' foundation (gender, sexuality, instincts, natural predispositions, etc.). Thus, while the attempt at organising the body/ego as a coherent, self-transparent unity always fails, the 'natural' tendency of a bourgeois driven by the will-to-not-know is to passionately mask this failure and the Other's lack with her embodied conducts.

Using the body to cover up the lack necessitates a constant labour of making the body into what it is supposed to be according to the dominant ideology: the natural foundation of reality. And to the extent that it portrays the Oedipal drama as the original event determining each and every element of this reality, psychoanalysis supports this ideological operation. It is worth, therefore, starting this discussion of sexuation and reproduction as elements of the will-to-not-know with a critical analysis of the psychoanalytical discourse of sex and the family. After all, even a devotee of the Lacanian notion of sex difference as Žižek is cannot ignore the relationship between the operations of patriarchal ideology and the psychoanalytical Oedipal fixation:

> Numerous treatises have been written about the perception of a historical Real in the terms of a family narrative as a fundamental ideological operation: a story about the conflict of larger social forces (classes and so forth) is framed into the coordinates of a family drama. … (A Deleuzian cannot resist the temptation of pointing out how the main theoretical justification of such familialization is psychoanalysis, which makes it the key ideological machine). (Žižek 2008, 52)

More or less faithful to my self-imposed rules of avoiding lengthy academic debates, I will cursorily point at some of the pitfalls of the psychoanalytical insistence on the Real as the unsurpassable anchor of sex difference, and of its related insistence on the axiomatic inexorability of gendered desiring structures. And I will exemplify the political consequences of the psychoanalytical insistence on submission to the paternal law as our only guarantee against social chaos. After which I will engage in a discussion of reproduction as a practice of the will-to-not-know.

Propping Up Daddy's Phallus

Lacanian psychoanalysis continues to derive the adult's psychic structure from the Oedipal complex understood as the universal and original mould. The Lacanian subject enters the symbolic and acquires desire with the successful resolution of the Oedipal family drama. This entry depends on the subject's 'correct' assumption of sex difference, which is therefore posited as the fundamental symbolic polarisation. From this moment on, the subject is definitively positioned not only on one of the mutually exclusive paths of neurosis or psychosis but also on those of masculine or feminine desire and jouissance. Thus, while Lacan understands gender/sex as symbolic positions rather than biological givens, his theory inscribes this polarity into the subject's psyche and reality in manners as definitive and mutually exclusive as if they were a biological destiny: one's original positioning in relation to the Name-of-the-Father immutably shapes her psychic structure. This ineluctable splitting of all subjects into two positions, feminine and masculine that can never merge, hybridize, vary, or transform, is to a great extent dependent on the Lacanian positing of sex difference as 'Real', where the Real is understood as an ontological form external to the symbolic and the imaginary. Following a line of feminist argument most prominently articulated by Judith Butler, I take issue here both with this concept of the Real and with the usual Lacanian mobilisation of this trope of the Real to insulate 'sex difference' from any possible critique.

The only reading of the Lacanian Real that has significance for social critique is, to my mind, the one starting from the axiom that 'all of the Real is nothing but the Real-of-the-Symbolic' (Chiesa 2007, 122). Otherwise, the ideology of a 'non-representable' lying outside the symbolic easily mutates into the realist modern fantasy this analysis critically deconstructs, a fantasy of an Other of the Other that, even if non-representable, shapes what can be known and said. Laclau (in Butler et al. 2000, 68) designates the Real as a 'retroactive effect of the failure of the Symbolic' to achieve fullness: a *re presentation* of the unnameable/nameless. In this reading, the Real is produced by a process of figurative substitution (ibid.) that attempts to symbolise that which the symbolic cannot represent, that is, 'symbolic failure' or the Other's lack, and in the same process to project this threatening failure outside the symbolic field. The Real is, then, a necessity of the symbolic, which cannot account for its lack without representing a radical heterogeneity that is external to it, a field of the un-representable. The Real cannot be meaningfully integrated into the symbolic precisely because it is a representation of its own lack, of its failure to create full meaning. What we repress and exclude as the Real cannot be understood as a universal Oedipal law but as the encounter with the Other's lack, with the lack of closure of our reality and of any object within it. That is: the Real is that which impedes the closure of any identity, perpetually disrupting and making unintelligible our systems of difference, and it is in this guise, as that which exposes the lack that it is represented as a trauma by a subject, the bourgeois, whose enjoyment depends on denying the lack.

It is interesting to notice that when certain Lacanians discuss sex difference, they use the Real exactly in the opposite manner: as some sort of impossible to represent kernel that impedes the disruption of the binary system of differences we know as 'sex'. To insist: for many Lacanians, when sex difference is concerned, the Real stops being a threatening non-representation of the Other's lack and becomes its opposite, that which secures the stability of the symbolic system of differences, making them as immutable as nature. In this account, the Real mutates from a negative limit with no ontic content to a 'transcendental limit with an ontic determination of its own' (Laclau in Butler et al. 2000, 184). Little wonder that the effects of this almost religious insistence on heterosexual difference as being foundational of all meaning because sex difference is Real regularly results in fascist claims, for example, the concerted campaign of French Lacanians like Sylviane Agacinski, Irene Thery, Francoise Héritier, and Jacques-Alain Miller against the extension of legally sanctioned alliances to non-hetero people (cited in Butler et al. 2000, 146–147 and notes 10 and 12), which successfully promoted legislation denying a gay couple's right to adopt. Their justification is the mantra that patriarchal Lacanians wheel out whenever they feel daddy is under threat: without a strong father that can block the mother's unbound desires to devour her child, psychosis threatens the latter. As these Lacanians write their arguments, a new generation of adolescents raised in gay families is about to unmask the scarecrow of an assured disaster following the Father's decapitation ('pèreoupire') as a patriarchal fantasy, not different from the nineteenth-century myths that education will make women sterile.

Tim Dean's (2000, 87) argument is more nuanced, and one of its interesting premises is that there is no signifier of sexual difference in the unconscious.[1] Which, of course, means that there is nothing heterosexual about desire ('…desire is originally independent of heterosexuality' [88]), prompting Dean to propose a 'shift beyond sexuality as the primary register in which we make sense of ourselves at all' (ibid.). I would no doubt agree with this, but I find confusing Dean's further description of sexual difference and his intellectual alliance with Catherine Millot, which in the light of Dean's attack on the Lacanian theory of the gendering of desire/jouissance seems rather strange. What is suggested—although Dean does not dwell much on the details of the Lacanian description of the Oedipal phase—is that, while desire and the unconscious are not gendered, there is nevertheless an immutable gendering of the subject. Thus, Dean ends up reiterating the Lacanian argument that sex difference belongs to the field of the Real understood as a traumatic resistance to meaning-making and change.[2] How is gendering produced in Dean's scenario, I am left wondering, is it still through the classical positioning of the subject in relation to the phallus? How does the ungendered phallus regulate the formation of gender dichotomy? And if sex difference is generated by symbolic and imaginary processes, then how and when is it transferred into the field of the Real or non-meaning? These processes remain shrouded in esoteric secrecy. Once the transfer of sex difference to the domain of the Real happens, though, it places sex difference outside symbolic or imaginary intervention: 'No matter what one does or says, there is a sense in which transcending gender remains impossible' (87).

Starting from these premises and following the arguments of Catherine Millot, Dean (78, 81–82) argues that an attempt to transcend the sex/gender difference often signals a desire to step 'outside sex' and to enjoy fully, without symbolic or imaginary boundaries. In other words, desiring to transcend the gender/sex dichotomy is a desire to abolish the Real and the unconscious altogether and to transcend castration by becoming the ungendered phallus; this is a desire that diagnoses a psychotic structure (ibid.). It seems bizarre, to say the least, that Dean and Millot select gender difference as the barrier to bourgeois enjoyment, as if we were not experiencing today the obsessive and omnipresent activity of dispositifs that correlate full enjoyment with the subject's assumption of her gender as fullness, that is, as inexorable, natural difference. In this, Dean and Millot follow a Lacanian stream of thought that makes castration synonymous with the institution of sex difference and that equates any effort to contest gender dichotomy with the effort to transcend the castration. Since Dean equates the phallus with the instrument of castration, and since he follows the Lacanian understanding of gendering in relation to this phallus: '[the phallus installs] in the subject ... an unconscious position without which he (sic) would not be able to identify himself with the ideal type of his sex' (86), he is literally equating castration, the barring of one's access to fullness, with sex difference. To insist: if one posits, as Dean and Millot do, that the fantasy of transcending castration takes in the modern psyche the form of the fantasy of transcending sex difference, then one makes castration equivalent with the installing of sex difference. In this case, any contestation of sex difference is read as a fantasy of transcending castration. I think this is a too literal understanding of castration that, in itself, has nothing to do with sex. I have already argued that castration remains an interesting concept only in as much as it designates the anxiety-inducing gap between the phallic signifiers that institute our being and our relationship to the Other which constantly undermines the solidity of these signifiers. In Žižek's (2006, 34) words:

> This gap between my direct psychological identity and my symbolic identity (the symbolic mask or title I wear, defining what I am for and in the big Other) is what Lacan ... calls 'symbolic castration,' with the phallus as its signifier ... Castration is the gap between what I immediately am and the symbolic title which confers on me a certain status and authority. In this precise sense, far from being the opposite of power, it is synonymous with power; it is that which confers power on me.

If adopting this understanding of castration, it makes more sense to argue that the bourgeois does not experience castration as the division of all humans into two antagonistic categories, men and women, but as the impossibility to be a 'real man' or a 'real woman'. In other words, it is not the gender binary that the bourgeois experiences as a barrier to symbolic and imaginary enjoyment but, on the contrary, the impossibility to ever completely be one gender. When Dean (88–89) describes the mythical patriarchal figures of prohibition that in the gendered bourgeois' imagination are enjoying without limit, the phallic Mother and Father, he oddly insists that, since these figures embody the 'real phallus' (whatever that means), they are ungendered, not subject to sexual division. I would think that on the contrary, in the realist modern fantasy (and fantasy is a term that Dean does not use much in his analysis of desire), the attempt to become the phallus takes the form of efforts to become a 'true man' or 'true woman', exempt from castration like the exceptional Father or Mother. Not in the sense of being exempt from gendering, but of being exempt from the gap between 'name' (man) and 'being' (lived masculinity with its imaginary and symbolic dimensions and the power relations they determine). In other words, in the gendered and gendering modern fantasy, the subject will try to become the non-castrated ego-ideal by identifying with the always gendered phallic figures of the Mother and Father, be they Marilyn Monroe or Elvis, and not with a bigendered or ungendered phallic figure. Thus, to the extent that desire is guided by the modern fantasy, sex reassignment surgery fails to provide full jouissance for the transsexual by failing to close the gap between name and being, rather than by erasing the name (man or woman), which the transsexual supposedly fantasises would free his or her jouissance from the shackles of gender. When Dean (89–90) gives the example of trans black model Octavia Saint Laurent's identification with cis white model Paulina Porizkova, he argues that what Octavia really identifies with is the phallic mother, woman, that is, a position 'outside sex'. I find it more plausible to say that her identification is with an equally unattainable ideal femininity, which explains why this ego-ideal, being a figment of the modern bourgeois fantasy, is always cis, white, rich, and spoilt. And if Dean (90) illustrates the effects of the lure of full jouissance/the phallus with the transsexuals' willingness to sacrifice their own genitals, I would illustrate it with the cis believers' willingness to engage in gender violence.

It is the quest for 'true sex/gender', the disavowal of the lack in the subject and the Other that results in the violence typical of 'true masculinity'. We should maybe concern ourselves more with the effects of this quest rather than obsessing, yet again, about the alleged pathology of the transsexual. This masculinist violence can reach levels that surpass the wildest paranoid fantasies of psychotic and homicidal transsexuals/homosexuals whipped up by our bourgeois patriarchal order and illustrated by Bruce Fink's statements (see below). Consider, for example, the global ritual of men aggressing passing women through sexual comments, whistling, stares, and so on, reiterated as systematically as drooling is when a bell is rung. The function of this conduct is to sustain the bourgeois symbolic law that stipulates that gender is natural and the penis is the phallus. The aggression is meant to signal to the Other that the aggressors really are what their label says ('real men') and that their limitless penile-heterosexual enjoyment springs from their lack of castration, translated in this case as their inborn superiority over and desire for women. The ritual is reiterated compulsively because it constantly fails to fulfil its function, reflecting the irony of a phallic law that incessantly stages the humiliating impossibility of the penis to rise to the status of absolute embodiment of full jouissance/non-castration. Little wonder that men cannot be convinced by the 'size doesn't matter' argument and that the penis enlargement industry continues to prosper: a penis is never large enough to prove to the Father, the real sex partner of any male, that one really is a man.

If we want to transpose this discussion of the search for the phallus-qua-gender-fullness at larger scale and intensity, then we can argue that the systematic violence of modernity is an attempt to cover the lack with phallic objects ('gold', 'profit', 'capital', 'victory', and 'sovereignty') or metaphysical substance ('masculinity' and 'racial purity') and thus attain full jouissance. In its modern instantiations, mass violence is a very much gendered and heterosexual attempt to become the phallus, and for example, Sarah Kane's (2001) play 'Blasted' acutely draws out the always-intimate connections between gender violence and militaristic atrocities.

The so-called 'Lacanian left' also seems prone to theorising events that would bring about the radical transformation of the bourgeois regime while leaving intact its heteronormative dispositifs. Destroy all masters, in other words, but not the Father. Justifying this postulation of the absolute intractability of sex difference in any imaginable regime, pre- or post-revolutionary, is the usual Lacanian line or defence against sex/gender destabilisation: sex difference is the polarity making operational the symbolic order. Thus, deploring the dangerous 'post-modern' desire to do away with master-signifiers and create an 'atonal', unravelling world, Alain Badiou (in Žižek 2008, 30)—surprise—selects sex difference as the exemplary such master-signifier. Applauding Badiou's 'perspicuous' choice, Žižek projects the implications of this effort to keep the sex/gender master-signifier safe on his other academic foe—besides 'post-modernism/post-structuralism'—namely 'gender studies':

Badiou's perspicuous example of such an 'atonal' world is the politically correct vision of sexuality, as promoted by gender studies, with its obsessive rejection of 'binary logic': this world is a nuanced, ramified world of multiple sexual practices which tolerates no decision, no instance of the Two, no evaluation (in the strong Nietzschean sense). This suspension of the Master-Signifier leaves as the only agency of ideological interpellation the 'unnameable' abyss of jouissance: the ultimate injunction that regulates our lives in 'postmodernity' is 'Enjoy!'—realize your potential, enjoy in all manner of ways, from intense sexual pleasures through social success to spiritual self-fulfillment. (Žižek 2008, 30)

And so we witness theorists of the communist revolution serenely arguing that the responsibility for: our falling into the cruel hands of the superego's injunction to enjoy that removes any possibility of enjoying; the reproduction of the cynical liberal culture accompanying this injunction and the paralyzing guilt associated with this shift have nothing to do with the patriarchal, obstinately gendered liberal-capitalist governing technologies. On the contrary, the responsibility squarely falls with those that misguidedly critique these technologies. The tiresome, if indefatigable, repetition of this argument in Lacanian studies finds a brother in arms in masculinity studies' blaming of the castration and loss of jouissance of Western white men on feminism.

Finally, in Bruce Fink's theorising, the injunction to submit to the paternal authority reaches apocalyptic tones. Fink follows the traditional psychoanalytic text to the letter: subjectivation is equivalent with the successful (i.e. neurotic) resolution of the third phase of the Oedipal complex, framed as the child's realisation of the mother's castration and the neutralisation of her devouring desires for the baby by the paternal law. This symbolic castration saves the child from the imaginary lock with the mother and introduces her to the symbolic world of difference and desire. I find such forms of describing subjectivation over-deterministic and static. When infants and young children manifest desirousness towards objects that are not the m/Other—towards cartoon, film, book, video game characters, the TV screen, toys, the nanny, an aunt, or a random visitor—a desire that seems to have no precise temporal starting point, the argument that the necessary and sufficient condition for such libidinal investments is the paternal prohibition seems rather slender. Fink, however, seems to trust the old patriarchal dictum that the mother is irrational, carnal desire while the father is the abstract law that regulates it for the common good and that the child's psychological 'normality' depends on her internalisation of this patriarchal order and waves around the usual threat: incomplete submission to the figure of the father and his law is equivalent to the absence of an ego-ideal and to psychosis (Fink 1999, 89). Here, the only game in town seems to be paternal domination: there can be no symbolic order unless it is ruled by the Father and contesting this 'symbolic = patriarchal' equivalence is madness. The examples of the dire consequences of refusing the paternal law we are offered do not stray very far from the rhetorical mix of castration anxiety and despotism characteristic of patriarchy in general. Not submitting to the Father means that one: is unable to properly establish desire, which results from the paternal prohibition (92); cannot have a social life (89); cannot exert control over one's body (90); has no ability to create metaphors, thus new meanings (90); does not establish properly the link between language (signifier) and meaning (95); and is left with chaotic, non-hierarchised, and uncontrollable drives (96), meaning a lack of morality and a conscience characteristic of the psychotic.[3] The unreasonable demands of an excessively authoritarian father[4] are the cause for another familiar patriarchal panic, the boy's 'feminisation'. While 'in certain other cases of psychosis, we see a tendency toward transsexualism, repeated requests for sex change operations, and homosexual activity' (98). Like the other Lacanians mentioned in this section, Fink ties in psychosis, femininity, homosexuality, and trans-sex/gender with perversion, pathology, and social dissolution.

The moral warnings that Fink volunteers are more easily identifiable as the classical fears of US conservatism: families without a father/father-figure are more likely to produce psychotic structures in the child (98); petty crooks and criminals are unfit fathers that will encourage psychosis in their sons (103); single women deliberately having children, lesbian couple raising children, increasing divorce rates, and anti-authoritarian parental roles amount to a weakening of the father's authority (thus paternal function) and will lead to an increase in cases of psychosis and mass chaos (110–111). We seem to be in moral panic territory:

> Given how frequently the traditional family structure already fails ... what are the chances that both roles will be played by one parent alone or by two parents raised into similarly codified sex roles? Isn't the incidence of psychosis likely to rise in such cases? (253, note 71)

Or:

> Can something like the paternal metaphor ... be instated without the father as symbolic function? If so, how? ... If not, is there some other way to introduce an outside – that is, to triangulate the mother-child relationship and stave off psychosis? ... Doesn't one sex [the man, obviously] have to play the part of the symbolic representative? (Fink 1999, 111)

Finally, submission to the law in all its forms, including to the liberal-capitalist legal system and the careful avoidance of social change, is proposed as the only modality of saving the imperilled US social space:

> If we are to preserve some notion of a just Law ... that is equitably and uniformly enforced, we must have an experience of Law at home which at least approaches that ideal to some degree. As rare as this experience is in the stereotypical nuclear family, practices currently being advocated seem likely to make it rarer still. As Lacan once said in a pessimistic vein: 'I won't say that even the slightest little gesture to eliminate something bad leaves the way open to something still worse – it always leads to something worse. (254, note 71)

The usual Lacanian argument that sexual difference does not stand for 'man' and 'woman' but for a deadlock, a kernel of Real that cannot be translated in any fixed subject-position and that, consequently, proves the impossibility of binary identification (see e.g. Žižek's intervention in Butler et al. 2000, 9), seems to work as a disingenuous subterfuge whose purpose is to preserve intact the bourgeois gender fantasy. These theorists' insistence that they treat gender/sex difference as a form without content comes at the price of refusing to recognise how difficult it is to void the form of Freud's concept of 'sex difference' from its content of 'normal heterosexual psychic structures in men and women'. It therefore contributes to placing sex difference beyond critical analysis, making it into 'a truly felicitous instrument of power' (Butler et al. 2000, 147). Butler's critique is pertinent: the claim that sex difference is merely formal or empty alludes at the pre-discursive, transcendental status of this dichotomy and thus obscures the exclusions performed in order to enable this very illusion of formalism. Any

> ideality that pertains to sexual difference is ... constituted by actively reproduced gender norms that pass their ideality off as essential to a pre-social and ineffable sexual difference. (Butler et al. 2000, 144)

The production of gender differences is shielded from critique by the argument that formal sex difference precedes any 'given social operation of sexual difference' (ibid. 145), absurdly suggesting that sex dichotomy is fully independent of heterosexist prescriptions and descriptions. Indeed, if sex difference is instituted by the law's injunction to make a piece of flesh into the symbol of one's being, then what precisely in this process escapes language and the social, what is this non-symbolic remainder in sex difference?

My suspicions are that all these theoretical defences built around the Father's throne aim to protect the privilege of this well-loved figure rather than to critically discuss the construction and effects of binary sex difference. This suspicion is amplified by some Lacanians' assertions that any disruption of the process through which the child internalises the masculine position as 'one' or 'plus' and the feminine position as 'zero' or 'minus', in other words, internalises the 'feminine' as symbolic and imaginary incarnation of castration and the 'masculine' as non-castrated, leads to psychosis at individual level and to chaos and destruction at social level. Fink (1999, 99) states that femininity or a 'feminine psychic structure' is equivalent to a passive position and is ineluctable for most subjects defined as 'woman' (i.e. lacking a penis). According to his argument, the social inferiority of the majority of women reflects their unchangeable psychic structure, which all of a sudden seems to acquire a very precise content indeed, one reiterating the traditional bourgeois patriarchal discourse: inertia, lack of dialectic movement, repetition in one's thoughts and desires (Fink, 101), irrationality, instinctual nature, weakness, apathy, and psychosocial deficiency in relation to 'man'.

Despite claims to the contrary, the Lacanian equation of the feminine with castration is not performed so as to expose lack as a constitutive feature of any identity and any state of being, but so as to fix gender in invariable and inescapable structures and to portray 'women' using the customary, coarse patriarchal strokes. According to these descriptions, once she adopts a feminine structure of desire, which happens in the unique and unrepeatable window of opportunity opened by the Oedipal drama, any woman ineluctably obeys these libidinal circuits for the rest of her life, with as little chances of becoming otherwise as the colonized subject described by the modern fantasy has. These are the same tropes used by colonial discourses for placing the 'black man' in relation to white civilisation, where 'The Negro symbolizes the biological' (Fanon 2008, 167). And like 'the Negro', the 'feminine desiring structure' symbolises everything the proper white man is not: mystery, strangeness, unfathomability, exoticism, insularity, primitiveness, carnality, nature, rhythm, mysticism, musicality, sensuality, possession by telluric/life energy, and so on. This is complemented by another classical colonial argument, that of the colonised as disruption of the white male's law:

> [The] scapegoat for white society – which is based on myths of progress, civilisation, liberalism, education, enlightenment, refinement- will be precisely the force that opposes the expansion and the triumph of these myths. This brutal opposing force is supplied by the Negro. (Fanon 2008, 194)

The similarities with the Lacanian description of femininity are significant: classical Lacanian theory presents femininity as the element that disrupts patriarchal order, since the law incompletely determines her. This incomplete symbolic determination allegedly gives woman access to some extra-social and extra-linguistic sources of being and thus to some non-totalisable, non-symbolisable enjoyment. This Lacanian mysticism of female jouissance, like the colonial mysticism of the primitive's jouissance, further subsumes 'woman' to the law in the process of affirming that she escapes it, making woman into Woman, an eternal and mysterious not-quite-social being. While the Lacanian axiom: 'man wants to have the phallus, woman wants to be the (the man's) phallus', in not only unsophisticated (any attempt to possess the phallic object is also an attempt to be the phallus, beyond castration) but also too close for comfort to the old-school patriarchal formula 'man does' (disembodied, abstract, public, and civilising acts), while 'woman is' (a body, sensuous being, and object of desire).

There is a lot left unexplained by the psychoanalytical proclamation of this cosmic coincidence between an ahistorical foundation of human reality (being in the symbolic i.e. having no other existence but linguistic) and a historically contingent form of the symbolic (dichotomous gender). This lack of explanation means that psychoanalysis describes the founding elements of the patriarchal symbolic order (gender and sexuality) using the founding assumptions of this very same patriarchal order, as they silently gestate in the psyche of theorist and reader alike (penis envy, sex difference, woman as body and the man as rationality, the passivity and stagnation of feminine subjects, the heteronormative family and sexuality, maternal/paternal roles, and so on). What in the linguistically instituted male/female dichotomy escapes linguistic expression and how is this symbolic split different from others, for example, white/non-white or hetero/gay? Especially since

> Sex doesn't subsume race, ethnicity, nationality, or sexuality; these attributes of identity intersect in ways that need to be specified. To restrict our view to sexual difference is to miss the always complex ways in which relations of power are signified by *differences*. (Wallach Scott 2011, 36)

If some Lacanians assume that it is impossible—at the risk of losing one's mind—to move away from our binary gendered and heterosexist order, are we to understand that the Real would block any change in the current dichotomous symbolic order? Are, then, any attempts to dismantle capitalism, colonialism, racism, homophobia, and so on plagued by the same predicament of either representing psychotic delusions or opening the gates for something much worse than the dispositifs we are attacking?

Bourgeois Sex Fantasy

Arguably, no Lacanian theorist would openly defend a concept of fullness or of an undivided subject, but the authors critically discussed here implicitly propose the next best thing: a stable, repetitive, and inalterable gendered enjoyment obtained by submitting to the patriarchal law of the Oedipus. Isn't such a devoted and devotional support for the paternal order a symptom of gender-related anxiety? When it defends the F/father's authority against attacks from a variety of hostile anti-paternal forces—gays, queers, single mothers, feminists, post-structuralists and, one presumes, anarchists, and other such—isn't psychoanalytical discourse defending male privilege and its spoils: heteronormativity; the subordinate social and symbolic position of women; and the bourgeois nuclear family with all its blessings: authority-sanctioned coupledom, transmission of physical and symbolic resources through male blood lineage, biological ties as the primordial social ties, the reduction of responsibility to responsibility for one's blood relatives and of politics to familial well-being, prudentialism, comfort, career, work ethic, propriety, consumption, private property, and so on? Isn't it, then, also defending the conducts associated with the Father in the modern fantasy: colonialism, nationalism, militarism, respect of the socio-political hierarchy, and more generally fascism?

I think that, on the contrary, psychoanalytical tools should be employed to challenge any technologies that make reality dependent on the rule of the Father. And the patricide could start by representing sex/gender as a phallic signifier that organises a fantasmatic narrative structure. Here, patriarchy is revealed to be not a specific set of indelible and rigid traits (femininity and masculinity) to be retrieved in any psychic structure, but a framework that orders each and every subject's desire in relation to the signifier 'penis', with variable rates of success. The patriarchal order's conflation of the penis with the phallus (the signifier of fullness-qua-desire-of-the-Other) shapes scenarios where castration is resolved by becoming a 'real' man or woman, by the chasing of phallic objects that confirm one's gender, by heterosexuality, by metonymic slides between the penis and power, and so on. Otherwise phrased, the sex fantasy provides us with an elementary answer to the question of the Other's desire: whatever it might want you to be, it is fairly soon evident that first and foremost it wants you to be a proper boy or girl.

This understanding of sex/gender difference as fantasmatic rather than as a structure of desire imprinted as ineluctably as a neural path is slightly less inflexible, while at the same time accounting for the intractability of gender: as is the case with all modern fantasies, it is protected by the bourgeois' will-to-not-know. Gendered libidinal structures remain in place because adults are enjoying them so much, because we have a stubborn commitment to the binary law of gender as a mechanism of hiding the Other's lack. In other words, the intractability of sex/gender is not due to a Real kernel that sex, unlike any other symbolic/imaginary dichotomy, miraculously contains, or to its definitive implantation in the psyche that is synonymous with the entry into the symbolic, but to our gendered fantasies of fullness and to the thorough genitalisation of jouissance and reality they produce.

Like any modern ideological operation, sexuation happens in two consecutive steps, and during its second step, the subject is not quite the passive recipient of the law. First, we are all introduced into the world of sex difference without any possibility of resistance—it is a situation of domination. However, domination cannot really dupe one; the true success of ideology requires the subject's libidinal investment in it. Gendering is, in other words, a game of power. In the second step, while able to do otherwise, we try to escape anxiety by accepting the patriarchal law as natural, unavoidable, and inalterable: 'the absence/presence of penis signifies the fundamental human difference'. At this moment, the subject invests high libidinal charges in the various technologies of gender, at both imaginary and symbolic level and subsequently refuses to betray them, and gender ideology in general, no matter what evidence he is presented with.

Sex/gender, then, shapes desire but only to the extent that the subject is unwilling to abandon the jouissance gender offers, just like one resists abandoning the jouissance of one's symptom. In this reading, sexuation is a lifelong and never quite perfect endeavour that can be narrativised as a fixed moment, period, or stage only retrospectively and as an attempt to achieve mastery over one's lack. Like all bourgeois forms of submission to authority, gender/sex provides relief from the anxiety of castration. The function of the gender/sex fantasy is to allow one to believe that behind the operations of language that shape reality and desire, there is a true essence: femininity is what men desire in women; masculinity is what makes men desire women (and vice versa); and heterosexuality is the natural law that channels our desire for men/women. As long as sex/gender shepherds our desire, it is akin to one's destiny, predicted at birth by the phallic fates but fulfilled only to the extent that the subject obeys the symbolic law that makes the prophecy meaningful and binding.

And so, sex/gender succeeds in explaining and governing each and every person and conduct, from intelligence to sexuality, from democracy to progress, from social hierarchies and structures to colonialism, and from taste in music to the type of chocolate or alcohol one prefers. This commitment to gender and the subsequent genitalisation of reality are only enhanced by the fact that, as Foucault (1990) argues, modernity offers the vocabulary of sexuality as the most accessible and intelligible language into which to phrase questions to do with the innermost, hidden, natural, and authentic self and, of course, with true, natural, and consuming pleasure. The waves of sex revolution we have experienced since the Victorian age managed to place sex at the core of our subjectivity just like capitalist economy did with money. Today in the West, sex functions as the currency or symbolic measure of one's jouissance, as demonstrated by the expressions: 'as good as/better than sex...' or 'orgasmic' used to denote one's enjoyment of anything, from shopping to eating. However, and here I agree with Tim Dean, there is nothing particularly sexual about the bourgeois unconscious or jouissance besides their thorough genitalisation by the modern fantasy,[5] which offers sex and reproduction as the answers to all of bourgeois' anxieties.

The Mother as 'One'

Some feminists take Lacan's sexuation formulae to represent a celebration of the feminine as that which escapes the phallic law, opening the path towards a new, unbridled, or revolutionary form of enjoyment. I am less optimistic about the escape routes these formulae open and will argue that, while the modern fantasy might indeed represent 'feminine jouissance' as dangerous, this masculinist fear triggers a deployment of dispositifs that invite femininity into the seductive palace of reproduction, motherhood, and unbridled sensuality which, no matter how gilded, domesticates any radical contestation of the Father's law.

A Freudian might argue that the female body threatens the male because it irrationally reminds him of the Father's castration threat, but there is more to it. A man's greatest fear is not even about his own castration, I would argue, but about the Father's castration being exposed, which is a higher danger to his fantasy of wholeness. After all, men are often happy to publicly perform their own castration—as for example in the humiliating rituals of the army of frat house hazing—if this supports the myth of the non-castrated Father (army, superior, homosocial hierarchies, and in a word, the natural dominance of masculinity). The radical potential of the female body to destabilise the masculinized fantasy of obtaining/becoming the phallus, then, is not its staging of what might happen to the man if he loses the penis. But on the contrary, its feeding of the masculine fantasy that the female body enjoys fully, since this fantasy stages the *other* as enjoying not phallic completeness (she is naturally castrated) but her castration. There persists in any masculinised psyche the anxiety that the feminine possesses a special jouissance, the potential of having more fun than the 'non-castrated' male subject, more fun than the Father himself. The already mentioned Lacanian fantasy of 'feminine jouissance' as well as the related fantasy of desiring or writing 'like a woman' and so on are offshoots of this masculinised fear of the body that enjoys its lack. This fantasised form of enjoyment ridicules the Father's threat of castration, exposing him as impotent, and therefore is for the man one of the truest representations of the fascinating, terrifying, and unbearable 'jouissance of the *other*'.

The fear that feminine jouissance might expose the Father's lack fuels the common masculine desire to either violently curtail or completely destroy, erase, or debase the feminine/feminised body, which in turn fuels ritual misogyny, gender violence, and homophobia. We might re-interpret the modern ritual of mass rape in times of war not as aiming to spoil the goods of the male enemy, but as aiming to irreversibly defile those bodies and forms of enjoyment that, in the masculine fantasy, point at the ridiculousness of the war itself and thus at Father's castration, to the extent that any war stages masculine bodies in yet another attempt of superseding castration through submission to the Father's (or Fatherland's) command.

This should not be taken to mean that bourgeois women really enjoy in a different, unbound manner, but only that the modern fantasy, which represents them as castrated by birth, creates this unshakeable suspicion in the minds of most men and of some women too. Indeed, the bourgeois woman's enjoyment does not per se represent a threat to the patriarchal symbolic order, since it is also generated by submission to the masculinised fantasy, that is, derived from the ontological security that submitting to the gendered ego-ideal provides her with. The feminine masculinised fantasy is thus symmetrical with the penile one (penis = man = having the phallus) and replaces it either with the classical 'no penis = woman = being had by the phallus' fantasy, or with the 'rebellious' fighting for the right to enjoy like a man, that is, with the fantasy that full jouissance is obtained by 'attaining equality with men' (which assumes that the bourgeois man, or at least the Father, enjoys fully). This feminine masculinised subject can thus occupy various positions in relation to the phallus, but her identity/symbolic position as 'woman' remains secure, like that of a planet moving around the sun. This is illustrated by Millot's argument that, first, one needs to be defined as '+' (man) or '–' (woman) in relation to the immobile phallus and only once locked into its gender/sex identity can it start gyrating through various successive positions in the phallus' gravitational field—sissy man, butch woman, and so on. This narrative reaffirms the fixity and supremacy of the penis/phallus as definitive anchoring point of the symbolic universe, making the absence of lack of the Other into a sine-qua-non condition of being.

However, even if the bourgeois woman's jouissance is not per se a liberating force, it has potential: the simple fact that the patriarchal fantasy creates the myth of the woman's unbound jouissance opens the possibility of this fantasy's demise. In other words, the fantasy that feminine jouissance can destabilise the masculinist order creates the possibility to destabilise masculinist order. In its representation of feminine jouissance, the patriarchal fantasy forges a potentially devastating weapon against the Father: the perpetual risk that the subjects designated as 'women' will start acting as if they know that they will not lose any jouissance by cutting off the Father's head. This threat of a subject that enjoys her castration—although unrealistic at the moment—can nevertheless reach the proportions of acute paranoia for anyone committed to hiding the Father's lack. It is symptomatically expressed in the fear and hatred of militant feminism—the feminism that aims to make the Father irrelevant or expose his castration—exhibited by so many 'real' men and women.

There is, however, in the masculinised bourgeois fantasy a form of femininity that neutralises this threat to the Father because it is firmly tethered to the masculinist gender schema: the mother. It is for this very reason that patriarchy attempts to impose motherhood on each and every woman and that we do not really have any critiques of motherhood as a symbolic position coming from patriarchs, but only from feminists. This is an insight that the authors of the Bible, a manual on the implementation of the Father's law, also intuited:

> It was the woman who deceived and became disobedient, even though she will be saved through the birth of the Child, if they continue in faith, love and holiness, along with good judgement. (New Testament, Timothy 2:11)

Todd McGowan's (2013, 156–157) reading of the Lacanian story of sexuation is the orthodox one: men identify with the unitary ideal of the Father of the horde, which is uncontroversial, universal, and homogenous. In opposition, women are offered only partial and contradictory models and therefore cannot identify themselves as a unified category but only as unmarked, singular exceptions. As repeatedly stated, I am not certain that we can explain the operations of the modern sex/gender fantasy using such a model. What is much more interesting in McGowan's story is that it points towards a model of Woman that rivals that of Man and that, I would argue, is more unified and universal than that of the Father: the Mother. The reproductive female body and the nurturing, caring, and self-effacing feminine soul are the ideal in relation to which all other feminine models—chthonian goddess, witch, virgin, princess, saint, queen, warrior, and so on—gain meaning. McGowan (ibid. 268) himself comes back on his earlier pronouncement to acknowledge that, in the guise of Mother, the woman is fully integrated in the symbolic order rather than representing its point of failure: the mother is 'woman as a present identity …the complement of the master or father figure'. We could even argue that 'man' is a more fragile identity than 'woman', since the signifier 'father' does not manage to secure it so completely. While necessary, biological fathering is not sufficient to prove one's status as a 'real man' and even less one's status as an exceptional, non-castrated man. 'Motherhood', on the other hand, does accomplish this purpose for the woman. Indeed, the argument I will put forward in what follows is that the most pernicious operation of the phallic regime is not to erase woman, although it does that too, but to offer her motherhood as the unitary position through which she can obtain an exceptional symbolic presence: 'the truth in a woman, in Lacan's sense, is measured from her subjective distance from the position of motherhood. To be a mother, the mother of one's children, is to choose to exist as Woman' (Jacques-Alain Miller quoted in McGowan 2013, 269).

In the modern fantasy, motherhood promises woman to make her into the phallus,[6] beyond castration, beyond anxiety, and enjoying fully. And to the extent that motherhood represents an attempt to transcend castration by fully becoming one's sex/gender, the motherly subject is enjoying according to the masculine fantasy of wholeness and exhibits the same castrating fears and shame as a 'man'. The fact that many recent mothers describe their new symbolic status as 'I feel whole, I feel complete, blessed', and so on seems an attempt to express that from now on, they experience the threat of losing the penis. The mother is therefore perceived in the masculinist framework as returning privilege to man: she desires to transcend castration, in other words and somehow paradoxically she desires to be a man as defined by the patriarchal fantasy. For man this is the ultimate source of flattery ('I want to be you') and enjoyment of the *other's* debasement ('you can never be me, you will always be a cheap copy'), the same enjoyment that the coloniser experiences when the colonized wants to become 'him'. The strands of maternalist feminism that aim to replace the repressive Father's law with the caring and empathic Mother's law seem to remain within this framework, since their aim is to displace not patriarchy but men and to occupy a position of phallic authority opened by the law itself. While feminists of this persuasion would insist that the maternal is oppressed and suppressed in the patriarchal regime, I will suggest the opposite: patriarchal dispositifs create the subject 'mother' and use it to secure the appeal of patriarchy.

On the other hand, the enjoyment of the woman that refuses motherhood is associated with the danger, inscrutability, and pathology that patriarchs ascribe to any subject they cannot subsume to their imperial schema of desire: the subaltern, the colonial, the homosexual, the racialised, the poor, the immigrant, and so on. The woman that refuses motherhood is the ultimate threat to patriarchy, the proof that the Father's offer of fullness is void and undesirable, which explains the systematic violence directed against her in the bourgeois order, ranging from symbolic to physical debasing.

McGowan (2013, 233) is right to argue that anti-abortionists want to inflict on women a form of death by denying her abortion: it is the death (*fatum*) of being instituted as Woman through motherhood. If motherhood is the ultimate modality of forcing one under the signifier Woman, then free abortion is the right to embrace the lack and refuse patriarchal identities. More generally, the pressure put on women to become mothers by such a wide variety of liberal dispositifs that tactically connect children's toys, biology books, media, art, the State, the medical establishment, husbands, other mothers or women, and so on must be explained not simply sociologically but also as an attempt to neutralise the threat posed to masculinity by the jouissance of the castrated subject that refuses the Father's promise of fullness. The concerted push for motherhood is an attempt to masculinize each and every desire.

While finishing my PhD, I started to read the acknowledgements of the books I was consulting, in their majority critical feminist studies of maternity and welfare in the USA, more than half of them written by women. Almost systematically, those scholars were thanking their children on the front page, and these dedications are symptomatic: most of these 'feminist' social policy books attempt to make 'woman' synonymous with 'mother'. To take but an example, Solinger's (2001,22–23) book, which presents itself as a defence of women's rights, frames the issue of foreign adoptions in the USA as a symptom of the 'choicelessness' of women in those deprived, backward countries from which children are imported: Romania, Russia, Mexico, and Vietnam. International adoptions 'almost always depend on extremely poor and/or culturally oppressed mothers who utterly lack choices' (22). Even if it is true that the children that 'affluent' US women adopt are almost always taken from 'poor' women, there is in Solinger's text an interesting slide between motherhood, choice, and emancipation that the financial dimension of the international adoption business networks does not suggest. This slide rather reflects the maternalist ideology of the US academic, who uses a sociological observation in order to make a political-ontological statement: the only emancipated choice for a woman is motherhood. And here one needs to be aware of the special valences of the term 'choice' in liberal discourses, where it signifies the defining characteristic of a free, rational, autonomous, sovereign, and educated subject, of a 'proper human'. As well as signifying the natural behaviour of this human, a reflection of her inborn propensities, uniqueness, character, and so on, in other words of everything that makes her an individual, the fundamental liberal form of humanity. For Solinger, only culturally oppressed and financially destitute (another sign of ontological destitution in liberalism) women that do not have a choice, thus lost their humanity, can give up their destiny as mothers. That one could choose voluntarily to renounce motherhood, for financial gain, for example, is implicitly presented as the characteristic of a person reduced to 'subhuman' status. I am not arguing that these 'choiceless' women sold their children voluntarily; the voluntary or not nature of their conducts is irrelevant for my analysis; and I am not contesting that maternity is a most powerful tool of subjectivation in patriarchy. I am arguing that Solinger presents motherhood as the only proper choice for a woman that aspires to the status of 'proper human', which is exactly what the Father's law tells us. This is confirmed further on, when Solinger argues that 'dignity and independence are, in fact, the life-enhancing ingredients that tend to be incompatible with relinquishing a child' (23). Refusing motherhood not only indicates a human without dignity but, ironically seeing how minutely governed motherhood is in the West, represents a sign of dependency; and the connections between dependency and a subhuman status in the US social policy discourses are systematic. What Solinger posits here, using as pre-text the situation of poor mothers that give their children up for adoption, is that a woman that refuses the position of mother in the liberal understanding of this subject-position, and especially after giving birth, lacks the basic traits of a 'free human being'.

It comes as no surprise that, when discussing the practices of removing the children of illegitimate mothers in the USA between 1945 and 1973 or so, Solinger (65–103) argues that those women were denied 'choice, rights, and motherhood' (71), putting on the same level of motherhood and the liberal markers of freedom: choice and rights. In the same logical move, Solinger defends the right of adopted children to find their 'real' parents, placing the biological (blood, genes, sperm, and egg) as the founding element of one's identity and of social relations in general and depoliticising parenthood as a social practice by reducing its meaning to insemination, pregnancy, and birth-giving. The US 'adoptees' movement ALMA (Adoptees Liberty Movement Association), founded in 1971, pushes this biological determinism to fairly tasteless extremes by defining themselves as part of the 1960s liberation movement and as sharing the same premises as the African-American struggle. In fact, ALMA made explicit analogies between adoption and slavery. These statements, as well as the declarations of the adoptees themselves, illustrate the emprise that submission to the realist modern fantasy, to one's name/identity as biological ('inch of life') has on the bourgeois subject; and the extent to which the bourgeois' love of submission combines with his mobilisation of narratives of martyrdom. One such adoptee declared that his past has been buried through adoption; another thought that being prevented from knowing 'the name I was born with' and whom his biological parents were made him feel like a second-class citizen (83). Most presented their desire to look for their biological parents as 'natural' (84). These accounts resonate with the theories about the psychological effects of a child's separation from his biological mother produced by Melanie Klein, Anna Freud, or John Bowlby (83) that still inform contemporary debates and have mutated into a brand of genetic determinism whose political effects are dubious. On the mother's side, most of the young women who had their baby being removed from them describe the event as the terrible experience of losing 'all that [one] has left in the world' (100). The same type of declarations that place motherhood as the foundational stone of a woman's being are present in the accounts of welfare recipients and activists (see Solinger 2001, 149, 157, 166, and 172):

> I would just like to say that it is time for our society to wake up and recognize [the] truth. I am a professional. I am a mother and motherhood is the most honorable and revered profession this world has ever known. It is also a position that is deserving the utmost respect. (Suzanne Murphy, welfare recipient, cited in Solinger 2001, 175)

And, on the law's side of the maternalist dispositifs, here is the statement of the director of reproductive endocrinology at Yale about the inability of some rich women to reproduce: 'They mourn the loss of personal growth, there is tremendous personal growth associated with having children' (201). Legal scholar Dorothy Roberts declares that 'denying someone the right to bear children deprives her of a basic part of her humanity' (210). Motherhood is thus offered as fundamental proof of a woman's humanity; as a woman's fundamental right to sovereignty, happiness, and fulfil-ment; and as a conduct defining what a woman naturally is, once again implying that the woman that chooses not to become mother is 'unnatu-ral', 'inhuman', or 'subhuman', the ontological categories that modernity usually reserves for the threatening *other*.

It is as if these advocates for women's rights never considered the hypothesis that liberal-capitalist State uses reproduction and the family as central pillars of its dispositifs and correlates motherhood with eugenic governmental impulses:

> Any Jewish woman who, as far as it depends on her, does not bring into the world at least four healthy children is shirking her [sacred] duty to the nation (he famously offered one hundred lirot to any woman on the birth of her tenth child). (Ben Gurion, cited in Rose 2005, 51)

In a fetishistic inversion, the instrument through which a potentially threatening subject is made governable by patriarchy, in this case moth-erhood, is understood as the most defining element of her being (her 'humanity') and as the main tool for emancipating herself from the patri-archal grip. The fastening of one's jouissance to the identity bestowed upon her by the phallic authority of the Father, here motherhood, and the efforts to protect this jouissance are illustrative of the way in which the will-to-not-know operates.

Reproductive Will-to-Not-Know

In the bourgeois fantasy, becoming a parent is another strategy for tran-scending castration: the child is an offering to the Other in exchange for which the parents expect full jouissance and recognition, the cancelling out of their anxiety. Evidently, the parental strive for full satisfaction is presented by the bourgeois reproductive rhetoric as an eminently altruistic, self-deny-ing conduct. However, as expected, the relationship with the modern Other is complicated by the psyche's inability to completely obliterate the memory of an obscene choice, trapping the bourgeois parents between two types of shame: a modified form of the classic 'submission shame' and, interestingly, a form of 'jouissance paranoia', the nagging suspicion of having made a bad choice jouissance-wise. This makes parenting a most difficult situation for the bourgeois subject, one that requires the compensating mechanisms of the will-to-not-know.

On the side of the 'submission shame', as is well known, reproducing means for the bourgeois opening themselves even further to the gaze of authority: a myriad of social institutions clamp down on the parent and child with microtome eyes, dissecting and judging. The school, social services, psychologists, doctors and nurses, child-raising manuals, media, fiction, other parents, the baby fashion police, the grandparents, uncles and aunts, and so on have the right to comment on and even intervene upon the bourgeois nucleus. Moreover, in the bourgeois sex/gender fantasy, good parents are conforming parents. For prospective parents, the normative templates of parenthood so abundantly exhibited by the Western dispositifs must be the only possible horizon of expectation. To be 'proper', the pre-reproduction bourgeois couple must expect nothing less (or more) than this regulated form of parenthood: the repetition of mass-produced symbolic gestures. Part of this regulation is the injunction to disinvest in the social, which is represented by the masculinist fantasy as a realm of frivolous practices of self-satisfaction and to focus one's energies on the responsible governing of the family, the 'selfless' fulfilment provided by the child, and the preservation of the womb-like, sanctuary qualities of the bourgeois home. All this compels the modern parent to cope with the shame of craving for the jouissance of parenthood and thus of eagerly submitting to the patriarchal blueprint of normality and respectability. Once bearing the mark of phallic enjoyment represented by the child, the bourgeois parent's effort to contest patriarchy is forever suspect of being counterfeit, making the necessity to appear as if rebelling against the law both more difficult and more pressing.

As to the mentioned 'jouissance paranoia', it stems from the same equating of reproduction and parenthood with full jouissance which makes these practices so alluring, a promise staged by the double symbolism of the child: as messianic promise for the future (see Edelman 2004) and as the parent's guarantee of full enjoyment (McGowan 2013, 41). However, in practice accessing this jouissance is not that simple. The mother faces a particular conundrum, since she finds herself stuck in a carnal relationship with the child. And however enjoyable this might be, in the realist modern fantasy, being a proper human means much more than enjoying one's body, making the bourgeois mother's enjoyment of the 'biological' relationship with the child similar to the irrational, animalistic, and primitive bodily jouissance that modernity ascribes to the colonised, racialised, lower classes, and the feminine. Having one's enjoyment equated with the enjoyment of the nonmodern *other* that is supposed to be everything the bourgeois is not is shameful indeed.

Related but not reduced to these anxieties of submission or regression to primitivism is the parent's anxiety that the child is actually not the ultimate phallic object, and therefore he/she did not really overcome castration. Due to the contradictory structure of the modern fantasy, the bourgeois parent can never fully convince herself that she did not miss on jouissance by having children. Having such dilemmas is a serious risk for both parents and child if we accept that by being stripped of the phallic aura the desiring subject invests it with; the object of the drive transforms into the terrifying Real object we cannot risk getting too close to. The Real object of the drive, then, remains fully within the symbolic/imaginary realm (rather than appearing to the desirer 'as it essentially is') but without its initial libidinal charge, and this is precisely why it looks horrible. If the phallic aura that the parents project on the offspring fades away, what will appear is not a 'real human child' in her natural form but a monstrous being that terrorises one's life, not dissimilar to the infant portrayed in David Lynch's *Eraserhead*.

From these dilemmas of parental jouissance—'does my child represent my sanctification or my debasing, full jouissance or a loss of jouissance?'—result further mechanisms of the reproductive will-to-not-know. The classical one involves the parent's and, again, disproportionately the mother's attempt to merge with the patriarchal ideology of parenthood that postulates 'children are both a holy duty and the ultimate fulfilment'. To make motherhood pleasurable under conflicting circumstances, the bourgeois woman must embrace the patriarchal fantasy of the sacred and primordial nature of the mother-child relationship that comes before the law, words, or the social and must attempt to convince herself that this bond is her developmental destiny and the most important contribution she can make to the world. Of course, this fantasy reiterates the modern patriarchal ideology that nurturing is the most natural and yet the most heroic of all conducts and the parent-child relationship is the most inspiring of social relations. Such merger with ideology immunises the parent-child bond from a critical analysis that can reveal it as less than what the patriarchal order promised, which would be a difficult realisation since the parent-offspring bond is irreversible.

The fantasy of instinctual *and* heroic motherhood gives the parents some respite by allowing them to present their loyalty to the Father's law as being its opposite: a unique opportunity for social and personal experimentation and transformation: 'there is something extraordinary, revolutionary, radically subjectivity-changing in parenting that you will miss on unless you have children'. Paralleling the mechanism, discussed in the second chapter, through which the will-to-not-know attempts to re-enchant the bourgeois universe, the regimenting of jouissance under the sign of the phallus that parenthood performs is presented as magic: retrieving one's true essence, seeing the light, blessing, miracle, fullness, and so on. Little wonder, then, that the maternalist bourgeois rhetoric is organised by catchphrases like 'putting in perspective', 'recalibrating' and 'reordering of priorities', sometimes radical enough to erase life before motherhood: 'I cannot even remember what my life was like before the baby'; and to engulf the mother completely: 'my life *is* the baby'. Such defence mechanisms, as mentioned, while insulating the mother against the lack in the Other (and replacing it with the terrifying threat of the disappearance of the baby's phallic aura), also perform the usual operations of the will-to-not-know, refocusing the subject's social horizon on the personal and her responsibilities and solidarity on the offspring.

Of course, this rhetoric is not enough to convince the patriarchal superego that the mother really enjoys fully. To achieve that status today, the bourgeois woman needs to be a mother; be desirable as a woman; and exhibit phallic jouissance, that is, some form of successful liberal career. This is yet another schizoid demand from the superego to demonstrate both feminised (passive) and masculinised (active) enjoyment, both submission to and rebellion against the sex/gender blueprint, and a particularly difficult task since the contemporary bourgeois order creates a tension between the attributes of proper feminine desirability and those of proper maternity. The maternal desire (for the phallic child) is supposed to be so supreme that no other desire should persist in that woman. Loss of desire is, thus, one of the law-stipulated conditions of motherhood: once obtaining the child, one has to feel fulfilled, complete, serene, ecstatic, beyond lack, and beyond desiring. Under this law's emprise, the mother feels that she has lost her want for more in the eyes of the Other, that she has obstructed the lack with the child and is out of the 'market of desire'. Otherwise put, the mother feels that she has lost desire as *objet a*, as cause of desire, and as source of jouissance (Stavrakakis 2007, 253): she has lost the pleasure of desiring. She therefore lost her attractiveness. This lack of attractiveness is not necessarily what men perceive; in fact, the unself-confident libidinal status of the mother makes her attractive to men, as illustrated by the emergence of the MILF category. Maternal insecurity has therefore more to do with the mother's own shame and anxiety at having abandoned the potentially unpredictable nature of her desire by having tethered it so univocally and irreversibly to the patriarchal machine.

This tension is illustrated by Renata Salecl's (2004, 100–102) dramatic example of Susan Smith, a US woman who in 1994 drowned her children in her car, apparently so as to secure the desire of her love interest, 'as if she wanted to abandon motherhood in order to reclaim some part of femininity [he] might find attractive' (101). As well as by the less dramatic but by no means less tragic efforts of the media to make motherhood glamorous. Here is how the website InStyle (http://www.instyle.com/celebrity/celebrity-moms, accessed 4 December 2015) presents its extremely well-stocked 'Celebrity Moms' page:

> Get an inside look at how celebrity moms are redefining maternity style – and dressing their stylish babies and kids for life in the spotlight. See the chic pregnancy clothes of Hollywood stars like Kate Middleton, Blake Lively, Angelina Jolie and Jennifer Lopez, and then shop our clothing picks to make their best mom-to-be outfits your own. Plus: click through the cutest instagram photos of celebrity moms and their fashion-forward tots.

The reverse side of this discourse of the child as the object that erases castration is the parental paranoia that everybody else is trying to steal their baby so that they experience this full jouissance themselves. This paranoid will-to-not-know produces jouissance through conjuring the figures of the contemporary ogres: the paedophile, the child molester, and the child kidnapper. These figures' promotion to the rank of major anxiogenic and phobic images of contemporary liberal-capitalism has to do with their role in the reproductive will-to-not-know, that is, in reassuring the parent that the child is indeed the supreme phallic object that everyone else desires and that therefore reproducing was the proper choice, which guarantees full jouissance rather than its loss. The representation of any adult's intimacy with someone else's children and even with their own children as terror feeds the fetish of the child's forever-endangered sexual innocence[7] and of the child as the ultimate object of desire that currently dominates Western culture. This is not to say that there are not people sexually turned on by children or that there are not people trying to impose themselves on children. But their existence does not in any way infirm the mechanism through which the existence of the paedophile becomes a dominant parental and State paranoia (Lacan says the same about jealousy: it is pathological even if the partner does indeed cheat on you).

I will conclude this subsection with some quotes from celebrity mothers retrieved from the Internet—the websites and pages of women's magazines are filled up weekly with hundreds of such quotes—that illustrate most of the reproduction-related will-to-not-know tactics described above. I will just insist on another rhetorical strategy featured in these quotes, what Barthes calls an 'Operation Margarine' (a concept which bears more than a passing resemblance to the concept of suture):

> To instill into the Established Order the complacent portrayal of its drawbacks has nowadays become a paradoxical but incontrovertible means of exalting it. Here is the pattern ...: take the established value which you want to restore or develop, and first lavishly display its pettiness, the injustices which it produces, the vexations to which it gives rise, and plunge it into its natural imperfection; then, at the last moment, save *in spite of*, or rather *by* the heavy curse of its blemishes. (Barthes 1972, 41)

Barthes' literary and film examples are of bourgeois institutions tightly connected to the family: the army, which in Fred Zinnemann's *From Here to Eternity* is first presented as a tyrannical, narrow-minded, and unfair institution before being displayed triumphant, flags flying, in an image that makes it irresistible to the viewer (ibid.). Or the church, which in Graham Greene's *The Living Room* is displayed in all its bigotry and its potentially murderous effects only to be redeemed at the end by the demonstration that 'the letter of the law … is a way of salvation for its very victims', which justifies the church's shortcomings through 'the saintliness of those whom it crushes' (ibid.). Barthes' final and equally compelling example is that of margarine ads. This tactic works homoeopathically, presenting the ills of an institution only to neutralise any potential revolt against the established order, precisely by showing to the subject how her revolt might look like. Representing to the viewer, the ills of the established order suggests that such revolt against it is a common affliction that needs to be exorcised and represents the established order as both marginally evil and supremely good, inevitable, and beneficial: 'The immanent evil of enslavement is redeemed by the transcendent good of religion, fatherland, the Church, and so on. A little "confessed" evil saves one from acknowledging a lot of hidden evil' (42). What are the little deficiencies of order compared to its advantages, to the gift of identity it bestows on the bourgeois subject? Wouldn't acknowledging the far-reaching effects of the governing technology of motherhood be considerably more detrimental, costing us too much in 'scruples, in revolt, in fights and in solitude' (ibid.), than the comfort of surrendering to its lure, especially if one can mimic revolt and reflexivity through this operation margarine?

Declarations by mothers, famous or not, all similar to those presented below, indefatigably forge a panoply of standardised utterances, acting as an armour against any troubling questions about jouissance, desire, and submission. I did not mention the name of the blessed celebrity mothers making these declarations so as not to unnecessarily feed anyone's celebrity fetish (except mine). The first batch is taken from the Red Book website (http://www.redbookmag.com/life/mom-kids/interviews/g392/celebrity-moms/?slide=1, accessed 4 December 2015):

> I was confident before I had my children, but maturing and becoming a mother enhances that self-confidence. You learn that you can take on quite a lot and make it all work. When your kids need you to be strong and secure, it's very natural to be.

You make sacrifices to become a mother. But you really find yourself and your soul when you are one.

[Being a mom made me...] realize something that no one tells you: Sometimes it's incredibly boring, but most of the time, it's wonderful.

[Being a mom made me...] calm — in a way that I would never have thought. I can get ready so quickly now. I'm shocked: It used to take me two hours to get ready for everything, and now I'm like, 'We're leaving in 10, let's go!' As long as my son's okay, we're good.

Being a mom made me stronger. I'm a warrior!

Being a mom has made me so tired. And so happy.

The second batch, from Babble (from http://www.babble.com/entertainment/celebrity-moms-on-motherhood/):

As a mother I always have something better to be doing. I love work still but I'm less tolerant of my time being wasted.

Becoming a mother has helped me to realize who I am aside from my career.

[7-year-old child's name] is the best part of my life. I love everything about being a mom, but our walks and talks on the beach are my favourite moments.

'Oh, I'm just a mom' you hear women say. Please! Being a mom is everything. It's mentorship, it's inspirational, and it's our hope for the future.

Your children teach you so much. It's a real mirror of yourself.

The natural state of motherhood is unselfishness. When you become a mother, you are no longer the center of your own universe. You relinquish that position to your children.

Finally, the most margarine-friendly of the lot, from the website BuzzFeed, which grouped them under the title: '19 Celebrities Who Were Refreshingly Honest About Motherhood' (from http://www.

buzzfeed.com/kimberleydadds/inspiringly-honest-celebrity-comments-about-motherhood#.usMXn6naG):

> I think if you ask any pregnant mom, they're like: 'I want my body back'... The second I start to get down like 'What happened to my body?' I look at my beautiful baby – and I've never been more appreciative for this body that I have.

> Nobody told me it would be this hard ... But I love it, I really love it.

> You're participating in the most beautiful cycle this Earth has to offer – who cares if you put on weight for a few moths or a year or two years? In the grand scheme of things, I refuse to let it bother me.

> It gets you down sometimes, I'm not going to lie. I've had days when I'm like 'Ugh, I wish this was easier'. But it's not, and that's ok.

> It's one part of my life I'm learning about every day. I've been challenged a lot by it, but it's the most rewarding part.

> I feel incredibly lucky and blessed. But I do sometimes I feel like that exorcist lady!

> It's exhausting, but my daughter is the light of my life ... It's just so hard trying to express that verbally.

> When you're having dinner with your kids and husband and someone says something funny or you're dying laughing because your three-year-old made a fart joke, it doesn't matter what else is going on. That's real happiness.

Attaching the Libidinal Cord

There are more facets to the difficult position of the mother within the bourgeois sex/gender fantasy since, according to this framework, she adopts a masculinised structure of desire while lacking the essential attributes that entitle one to such phallic forms of being, that is to say, while lacking a penis. Thus, the patriarchal order introduces another impossible to solve contradiction in the psyche of the woman-mother: while the

Mother represents for a woman the phallic position, the position and experience of motherhood are forever insecure and remain marked by the woman's symbolic castration. In psychoanalysis' own retelling of this paternal narrative, it is the instinctual, non-symbolic nature of mothering that turns her into a danger to the child, a crocodile ready to engulf and re-assimilate her within her body. I would suggest a reversal of this typology: assuming that we can observe such saurian conducts in mothers more frequently than in fathers, we should not take them as an indication that this is how sexualised structures of desire are implanted in the mother and the father's psyche. Rather, this rapacious conduct is a reaction to the impossibility of being a mother in the patriarchal order.

These dilemmas are less acute in the case of the paternal position: once the baby is born, the man considers himself consecrated as father for all eternity, having proven to the Other his virility and bestowed on the child his name, bloodline, identity, inheritance, and an ego-ideal without the need to have an embodied bond with the infant. Fatherhood, thus, remains secured by its positioning in this abstract, superegoic field from which no one can dislocate it. The man can more easily annex the child as his masculinity-enhancing phallic object even in the absence of a direct relationship with the child, which is maybe why men can more easily run away from the child without jeopardising their selfhood. The amount of Hollywood artistic productions[8] dealing with this abstract, fetishistic relationship with the 'shadow of the father' that does not need his constant physical presence, from Chris Nolan's 'Batman' films to Paul Thomas Anderson's 'Magnolia' and to 'Iron Man', 'Thor', 'Kung Fu Panda', or even 'Star Wars', is illustrative.

The women's position as mother, on the other hand, becomes less secure after giving birth than while pregnant. Once her bodily performance is over, claiming the child as 'hers' is less self-evident, since the bourgeois sex fantasy gives her no right to phallic ownership. After all, she is 'minus', the castrated subject that cannot assume phallic valences. Symbolically, the State, market, army, bloodlines, grandparents, and so on have more grip on the child than the mother. The mother is body, caring, nurturing,[9] imaginary, not bestowing symbolic identity. Her efforts to assert symbolic rights, being shaped by the Father's law, are therefore compelled to take the form of disciplines in the Foucaultian sense—the woman demonstrates she is a mother by cajoling the baby, playing with her, reading her children's stories, and teaching her to go to the potty, not to eat dirt, to wash, to walk, to talk, and so on. When affluent bourgeois women quit work using the line: 'I have to stay with my baby while she is growing, otherwise I will miss these most important moments', their fear is that they will lose this opportunity to assert symbolic, if carnal, ownership of the child: 'I remember your first tooth; when you were suckling my teat; your first word was…'

While crucial to the functioning of patriarchy, this embodied relationship between the mother and the child is, at the same time desirable and fragile, venerated and reviled in the contemporary bourgeois world and therefore needs both validation and policing. And is not the governmental function of 'Attachment Parenting' as a network of knowledge, discourses, and practices that shapes subjectivity—I refer to the parenting dispositif promoted by a network of predominantly North-American non-governmental institutions, of which I will discuss below the Attachment Parenting International (API)—to confirm the bodily, instinctual, disciplinary bond between the mother and the child as the only possible and relevant one?

One piece on the topic by a Richard V. Reeves on the website of the Brookings Institution (http://www.brookings.edu/blogs/social-mobility-memos/posts/2015/04/21-attachment-theory-parents-reeves) marks from the beginning the interesting position that the governing of motherhood occupies in the network of liberal dispositifs, if only because of the author's background: his CV blurb informs us that he is a senior fellow in Economic Studies, co-director of the Center on Children and Families, and editor-in-chief of the Social Mobility Memos blog; that his research focuses on social mobility, inequality, and family change; and that prior to joining Brookings, he was director of strategy to the UK's Deputy Prime Minister. The State, the economy, social stratification, bourgeois reproduction, and the mother's body are tightly connected in neoliberal governmentality. This short piece discusses a three-decade longitudinal study of low-income children performed by a team of psychologists from the University of Minnesota that, according to Reeves, clarifies a lot about the topic of 'opportunity and equality today'. According to this study:

counter-intuitively, the infants who have a reliable caregiver are also most likely to become self-efficacious later ... But this virtuous learning cycle breaks down if the caregiver fails to respond adequately.

The window of opportunity for the creation of these self-efficacious citizens through the complete 'responsiveness' of the mother[10] to the child's needs, seems to be the 9–18 months of age, somewhat overlapping with the psychoanalytical timeline of the Oedipus. There is nothing new introduced by this 30-year-long study, whose only purpose is to reiterate much older ideas about the mother's duty to the young child: the injunction that the mother has to become the one and only significant presence in the life of the toddler. And the only mother-child interaction this research classifies as 'secure attachment' is that which makes the mother into a threatening crocodile without whose presence the child experiences immediate distress:

> When the caregiver (mom, in this study) is present, the infant explores the room and interacts with the experimenter, occasionally returning to the caregiver for support. When the caregiver leaves, the child becomes sad and hesitates to interact with the experimenter, but upon their return, is visibly excited.

The psychologists also taxonomise an 'anxious/resistant' type of attachment, where the child is generally afraid of novel situations and resentful of the mother's departure, which seems not much more than an exacerbated subset of the 'secure attachment' category. And, at the other extreme, a third, 'anxious/avoidant' type of attachment where the child manifests no preference between the mother and a stranger:

> Infants play normally in the presence of the experimenter and show no sign of distress or interest when their caregiver leaves and returns. The experimenter and the caregiver can comfort the infant equally well.

The latter, anxious/avoidant type, is considered the most problematic one, the one that presumably will not yield 'efficacious citizens'. Which can be read as this psychological study's claim that a child with no particular attachment to the body of the biological mother, that is, a child that remains unaffected by the Oedipal conditioning and thus unaffected by the symbolic weight of the bourgeois family triad, is a liability, or at least inadequate for functioning in the bourgeois order. In other words, what this lengthy study seems to claim through its 'objective taxonomies', and its entire design is that, to become a proper 'independent' bourgeois adult, the child needs to become fully dependent on the mother. Moreover I would go as far as suggesting that, in the framework of these Minnesota researchers as well as in Reeves' interpretation of it, the role of the mother as nurturing-disciplinarian authority in the child's early life is to create a pattern of love of authority on which the law of Father—represented by Reeves as liberal 'self-efficacy' or 'independence', that is, the ability to seize and maximise 'opportunity'—can easily graft itself, displacing the mother and her carnal presence and filling up the affective locus left with the letter of the phallic authority. 'Dependence [on the mother] builds [masculine, liberal] independence', in Reeve's words, revealing the Oedipus as an expert prescription rather than a natural occurrence.

These studies' governmental function is to correlate the bourgeois child's conditioning within the family, where her autonomy, in evolutionist terms her development, must exist only if guaranteed by the parent/master, with the general functioning of the bourgeois psyche and liberal-capitalist order. This governmental framework aims to shape a 'proper' bourgeois adult unable to think of herself as autonomous and self-determining unless within a space secured by an authoritative but familiar law, in the most obvious cases in the spaces made safe by the family and the State. In other words, the proper bourgeois is a subject whose personal freedom—and this is the story that Hobbes re-spins in his social contract fantasy—can only exist in spaces protected by a master. It is not only the expert networks that promote this idea of freedom-qua-submission; it has a capillary status, circulating freely through the spaces that liberal political philosophy wants to keep separate: the public and private, the collective and the personal, and the regulated and spontaneous conduct. For example, a recurrent educational tactic one observes among enlightened parents is to feign to abandon the child that shows signs of independent desire: 'Ok, mommy/daddy is leaving now, bye-bye baby, see you …', and so on. Here the parent threatens the child to give her the independence she craves and, in the same move, reminds her that by herself, independently of the parent, she is helpless. While reinforcing in insidious but violent manners of parental authority ('without me you're as good as dead …'), this threat of removing protection can also be read as a projection of the parent's own fear of being left without his master's protection (State, government, boss, military, etc.) and contributes to creating the same fear in the child. This is bourgeois parenting at its best, transmitting generationally the love and fear of the Father, 'a life cycle of compassion and connection', as the experts from API would argue (see below).

'Attachment Parenting', on which Reeves' draws, is a child-raising technique quite popular at the moment and developed by a paediatrician, William Sears and his wife Martha in the 'bible book' titled *The Baby Book*. API is a US-based non-profit association founded in 1994 whose board of directors and staff is 100 % women, a majority of them are professionals, from clinical psychologists to business women. The following comments are taken from their official website (http://www.attachmentparenting.org, 5 December 2015). I will not go into details when analysing the onto-epistemological construction of such studies, since I have done it elsewhere (see Panu 2009), but simply present some examples of their rhetoric to illustrate the points already made in this section. The API aims to strengthen the bourgeois family as a method of forging parent-child dependency or, in their own words, to foster 'parenting practices that create strong, healthy emotional bonds between children and their parents'. In other words, their aim is to secure and strengthen the Oedipal bond, the dissipation of which conservatives in the USA and elsewhere are in permanent fear of witnessing and which would mean for all these worried parents the end of bourgeois civilisation (on which point, I concede, they might not be far from the truth). Their aim is a self-reproducing system of Oedipal bonds, all in the name of that most defining trait of the bourgeoisie, compassion of course: 'A life cycle of compassion and connection … As a result, this strong attachment helps children develop the capacity for secure, empathic, peaceful, and enduring relationships that follow them into adulthood'. The benefits of this Oedipalisation of the parent-child relations are, apparently, nothing less than a bright bourgeois future:

> Through education, support, advocacy and research, API's principal goal is
> to heighten global awareness of the profound significance of secure attach-
> ment – not only to reduce and ultimately prevent emotional and physical

mistreatment of children, addiction, crime, behavioral disorders, mental illness, and other outcomes of early unhealthy attachment, but to invest in our children's bright futures.

The foundation of API's truths is, as customary for these satellites of the realist modern fantasy, nature itself, that is, human needs as 'hardwired' in the infant's brain and discovered by 'researchers studying the brain' (I will remind the reader that one of the favourite lines of the bourgeois will-to-not-know is 'Science has proven that ...'; see Chap. 2):

> These studies revealed that infants are born 'hardwired' with strong needs to be nurtured and to remain physically close to the primary caregiver, usu-ally the mother, during the first few years of life. The child's emotional, physical, and neurological development is greatly enhanced when these basic needs are met consistently and appropriately. These needs can be summarized as *proximity, protection, and predictability.*

From here on, the API discourse—summarised into their commandment-like 'Eight Principles of Parenting'—ineluctably clamps the body of the child onto that of the mother to transform the latter into a docile and useful tool of patriarchy. Once the mother is reduced to an appendage of the baby's body and vice versa, the woman's most important triggers will be the child's 'needs', which she needs to learn decoding and responding promptly. Here is a selection of such advice:

> You can build the foundation of trust and empathy by understanding and responding appropriately to your infant's needs. Babies communicate their needs in many ways including body movements, facial expressions, and crying. They learn to trust when their needs are consistently responded to with sensitivity. Building a strong attachment with a baby involves not only responding consistently to his (sic) physical needs, but spending enjoyable time interacting with him (sic) and thus meeting his (sic) emotional needs as well ... Understand your child's natural inner rhythms, and try to sched-ule around them. The more parents learn to identify and meet their baby's needs, the more securely attached the parent-child bond becomes. It is per-fectly normal for babies to want constant physical contact. High levels of stress, such as during prolonged crying, cause a baby to experience an

unbalanced chemical state in the brain and can place him at risk for physical and emotional problems later in life.

Breastfeeding is firmly promoted as the best method of infant feeding and comforting, as well as providing unmentioned benefits for the mother, and mothers are encouraged to continue breastfeeding for as long as possible: 'Breastfeeding continues to be normal and important nutritionally, immunologically, and emotionally beyond one year'. More recently, a scientific study hailing from Brazil (http://www.theguardian.com/lifeandstyle/2015/mar/18/brazil-longer-babies-breastfed-more-achieve-in-life-major-study) correlates the length of breastfeeding with the child's IQ and professional future including earnings, seamlessly linking the liberal favourite discourses of maternalism (maternal care determines adult socio-biological characteristics and success and adult character); eugenics (intelligence is a pre-social, biological given); and meritocracy (in capitalism, the most intelligent occupies the most prestigious and well-paid social positions).

Unsurprisingly, parental roles are strictly delimited, even if in that soft voice of the wise patriarch: 'Mothers flourish when nurtured by their partners. Fathers can develop a relationship with the baby in many other ways than feeding'. As the child grows, the mother remains an embodied appendage of her 'normal development' and the provider of the comforting master's gaze, the one that secures the bourgeois child's desire to 'explore', as this final selection of commandments and axioms illustrates:

> Support explorations by providing a safe environment for discovery and remaining close by. Show interest in the child's activities and participate enthusiastically in child-directed play. Instead of trying to fit baby into the existing pre-baby schedule, come up with creative ways to design new routines that include the baby. Consider taking a sleeping baby along on date night, getting exercise by taking walks with baby in a sling, taking a trusted caregiver along for long evenings or special events, and working with employers to create a schedule that maximizes both parents' time with their child. Different children are ready for separation at different ages, but research shows separations of longer than two nights can be very difficult for children under the age of three.

Portrait of Oedipus as a Bourgeois Fetish

In the light of this concerted, if always incoherent, attempt to keep the Oedipal drama as the decisive structure that shapes the bourgeois adult's conducts, it is probably necessary to put Oedipus to work in a more interesting way. My attempt is obviously inspired by Deleuze and Guattari's (2000) critique of the Oedipus as a strategy of bounding desire to capitalist dispositifs, but tries to reconcile their attack on patriarchy with the idea of lack (which they hate).

I will suggest that the Oedipus is not a temporally, spatially, and ontogenetically easy to locate event that, with clockwork regularity, causes the coming into being of the bourgeois psyche, but itself a fantasy that instructions bourgeois desire, soothing the contradictions of the modern cosmology with the ointment of the boudoir drama. Bourgeois enjoyment is not Oedipal because the paternal law of incest prohibition and gendered identification is imprinted in our psyche ineluctably since infancy; but because the Oedipal fantasmatic frame manages the bourgeois' relation to authority, helping her pretend that the enjoyment she takes in submitting to authority is actually a private, exceptional, and almost always tragic story about some mommy/daddy/me combo: 'My libidinal and social predicaments are not a result of my desire for and my efforts to be recognised by the patriarchal, colonial, liberal-capitalist authorities; but of the particularities of my childhood and upbringing'. In other words, oedipalising the bourgeois libidinal flows is an active effort to make reality less anxiogenic, by representing love of authority ('I desire to be a proper bourgeois; I deserve success; I desire wealth and comfort') as a unique family story ('because my parents asked me to make them proud; or sacrificed everything for my success; or denied me piano lessons; or were poor; or abusive', etc.).

According to the dominant modern discourses, and explaining the efforts of dispositifs like API to reclaim this classification, the child's power relationship with the parents is degrading, a type of 'dependency' such discourses attribute to abject *others*: slaves, colonial subjects, women, welfare recipients, and so on. For example, the first act of investiture that a child is submitted to after having been gendered is being given a first name, an act that in the modern fantasy and Western history is characteristic of processes of domination/submission: historically, the re-naming of the colonial subject or slave to reflect the symbolic and libidinal order of the master has been a powerful gesture of marking one's control over another. Think of the function of giving the master's name to the slave in North America or of the function of Catholic baptism in the South American colonies. The same is valid of renaming subjects upon their entry into a Christian group, be that a monastery or a Baptist group. In return for marking the child with the symbol of their enjoyment, the parents demand from her not simply obedience but the unconditional recognition, love, and respect due to a good master. From the obstinate insistence that the first words of the child should be mamma or dada to the never-ending questions—'Do you love mommy/daddy? Whom do you love most?'—and assertions: 'Mommy/daddy loves you more than anything. You are *my* baby forever', the dependence of the child's being on her libidinal relationship with the parent is relentlessly instilled.

Why, then, is it that once the offspring does obtain some relative agency in the relation with the parents, she finds it nearly impossible to break with the family, to refuse her given name, and to erase mommy and daddy from the position of sun and moon of her symbolic cosmos? Why are we constantly going back to the family? Hardly because the family leaves an indelible mark of the 'fuck one/kill the other' type on our psyche, I would argue, and more plausibly because the family gives the child the security of being permanently desired by the authority figures whose recognition she learned to desire. If the offspring represents for the parents an embodiment of their desire offered to the big Other, then for the offspring, after her voyage through the intimate corridors of the bourgeois family, the parents become a metonym for the enjoyment she obtains in return for submitting to authority. In the bosom of the family, the bourgeois adult feels constantly desired by the Other; she feels that her identity is grounded in something more than just language, in something pre-symbolic and natural: we always will be mama's or papa's boy/girl. Little wonder that the signifier 'son/daughter' is experienced as one of the most natural, profound identities.

The Oedipal fantasy, then, offers a scenario in which submitting to authority is rewarded with love/recognition. And isn't it that from the beginning of her symbolic life, the child understands symbolic hierarchies and the power relation with the parents in conjunction, in the sense that the parent is always understood by the child in the light of his or her position in a symbolic hier-archy? Within the bourgeois family, the father is invested with the author-ity of patriarchy: of the State, the army, or the nation, just like a sergeant is invested with the power of the (immortal) national army. And if, to invert the example, the soldier or the respectable citizens think of the army as daddy, it is because power has learned that this is a very important mechanism for obtaining docility. We are thus told: the army, the nation, and the state are like your father that loves and protects you and safeguards the family, even if the law we apply is sometimes severe. Respecting and loving the father and mother is a symptom of one's respect and love for the symbolic order that invests them with their weight: for the State, the president, the prime minister, the army, the nation, the flag, the boss, the doctor, the professor, and generally the expert; for the bourgeois entertainment industry; for the successful and famous; for gender/sex and (hetero)sexuality; for the private/public divide with the man ruling both; for blood as the most important tie uniting humans ('biological parents') and for purity of blood as signifying purity of being; and, related, for race as a defining feature of the self, since the purity of blood/lineage in the bourgeois family is correlated to the racial or blood purity of the nation (Germanness and Britishness).

Once this two-way relationship between submission to the symbolic authority and submission to the mother and father is achieved, the bour-geois tries to keep her jouissance within the confines of the family's elastic straightjacket. The Oedipus brings bourgeois anxiety on the terrain of the known and predictable, that is, of the loops of desire and aggres-siveness we are used performing within the bourgeois family, and shapes enjoyment in relation to the bourgeois' submission to a familiar/famil-ial authority whose desires and demands are manageable, replacing the threatening Other with the soothing figures of mom and dad. And since in the Oedipal scheme the imaginary *other* is the parent, it can be easily integrated in the self ('I am like mom' or 'mom traumatized/educated/shaped me'), making unnecessary the thinking of the non-kin *other-in-self* that constitutes us and thus allowing the continuation of the enjoy-ment the bourgeois takes in annihilating this *other*. Of course, this is not to deny that the Oedipus also allows us to compulsively extract enjoyable martyrdom and aggressiveness from the relationship with mom and dad, but the aggressiveness against the parents or child is usually less extreme than that against the *other*, since mitigated by the narcissistic fantasy that parents or children are a 'part of us'.

Today, the law tries to keep the libidinal circuits of the bourgeois parent-child relationship constantly present, to place them at the foundation of any and each explanation of subjectivity, pleasure, and desire. This is why, whenever attempting to explain her life and reality in general, the bourgeois returns to her familial trauma. The symbolic family album is flunked on the table whenever one gets into an intimate conversation with a bourgeois, with the same anxious eagerness and entitlement that parents have when showing everyone photos of their kids.

Conclusion

How can the body be utilised as an instrument for destabilising the compulsive reiterations of jouissance imposed by contemporary bourgeois dispositifs? It is difficult to provide an unequivocal answer to this question, considering that the modern fantasy's reality-shaping regime mobilises the body so extensively, strictly, and, so far, successfully. One possible experiment in this direction might be detaching the feminine and especially the pregnant body from motherhood. The connection between these elements, pregnancy and motherhood, although it seems to us the most natural thing, is a painstakingly constructed and maintained artefact of the patriarchal order. Indeed, motherhood as an individual, exclusively feminine code of practices does not make sense but within a patriarchal, bi-gendered system that describes the woman's natural fate as being reproduction and nurturing. Severing the connection between the feminine body and motherhood would thus challenge both the dichotomous gendereed system that partly rests on the figure of the mother and the ramified system of dispositifs that in the bourgeois regime mobilise and put to work motherhood, from public health and eugenics to differential gendered wages, welfare, or militarism. More importantly, severing this connection might transform the feminine body into the threat that the patriarchal order fantasises it already is: the threat of a subject that enjoys castration and that, therefore, is living proof that the Father is dead.

Notes

1. Dean considers the phallus, or its equivalent the Name-of-the-Father, to be ungendered (85, note 36).

2. The 'how' and 'why' of this blockage are left obscure. It remains surprising that, while many Lacanians insist on the cosmogonic function of the Real, they seem rather shy when it comes to defining what this extra-linguistic entity represents in relation to language. Dean (88) tells us that the Real can be defined only negatively, as a normative zone of impossibility: 'the real is what must be excluded. The real is not the effect of symbolic or imaginary orders; at most it is a theoretical construct that explains negatively the function and limits of these two orders' (ibid.). That the Real is the name we give to the impossibility of fullness is a tenable position, but the rest of this definition is less so. If the Real is born through exclusion, or if the Real is the name we give to that which cannot be expressed in symbolic or imaginary registers (Dean uses both definitions, although they are not quite referring to the same thing), then how can the ontological status of the Real be independent of that from which it is excluded? Moreover, how can the Real precede causally that from which it is excluded (the symbolic field)? That is, how can it precede causally the symbolic field if it is apprehended as the failure of symbolisation? Since Dean defines the Real using a language of obligation or necessity ('what *must* be excluded for the subject as a speaking being to constitute itself', my italics), according to what rules, if any, is this exclusion performed and according to what or whose necessities? Are these rules and necessities universal, ahistorical givens or are they contingent, as imaginary and symbolic content are?

   That these fundamental premises of the ontological status of the Real remain unelucidated do not prevent Dean (2000, 78) from making strong ontological statements, for example, that discourse is an effect of the Real and not the other way around, turning the Real into a God-like entity that brings into being the symbolic and imaginary world, a supernatural figure whose nature and existence cannot be known or contested but whose laws *must* be followed to the letter. A true fantasy of an Other of the Other. And when sex difference is made synonymous with the Real, the demiurgic qualities of the Real are transferred to it. Which, one would think, goes against Dean's project of detaching desire from heterosexuality.

3. Impervious to decades of critique of the modern framing of madness, Fink (1999, 98) describes psychosis, implicitly in its relationship to improper gendering, as the greatest social threat imaginable: '[the psychotic] is more

prone to immediate action, and plagued by little if any guilt after putting someone in the hospital, killing someone, raping someone, or carrying out some other criminal act'.

4. Proper fathering is a delicate balance for these daddy-loving theorists: either an excessively strong or excessively weak father will lead to deficient sons.

5. This genitalisation accounts for the symptomatic bourgeois attempts to transcend castration through sexual performances, as attested by Millot's memoirs of compulsive heterosexual copulation.

6. It is clear that, as already mentioned, the desire to be the phallus is in no way an indication of a feminine or masculine structure of desire but represents a constant of any subject that tries to fully become his or her gender. If a woman wants to become a mother so as to become the phallus, above castration and enjoying without limits, a man desires to possess a desirable woman—or a car, a gun, son, crown, and so on—for exactly the same reason.

7. See McGowan (2004, 143–145) for a discussion of the child as the 'subject supposed to not know'.

8. 'This ideology [of the family], of course, finds its clearest expression in Hollywood as the ultimate ideological machine: in a typical Hollywood product, everything, from the fate of the knights of the Round Table through the October Revolution up to asteroids hitting the Earth, is transposed into an Oedipal narrative'. (Žižek 2008, 52)

9. This was not always the case, since motherhood ideology in the West undertook significant historical reconfigurations; see, for example, Badinter's (1981) genealogy.

10. Although it is both parents that are supposed to serve the child's needs, the Minnesota psychologists performed their multi-decade research exclusively on mothers, making it fairly clear that they are in fact talking about just one of the parents.

References

Badinter, E. (1981). *The myth of motherhood: A historical view of the maternal instinct*. London: Souvenir Press.

Barthes, R. (1972). *Mythologies*. New York: Hill and Wang.

Butler, J., Laclau, E., & Žižek, S. (2000). *Contingency, hegemony, universality: Contemporary dialogues on the left*. London/New York: Verso.

Chiesa, L. (2007). *Subjectivity and otherness: A philosophical reading of Lacan.* Cambridge: The MIT Press.

Dean, T. (2000). *Beyond sexuality.* Chicago/London: University of Chicago Press.

Deleuze, G., & Guattari, F. (2000). *The anti-Oedipus. Capitalism and schizophrenia.* Minneapolis: University of Minnesota Press.

Donzelot, J. (1980). *The policing of families.* London: Hutchinson.

Fanon, F. (2008). *Black skin, white masks.* New York: Grove Press.

Fanon, Franz. 2008. *Black Skin, White Masks.* New York: Grove Press. Fink, B. (1999). *A clinical introduction to Lacanian psychoanalysis: Theory and technique.* Cambridge: Harvard University Press.

Foucault, M. (1977). *Discipline and punish: The Birth of the prison.* Hammondsworth: Penguin Books.

Foucault, M. (1990). *The history of sexuality volume 1: An introduction.* New York: Vintage Books.

Kane, S. (2001). *Complete plays.* London: Bloomsbury.

Lee, E. (2004). *No future: Queer theory and the death drive.* Durham: Duke University Press.

McGowan, T. (2004). *The end of dissatisfaction? Jacques Lacan and the emerging society of enjoyment.* Albany: State University of New York Press.

McGowan, T. (2013). *Enjoying what we don't have: The political project of psychoanalysis.* Lincoln/London: University of Nebraska Press.

Panu, M. (2009). *Contextualizing family planning: Truth, subject and the other in the US government.* London/New York: Palgrave.

Rose, J. (2005). *The question of Zion.* Princeton/Oxford: Princeton University Press.

Rose, Jaqueline. 2005. *The Question of Zion.* Princeton and Oxford: Princeton University Press.Salecl, R. (2004). *On anxiety.* London/New York: Routlege.

Solinger, R. (2001). *Beggars and choosers: How the politics of choice shapes adoption, abortion, and welfare in the United States.* New York: Hill and Wang.

Stavrakakis, Y. (2007). *The Lacanian left: Psychoanalysis, theory.* Politics: Edinburgh University Press.

Wallach Scott, J. (2011). *The fantasy of feminist history.* Durham/London: Duke University Press.

Žižek, S. (2006). *How to read Lacan.* New York/London: W.W. Norton &Co.

Žižek, S. (2008). *In defense of lost causes.* London/New York: Verso.

5

The Fantasmatic Revolution

My purpose in this final chapter is twofold: on one hand, to discuss critically the academic left's fantasy of the communist revolution in order to argue that it discourages revolutionary action rather than stimulating it. This discussion is relevant to the extent that academic discourses interact with and influence anti-capitalist political acts outside the academe. And on the other hand, to contribute to the on-going discussion of anti-capitalist tactics based on awareness raising, on protestor, which amounts to almost the same, on pointing out the adversary's shortcomings, of which the occupation of public spaces is a recent example. This discussion aims to question the implicit attachment that these 'politics of spectacle' have to the figure of fatherly authority and to the political-libidinal framework imposed by liberal-capitalism. Both discussions connect anti-bourgeois politics with the theme of a population profoundly devoted to its framework of jouissance, in this case to liberal-capitalism, and with the hypothesis, introduced in the previous chapter, that the task of anti-bourgeois politics is to 'turn its back' on this framework that serves so well the adversary's goals and to develop tactics and strategies that do not need the recognition or support of the master's gaze in order to function.

© The Author(s) 2016
M. Panu, *Enjoyment and Submission in Modern Fantasy*,
DOI 10.1057/978-1-137-51321-2_5

This analysis is not intended as yet another denunciation of the inadequacies of leftist thought and even less as a trial of the mistaken path chosen by whoever in the academic left does not share my own political fantasies. Even if it is presented in the form of a critique—clearly the most respected, expected, encouraged, and enjoyed form of academic interaction—and refers to academic discourses, this intervention is not conceived as an academic debate, but as a contribution to the experimental rethinking of tactics and of our own political imagination after the post-1990 'demise of the Left' as a hegemonic force. It seemed, however, timely to focus the first part of this intervention on the discourses of the academic left, not just because I am at the moment labouring within and thus propagating this sly State dispositif, but also because in contemporary capitalism, the relations between academic discourses and transformative political action are intimate and tense, and anxious even.

Most of today's Western political action is at some level inspired by academic productions, which since the rise of this State institution as the centre of anti-bourgeois thought seem to have monopolised the role of shaping our political fantasies. However, the gap between such academic work and radical political activity is wider than ever. Not only is it difficult to embed the socially deracinated narratives produced by the academic dispositif into relevant political tactics and strategies, but whenever the academic figures whose work tackles anti-capitalist action most confrontationally and uncompromisingly attempt to provide blueprints for action, or just illustrate their work with examples of such action, they come across as naïve in the best case, and as counter-productive or conservative in the worst. This chapter does not explain this theory-practice dynamic—such an explanation demands a book of its own—but discusses a particular aspect of the contemporary academic discourse's framing of the political.[1] That is, it tries to prompt a more serious reflection on the way in which Western academics self-defined as radical, including some with significant weight in shaping the contemporary leftist political imagination, put to use the fantasy of communist revolution as the sine-qua-non vanishing point of any relevant political tableau, since such prestigious imaginaries impact not just on academic politics but also on militantism outside the academe.

In a somewhat contradictory manner, I will initiate this discussion of the revolution with caveats. Firstly, I am not interrogating the fantasy of revolution in general—as a political horizon, this fantasy remains indispensable. My critical engagement is with the communist revolution as framed by academic discourses. And the critical aspect of this discussion does not stem from the hypocritical liberal position of refusing communist terror, violence, destruction, or authoritarianism as possible political tools for ending this centuries-long global capitalist crisis. If anything, such tools are already a habitual part of most people's lives, the routine instruments applied by liberal-capitalism to preserve bourgeois order (see e.g. Mbembe 2003). The principled distinction between violence and non-violence is one difficult to sustain when the definition of what counts as one or the other depends on partial, exclusionary, and contingent frameworks which make violence seep into non-violence and the other way around. While having recently given a series of lectures on the theme of non-violence, in a 2011 interview, Judith Butler expresses similar concerns:

> ... we are probably left with new quandaries about whether the line between violent and nonviolent resistance ever can be absolutely clear ... If one puts one's body on the line, in the way of a truck or a tank, is one not entering into a violent encounter? This is different from waging a unilateral attack or even starting a violent series, but I am not sure that it is outside the orbit of violence altogether. (http://blogs.ssrc.org/tif/2011/04/01/implicated-and-enraged-an-interview-with-judith-butler/)

What rather interests me are the political effects of defining the immediate task of the left as being that of taking power, or, which amounts to the same, the consequences of defining radical anti-capitalist activity around a ruptural event. In fact, my critique of contemporary communist revolutionary thought is that, despite its provocative vocabulary, it prevents the building of a different economy of enjoyment.

Revolutionary Events and Disciplinary Terror

Some time ago, Judith Butler was asking a crucial question: '...why does resistance appear in a form that is so easily co-opted by the opposition?' (Butler et al. 2000, 174). It will not come as a surprise that I suggest as one possible answer the will-to-not-know: whenever the symbolic authority—Father, State, government, army, economy, family, and so on—is in crisis, the bourgeois mobilises libidinal circuits that the modern dispositifs have most deeply implanted in his soul and most minutely monitored and nurtured, in an attempt to hide the Other's lack. For any form of political resistance arising from these libidinal circuits, co-option functions as an enjoyable fear of something that has already happened. These circuits try to refold whatever threat to authority into the comforting fantasy of submission to authority and range from embodied femininity to aggressive machismo; from familism to Hobbesian war of each against all; and from violence against the *other* to demands for the strengthening and perfecting of the liberal-capitalist governing dispositifs. In other words, resistance is easily co-opted because most of the customary forms of resistance we witness today represent a symptomatic enactment of our desire for authority.

This is, perhaps, why some of the most influential theorists of the contemporary left like Jameson, Badiou, or Žižek, came to theoretically depend on the trope, or hope, of a moment that definitively ruptures the bourgeois libidinal cycles of submission to authority, the event. The event they theorise, however, is not something that we can politically work towards since it is unpredictable, outside social control, seemingly unthinkable until it happens. Especially in Žižek's theorising, what is possible or impossible looks completely different before and after the event, since the latter's effect is to shuffle these very coordinates; the conditions of possibility of the event are a post-hoc effect of the radical symbolic transformation enacted by the event itself, not something strategically produced. My fear is that such theorising of a (communist) revolution triggered by the event works in self-defeating manners, reinforcing the libidinal loops it is supposed to interrupt.

Fredric Jameson suggests that the true revolutionary task is to re-invent our mode of dreaming by producing 'a set of narrative protocols with no precedent in our previous literary institutions' (Jameson in Žižek 2007b, xxix). Even if I am suspicious of institutions, pre- or post-revolutionary, I agree: the radical transformation of fantasising, desiring, and enjoying is the revolutionary task. However, what does it mean to make this transformation depend on an unsurpassable gesture of 'radical negativity' that erases the former blueprint for desire and identification (ibid. xxviii), especially if this negative moment is understood as the revolutionary taking of power? How does the narrative of a total purge affect our current political fantasies?

> ... the first moment of world-reduction, of the destruction of the idols and the sweeping away of an old world in violence and pain, is itself the precondition for the reconstruction of something else. A first moment of absolute immanence is necessary. (Jameson in Žižek 2007b, xxviii)

Similarly, Badiou (2003, 39) posits historical contradiction—from which the subject arises—as the dialectical antagonism between a pole of repetition that ensures the reproduction of bourgeois reality or the law, and a pole of destruction that is the non-law. What Badiou calls 'force' or 'more than real' is the thrust of this destruction which jams the mechanism of repetition of the law and precipitates its demise: 'In the place where the old coherence prescribed a mere sliding, we find instead an interruption that takes place through a purification that exceeds the place. This is the history of force' (ibid. 40). The force always surfaces as an event that cuts across lack and destruction (ibid.). The event imposes a new system of signification, a new master signifier, while the aim of revolution is to produce a crisis of reality by showing the whole truth of the symptom (42). Badiou's dialectic of repetition and destruction is an appealing model; I doubt, however, that this necessary destruction should be made to depend on the purifying event. Can we rely on a revolution predicated on a moment of truth, especially a truth as hard to accept for the bourgeois subject as that of the symptom?

As already mentioned, for Žižek, one of the definitions of the real act is 'transforming the very coordinates of the disavowed phantasmic foundation of our being' (Butler et al. 2000, 124). To the extent that any social or psychic structure is constructed around a disavowed traumatic kernel (or antagonism), the political act consists in intervening 'not out of nowhere but precisely *from the standpoint of this inherent impossibility, stumbling block, which is its hidden, disavowed structuring principle*' (ibid. 125, original italics). The true political act is generated by the conflict that shapes the symbolic order and its result is to dissolve the fantasy that maintains this conflict as the structuring principle of the symbolic. Žižek (Butler et al. 2000, 121) thus argues that the real political act is not the one performed within the symbolic structures, an attempt to 'solve the problems of the system', but the act that subverts and repositions the symbolic field's horizon of 'what is possible', retroactively creating the conditions of its own possibility. Here, we have to be realistic and demand the impossible.

In all these accounts, the necessary conditions for subverting the symbolic order are made to seem impossible precisely by our being within this order. To rupture our libidinal circuits, the act needs to intervene on the symbolic from outside it. But, as argued throughout this book, this outside position cannot be but an effect of the current symbolic order, even if an impossible to foresee one, just like a systemic error is in the scientific understanding of the term: a possibility undetectable from the theoretical or empirical system the scientists build but that nevertheless invalidates this system. Like any error, this act is experienced by the subject as an accident, that is, unpredictable and unwilled. Žižek's 'authentic act' is non-subjective and non-intentional, an encounter with the Real (Stavrakakis 2003, 122). I will reiterate that the necessity to restructure the symbolic field is not something that anyone committed to the radical transformation of the bourgeois regime would disagree with. What is questioned here is the possibility of a revolutionary event that intervenes on a mass of subjects for whom this event appears like an error.

The questions raised by such theorising of the event are, indeed, serious. For example, can we ever be certain that the moment of immanence that Jameson discusses, the devastating sweeping of the old world, coincides with the dissolution of the fantasy that supports the current symbolic order that Žižek writes about? Will the revolutionary event purge us of liberal-capitalist fantasies and forms of enjoyment or is the revolutionary purge, even while destroying the old idols in effigy, leaving these idols' erect fantasmatic position intact? Daniel Bensaid's critique (in Bosteels 2014, 16–17) is relevant:

> The philosophical hypothesis of the escape from the cavern by way of the event … does not allow the articulation of the event with history, of contingency with necessity, of the goal with the movement … for us there is no exteriority, no absolute outside of politics with regard to institutions, of the event with regard to history, of truth with regard to opinion. The outside is always within.

I am equally sceptical about the ability of an event to restructure a modern subjectivity particularly disposed to compulsively remember, re-imagine, and re-ignite its liberal-capitalist passions. Even if the event occurs, wouldn't the crisis of reality it engenders immediately intensify the mechanisms of the will-to-not-know? Isn't the bourgeois a subject whose jouissance is by now able to survive the demise of the old law and its dispositifs and face a new law intact? That is, if the bourgeois enjoys submission to authority and develops complex mechanisms allowing him to ignore any threat to this enjoyment, then it is difficult to imagine an event single-handedly effecting this subject's libidinal restructuring, even if this restructuring would consist in nothing more than the basic act of accepting that a ruptural event has occurred, that is, in taking responsibility for the event and thus traversing the (modern) fantasy. If psychoanalytical practice is anything to learn from, leading a subject to the moment when she can assume responsibility for an event that has already happened is a tenuous and lengthy process, rather than a ruptural event. It remains intriguing that cosmogonic events remain such a fundamental theme in Lacan-inspired theorising, as exemplified by the Nom-du-Père story; I incline towards understanding such events as the subject's post-hoc reconstruction of lengthier and more complex interactions between herself, *others*, and the Other.

Historical experience also suggests that prudence is justified when correlating desubjectivation (or the traversing of the modern fantasy) and the event, since the latter's ability to affect the former is uncertain:

> ...and no sooner do revolutionary social transformation appear that these [communist party] apparatuses show an extraordinary facility to amalgamate themselves with the state machinery so as to reconstruct them in their exclusive function of expropriating the general will, which at the same time reinforces the logic of capitalist reproduction from which it emerged. (Garcia Linera cited in Bosteels 2014, 236)

The European revolutionary experiences of the twentieth century seem to confirm that the revolutionary event leaves bourgeois libidinal structures largely intact, making necessary the dictatorship of the proletariat. Badiou (in Bosteels 2014, 26) expresses the same worries about what he calls 'speculative leftism', which according to him is based on the theme of the absolute commencement, of a radical break introduced in the history of world that rejects the immanence to the 'structured regime of the count-as-one'. As he rightly argues, 'being does not commence' (ibid.); how much his own theory of the event escapes this critique is debatable.

If the event does not restructure fantasies, then will the aftermath of the purge be dedicated to engineering enjoyment through biopolitical techniques? Žižek argues that the task of communism is exactly this that 'out of revolt we should shamelessly pass to reinforcing a new order' (Žižek quoted in Boteels 2014, 194). This approach approximates the Bolshevik fantasy, in which the dictatorship of the proletariat is a protracted biopolitical regime replacing the liberal-capitalist engineering of the soul with the communist such engineering. The Bolshevik leaders never addressed the question of desire in a sustained or complex manner; for Lenin and Trotsky, the main determinant of subjectivity is the mode of production; and once the mode of production is transformed, the road is cleared for a biopolitical re-organisation that will lead to self-fulfilment and social harmony without encountering any libidinal obstacles:

> ...freed from capitalist slavery, from the untold horrors, savagery, absurdities and infamies of capitalist exploitation, people will become accustomed to observing the elementary rules of social intercourse that have been known for centuries and repeated in all copy-book maxims. They will become accustomed to observing them without force, without coercion, without subordination, without the special apparatus for coercion called the state ... we know that the fundamental cause of [individual] excesses, which consist in the violation of the rules of social intercourse, is the exploitation of the people, their want and their poverty. (Lenin 1982, 105–106)

> Under capitalism, democracy is restricted, cramped, curtailed, mutilated by all the conditions of wage slavery, and the poverty and misery of the people. This and this alone is the reason why the functionaries of our political organisations and trade unions are corrupted ... and betray a tendency of becoming bureaucrats, that is privileged persons divorced from the people and standing above the people. (ibid. 127)

An unequivocal disciplinary path leads from capitalist lack to the fullness of communism, a trajectory set in motion by the taking of power and financial redistribution and pursued through the disciplining of bodies and souls. In his *State and Revolution*, Lenin sets up a plan for the first post-revolutionary phase of Communism whose insistence on minute and pervasive regulation would not have been out of place in Foucault's (1977, 135–231) description of the modern training of docile bodies:

> Accounting and control – that is the main thing required for the 'setting up' and correct functioning of the *first phase* of Communist society. *All* citizens are transformed into the salaried employees of the state, which consists of the armed workers ... When the majority of the people begin independently and everywhere to keep such accounts and maintain such control over the capitalists (now converted into employees) and over the intellectual gentry who preserve their capitalist habits, this control will really become universal, general, national: and there will be no way of getting away from it, there will be 'nowhere to go'. The whole of society will have become a single office and a single factory, with equality of labour and equality of pay ... For when all have learned to administer social production independently ... the escape from this national accounting and control will inevitably become so incredibly difficult, such a rare exception ... that very soon the *necessity* of observing the simple, fundamental rules of human intercourse will become a *habit*. And then the door will be wide open for the transition from the first phase of Communist society to its higher phase ... (Lenin in C. Wright Mills, 233–234, original italics)

A society organised as a gigantic 'office' or 'factory' really is not the most appealing communist blueprint, especially when considering how closely it mimics the neoliberal fantasy of a globally integrated economy, that is, of a total management/production/consumption capitalist unit.

Trotsky, on the other hand, envisages a 'New Man' resulting from generalized and radicalized anatomo-apparatuses whose elegant, machine-like rigour will encompass all aspects of his life, shaping a rationalist-eugenicist yoga master of the future:

> Man at last will begin to harmonize himself. He will make it his business to achieve beauty by giving the movement of his own limbs the utmost precision, purposefulness and economy in his work, his walk and his play.

He will try to master first the semi-conscious and then the subconscious processes of his own organism, such as breathing, the circulation of the blood, digestion, reproduction and, within necessary limits, he will try to subordinate them to the control of reason and will ... The human species ... in its own hands, will become an object of the most complicated methods of artificial selection and psycho-physical training. (Trotsky in C. Wright Mills, 288)

The dangers of this biopolitical enthusiasm are obvious enough to warrant only a cursory mention: for Foucault (1977), the diffusion of such productive mechanisms of power transforms bodies and souls into obedient and productive forces servicing a modern regime that culminates in the murderous violence of Nazism and global colonialism. Dean (2010, 5) reads biopolitics from the lens of the drive, describing it as an ever-expanding field that endlessly creates new mechanisms, objects, and subjects of government, and as a process of capture of the subject within this pullulating network of apparatuses that cannot create it but as a passive element. And, paralleling Foucault's (2003, 240–258) analysis of State racism, Agamben (1998, 142) traces the horrors of contemporary Western politics back to the biopolitical impetus in the post-World War I exercise of State power, when the hystericised obsession with discriminating between the worthy political life and the bare life unworthy to be lived opens the body to every manipulation (ibid. 142). Agamben's conclusion is that any effort to transform bare life—what we have been taught to understand as 'biological' life—into the 'good life' is a dangerous exercise, one that 'tries to put the freedom and happiness of the man (sic) into play in the very same place that marked their subjectivation' (10). For Agamben, there is nothing in the body itself that can ground resistance to sovereign power—the biopolitical turn insures that any effort of grounding politics in the body will deteriorate into fascism, making the camp into privileged space of modern power operation, and the citizen and the 'homo sacer' become one (170).

This is not to dismiss en bloc the Soviet communist experiences but to point out that the Bolshevik planning of the revolution assumes that the dissolution of the bourgeois fantasy is something to be tackled after the event and assumes the strategic implications of such an assumption. That the theorists of the event, after complicated meanderings between the symbolic, imaginary, and Real or between symptom, repetition, and rupture, come up with the same strategic plan as Lenin and Trotsky as if it is the 1910s, is rather worrisome. This passionate academic embracing of proletarian terror as a universal requirement of radical social transformation decides to ignore Rosa Luxemburg's (Wright Mills 1962, 307–308) condemnation of the Bolsheviks' notion of the dictatorship of the proletariat for having transformed the contingent necessities of the Russian Revolution—that is, oligarchic rule—into a universal necessity. It also ignores the difficulties and eventual failure of the proletarian terror. The theory of the event becomes even less convincing when, finally, the subject is introduced into this revolutionary equation as an agent.

Strategic Preparedness and the Subaltern's Sacrificial Body

At some point, it becomes evident that the definitions of the event discussed above can a bit over-generously include developments like Nazism alongside communism, determining both Badiou and Žižek to try and establish a distinction between a 'real' event and a 'pseudo event'. The former is the type of act discussed so far: an opening that unleashes transformative potential, the collective moment that makes possible the radical transformation of the symbolic by opening up possibilities unavailable in the current order. The latter is a moment of enthusiastic upheaval that mobilises elements already dominant in the symbolic field, on the model of Nazism or anti-communism, leaving the basic coordinates of this field unchanged (Žižek 2004, 113). This separation of events into pseudo events and true events points out one of the tactical problems at the heart of the theory of event: if the event is irruptive, unpredictable, then we cannot be certain that a certain upheaval is an authentic event or not, that it creates a radical opening or a fascist closure, until it is too late. In other words, if the radical transformation is predicated upon the event, we will never be certain that what we are involved in is not a fascist reiteration of the most pernicious elements of the current symbolic order. This is the moment when the neo-communist philosophers reintroduce the subject in the revolutionary frame: Badiou (cited in Žižek 2008, 386) argues that, since the true event is not fully determined by its causes, the revolutionary subject can harness it. In other words, once the event irrupts, it is up to the revolutionary subject to stir it towards the 'authentic' side of the force, rather than its fascist dark side. This subjectivation of the event, however, considerably complicates the whole story of the symbolic purge, since the resources of a fragmented, self-opaque, and symbolically governed subject are a poor substitute for the purity of the structural event that, in these philosophers' imagining, so neatly cuts through the bourgeois fundamental fantasy.

One needs to ask once again: where are these revolutionary proletarian subjects supposed to emerge from and through what methods will they spontaneously escape their own obsessive libidinal repetitions so that they stir the event away from fascism and towards true revolution? Will the bourgeois all of a sudden shed his will-to-not-know when in presence of the event? This sounds improbable, to say the least, since bourgeois subjects are stubbornly self-gratifying and authority-loving creatures which, in this scenario, face the overwhelming risk of misinterpreting the event, just like liberals constantly mistake various happenings for the 'end of history', or face the temptation to stir it towards fascism. As repeatedly argued, if there is something to be learned from the history of the bourgeois order, it is that it developed efficient mechanisms for using any threatening proximity with the lack as fuel for the circuits of the bourgeois drive: left to themselves, the modern symbolic order or subject will never produce a true event.

What, then, should be the political strategy of a subject all of a sudden endowed with revolutionary responsibility? The academic theorists of the revolution are divided on the subject. To start with, Alain Johnston (in Žižek 2008, 391) describes the academic reliance on the revolutionary event as:

> the quietist patience of either resigning oneself to the current state of affairs drifting along interminably and/or awaiting the unpredictable arrival of a not-to-be-actively-precipitated 'x' sparking genuine change (Badiou's philosophy sometimes seems to be in danger of licensing a version of this latter mode of quietism).

This is a pertinent critique, but Johnston's alternative is not offering a clear way out. Since, before the event, the actors involved ignore the effects of their actions, be that reinforcing the current system or threatening it (ibid. 340), his answer is a line of political activity that moves beyond the duality 'frantic doing in the name of a poorly conceived notion of making things different' versus 'quietly waiting for the impossible to predict true event' and into a form of 'communist patience' that scrutinises happenings so as to distinguish the disguised weak points of the system and identify the minor gestures that might bring the system down (391).

Žižek (ibid. 392) returns the favour, describing Johnston's own stance as a form of 'active quietism' that waits for a miraculous leap from minor act to qualitative change while in the meantime pursuing bourgeois enjoyment as usual. Žižek (392–393) wants to supplement Johnston's account with a form of 'strategic preparedness' that will allow the revolutionary to leap into decisive action when the signs of the Big Change become visible, introducing a moment of active risk-taking in struggle or, if you prefer, of responsibility in bringing about radical change. But, I again wonder, who are these fierce combatants-cum-critical theorists that wait in the shadows to pounce on the opportunity of stirring an event towards the 'authentic event'? What will their 'strategic preparedness' training consist of? Who can read—under the already-mentioned conditions of a 'veil of symbolic ignorance'—the true signs of change? In tactical terms, none of these academics can provide useful advice. On the contrary, as the subsequent discussion will develop, the academic radicals seem rather ill-prepared to either recognise the signs of the Big Change or leap into action in any significant manner.

Johnston's and Žižek's critiques of each other bring into relief the puzzling premises of the presumption that the revolutionary situation must arise accidentally, as the effect of a structure working against itself. This presumption endows the Real with a (revolutionary) consciousness that remains random and unknowable to humans, bringing the theory of the event even closer to the Christian fantasy of God the Father. The critically trained subject awaits the signs of the Real's will but is prevented from engaging in any form of experiments that might create the potential for radical transformation. Anyway, anthropomorphising the Real into the Father is probably related to these authors' distrust in the subject's capacities to subvert, or even understand, the dispositifs that create her. Such distrust is not completely unfounded, but I do not think that it justifies a quasi-eschatological attitude towards the revolution, which allows modern dispositifs to gain the incomprehensible, transcendental qualities of an external force confronting the subject.

One of Žižek's (2008, 116–117) solutions to the conundrum of the revolutionary subject relies on the notion that the authentic event's enthusiastic unity will be driven by the 'part of no part', the subjects excluded from society while being part of it and that, because of their lack of social belonging, can assume the role of universal class. Thus, when trying to provide some concreteness to his grand narrative of the revolutionary event and after many elaborate theoretical loops, Žižek (ibid. 424) ends up putting his revolutionary hopes on the body of the subaltern at her most marginalised and immiserated, the slum dwellers from 'Mexico City and other Latin American capitals through Africa (Lagos, Chad) to India, China, the Philippines, and Indonesia'. Since slum dwellers are the ultimate excluded, the homo sacer abandoned in a twilight zone outside the disciplinary governing of the State, '[we] should be looking for signs of the new forms of social awareness that will emerge from the slum collectives: they will be the germs of the future' (426). This demand for emancipatory sacrifice from the capitalist subjects most deprived of resources and most exhausted by relentless violence is a rather lazy solution. Today, the Western left in general seems to have developed a technique of passionate appropriation of the colonised *other's* body as the entity to be doubly sacrificed: first by the liberal-capitalist dispositifs, and second because of this first sacrifice, by the communist revolution. In the process, the agency is sometimes removed from the subaltern's actions through the attribution of her revolutionary potential not to bravery and know-how but to the fact that she has 'nothing to lose'.

I wonder if Žižek's hypothesis does not deserve further elaboration, since slums around the world are far from being equivalent social environments. Moreover, while the slum is largely refused the spoils of the 'proper' bourgeois community, it is definitely inside the liberal-capitalist ideological and financial circuits. The process through which the slum dwellers, a heterogeneous group in terms of desires and lived experience of solidarity and political organization, will transform into the well-coordinated revolutionary force is not straightforward. What 'strategic preparedness' would the slum proletariat require in order to establish the global production and redistribution; to set up the dictatorship of the proletariat; to put in place systems allowing the flourishing of new, non-bourgeois types of subjectivity; and to engineer the new sublime spaces outside the grasp of the existing order?

As to the theory of the revolutionary class that Žižek's attachment to rudiments of Marxist-Leninism produces, I find it equally unconvincing: according to him, the feature that allows the slum proletariat to stand in for the universal and for equality is the lack of particular features that would make possible their legitimate inclusion into bourgeois society. But then, wouldn't any modern subaltern—the racialised, the gay, women, the poor, and the migrant—be able to occupy this position of universality since, while relentlessly catalogued by modern discourses in terms of their particularity, they are also positioned as the systematic block to bourgeois society's progress, the 'part of no part'? When Žižek tries to rescue the global slum proletariat as the universal class, he invokes the principle that this 'part of no part' cannot become a ruling class without abolishing itself as a class. But similarly, if women are successful in dismantling patriarchy, non-whites in dismantling racism, or gays in dismantling heterosexism, which means that they have successfully dismantled the dichotomous symbolic system that allows the division of all humans into two mutually exclusive categories: man or woman, gay or straight, white or non-white, and so on; then the revolutionary class—women, gay, or racialised—would dissolve as a group as well as dissolving their antagonist (men, whites, or straight).

There is more: when the anti-imperialist or anti-State struggle of subjects classified as nonmodern by the modern realist discourses—the Viet Cong, Maoism, Sandinistas, Zapatista, First Nations, PKK, 'Arab Spring', the Chavez government, and so on—is placed by the event-scouting academic radicals under the signifier 'global communist revolution', this placement flattens fundamental modern antagonisms—north-south, centre-periphery, master-subaltern, exploiter-exploited, producer-profiteer, colonizer-colonized, curating-curated, and rich-poor—into the fantasy of a common cause animating both the 'nonmoderns' and their oppressors. It thus plasters a thick universalist revolutionary discourse over the enjoyment fractures of the global capitalist regime or, if you prefer, over conflicts that cannot be solved but through a radical change of the current colonial order. This is a change that the neo-communist academic discourse, in its systematic dismissal of the decolonial problematique, cannot and does not want to deal with.

Such displays of solidarity with the struggle of the *damnés*, especially in the case of the *damnés* whose political struggles are against Western hegemony and the institutions that provide the Western leftist with enjoyment—modern fantasy, colonialism, nation-state, university-discourse and master-discourse, individualism, consumption, bourgeois family, or Europe—make the Western academic radical into the omnipresent centre of all political movements and subsume all political movements under her political fantasy. When Žižek or Jodi Dean take pleasure in using terms like global (as in 'global revolution'), to mean that towards which their writings are working, are we to assume that the universal revolutionary truths and tactics, valid globally, to any subject and political struggle, will be elaborated by European thinkers and applied by European expeditions? After teaching everyone how to become modern-capitalist, are we going to teach everyone about their true condition and the correct ways in which to liberate themselves from capitalism, namely through a revamped form of Leninist revolution?

These appropriations are an offshoot of the symptomatic blindness towards the colonial nature of modernity that most neo-communist authors exhibit, which indicates that colonialism is the true repressed of their philosophising. Žižek's[2] positing of anti-capitalist struggle as the most important contemporary struggle is illustrative:

> Here one should be as clear as possible: with the rise of the anti-globalization movement, the era of the multitude of particular struggles that one should strive to link in a 'chain of equivalences' is over. This struggle (the only serious opposition movement today) — whatever one's critical apprehensions towards it — is clearly focused on capitalism as a global system, and perceives all other struggles (for democracy, ecology, feminism, anti-racism, and so on) as subordinate. (Žižek 2003, 135)

With this assertion, Žižek subsumes all the significant political and theoretical movements of the twentieth century, from queer and feminist to anti-colonial and anti-racist, to the struggle against economic inequality and hides them under the fatherly mantle of proletarian struggle. It isn't clear if Žižek understands decolonial struggle as an element of global anti-capitalism, but, since decolonizing processes place claims over the symbolic and geographical spaces occupied by European invaders rather than just claims over the industrial means of production or redistribution of profits, it is safe to assume that decolonialism is one of the lesser struggles he subordinates to anti-capitalism.

On the other hand, the radical academic equally addresses his demand for sacrifice to the internal *other*, the 'people' within the Western core. When Badiou, Žižek, and Jodi Dean argue that we need to abandon the pathological following of the Kantian law for personal satisfaction that, in their minds, is specific of post-modernists, anarchists, aestheticizing left activists, anti-racists, feminists, and so on—when they urge us to follow the only true law, that of communist social transformation, not in order to obtain personal rewards but to attain a better social arrangement—what they in fact demand in the name of the communist law is the destruction of the *other's* body in the revolutionary process. It is the body of the people, the workers, the masses, the multitudes, or the enemies that will be sacrificed during the purifying bloodshed of the revolution or in the terror that will follow it. The strict discipline of the party, the dictatorship of the proletariat, and the armed struggle that these theorists marshal out seem to be always applied on the body of another. Indeed, these academic communists never shake this reader's impression that they fantasise themselves in the position of the master or the analyst. Their constant repetition of 'us' and 'we' to signify the revolutionary agents seems to me to be hiding the enjoyment these academics derive from the violent fantasy that stages a divide between the sadist and the victim's body.

While McGowan's (2013, 83–85) work does not share the neo-communist fantasy, he comes fairly close to this use of the *damné* as fodder for the libidinal revolution when he romanticises the enjoyment of the 'lower classes' as more unbridled than that of the upper classes, because less submitted to the social law. This romanticising of the subaltern parallels the description of the colonized and the pauper as 'bestial' in classical liberal theory (see Procacci 1991; Stoler 1995). Today's 'lower classes' are not the swinging, orgiastic, carefree, and bacchanalian classes that the middle/colonial class imagines, but subjects obsessed with prestige, consumption, sex/gender roles, race, sexuality, religion, hygiene, propriety, upper social mobility, the desire of the Other, and wealth accumulation at least to the same extent as the wealthier bourgeoisie.

However, Badiou, Žižek, and Johnstons' interventions bring up and critique a radical bourgeois posture, which mixes a declared desire to join the revolution with an apparent inability to see the revolution anywhere.

This is a valid characterisation of an increasingly popular brand of the will-to-not-know and gains, to my mind at least, additional relevance through its ability to turn around and point at the neo-communist academics that elaborated it. Perpetually arguing that the conditions are not there, bourgeois radicals can disguise as revolutionary their lack of desire for the revolution and their will to not see their own involvement in reiterating capitalist reality. This is the attitude that makes the 'revolution' such an appealing fetish in resolutely non-revolutionary bourgeois environments like the academic, fashion, advertising, or film industry: by declaring you are waiting for the impending revolution while at the same time denying its possibility, you can be a revolutionary while calmly pursuing authority-worshipping rituals.

In the academic field, this fantasy prompts an obsessive circling around the privileged object, revolution, fuelled by one's faking of the revolutionary desire expected from the trendy academic and by the fear that, if deprived of this revolutionary objective, the life of the academic radical will be revealed as a collection of habits not different from those of the 'civilian' bourgeois. This diagnostic, however, also applies to its producers: the neo-communist academic radicals overcompensate for the radical bourgeois' inability to see the revolution anywhere by seeing it everywhere.

To my mind at least, the neo-communist theorising of the event seems a rationalisation of alienation (that is to say, of the subject's projection of her agency on the divine event) into a revolutionary attitude. Without taking part in any struggle that experiments with transformation but entitled to comment on all of them, hovering above all battles from an abstract meta-space, the academic promoters of the revolution encourage confrontation, sacrifice, and bloodshed without feeling the need to assume a direct responsibility in organising such processes.

Revolution without Desire

As the previous sections argued, recent writings in the field of the 'Lacanian left', to use Stavrakakis' (2007) term, try to revive communism as the universal signifier of social transformation and propose the revolutionary taking of State power as the most desirable manner of achieving it. I will further detail the tropes of this revolutionary fantasy by discussing a text on communism by Jodi Dean (2012) that I find illustrative in both tone and content. In this text, the communist revolution of our times should follow the Leninist template: a party-led anti-capitalist struggle aimed at redressing economic inequality. This type of insurrectionist academic discourse starts from specific assumptions: (1) the only proper manner to change capitalism is the popular control of the means of production and State apparatuses; (2) the revolutionary taking of power will be followed by the dictatorship of the proletariat, even if in a re-interpreted manner; and (3) these two actions will solve economic inequality and thus equalise all other power relations of modernity. I will discuss the imagining of power, subjectivity, and the social and of the necessary and sufficient conditions of revolution in Dean's arguments, since they provide important insights on how the neo-communist fantasy, despite its uncompromising rhetoric, fuels the academic will-to-not-know.

Jodi Dean (2012) starts her pamphlet by rejecting any discursive analysis of capitalist domination and repositioning the analysis in the 'material' field: a global system of economic appropriation that leads to a rich minority and an impoverished majority (5–6). Reopening the communist horizon consists for Dean in focusing exclusively on the field of economic exploitation and interests. The discursive and, implicitly, the libidinal field are considered separate from and antagonistic to the economic field, in a position of causal subordination to it. I will not comment on the revival of this dichotomy 'material'/'discursive' which, I assume, means to replicate the base/superstructure one, nor on this surprisingly coarse understanding of the ontological nature of 'material conditions' coming from a theorist cogent of Foucault's and Lacan's works. For present purposes, it is more fruitful to discuss some of the main concepts mobilised by Dean in support of her revolutionary template. My argument is that what this template either leaves out or uncritically assumes reflects a commitment to the academic revolutionary fetishism discussed above and leaves out the most urgent questions when rethinking anti-capitalist tactics and strategies. Dean (2012, 158–163) contrasts Wendy Brown's critique of left melancholy with Benjamin's deploring of the loss of revolutionary ideals among the intellectual left to argue in favour of the latter; my reading of Dean's work will be on the side of Brown's point that revolutionary ideals are for today's leftist a fetish that prevents more serious anti-bourgeois activity.

The first element to notice is that in Dean's work there persists the same dissociation between an often pertinent critique of the current bourgeois regime and a largely reactionary revolutionary rhetoric. Dean's critique of bourgeois radical politics is relevant: today signifiers like awareness raising, rights, inclusion, lifestyle changes, and so on are all fuelled by bourgeois narcissism and/or resentment rather than by a desire for radical change. I am in agreement with a great part of Dean's critique of the contemporary left, of its abandonment of transformative ideals and practices and its obsessive engagement in liberal-bourgeois political activities, and of its inability 'to break out of the circuits of drive in which it is caught, unable because it enjoys them' (175). I am however less convinced by the argument that a return to Marxist-Leninist political ideal of party, class, and revolution, not to speak of Dean's resolutely non-Marxist embracing of unionism and welfarism, is the answer to this leftist will-to-not-know. Marx's assimilation of the proletariat with the revolutionary class—which, if anything, is a projection of the model of the bourgeois class as revolutionary[3]—hardly maintains its relevance today. And I have already argued that Lenin's tactical writing in the fire of the Bolshevik Revolution cannot be easily applied to contemporary Western capitalism, since the past 100 years have hooked much more intimately the 'people's' enjoyment and identification to capitalist dispositifs. On the contrary, I think that such revolutionary rhetoric signals the Western academic left's retreat from transformative politics,[4] and a retreat from confronting the fantasy of fullness that Leninist revolutionary arguments rely on when using terms like the people, the working class, the party, economy, production, work, and so on.

The nostalgic Western left has for some time now tried to redress its fragmentation and regain its lost (fantasmatic) unanimity of goal, action, and subjects. Dean, joining the chorus of neo-communist academics, blames the failure of Marxist politics to create a revolutionary consciousness in the proletariat on the 'post-modern' focus on difference and diversity and suggests that, in order to redress the left's lack of popular appeal, we should return to 'militant opposition, tight organizational forms (party, council, working group, cell) and the sovereignty of the people over the economy' (Dean, 12). Despite this academic's visible enjoyment of the Leninist rhetoric and especially of the theory of State terror, drawing on a revolutionary model never experimented with by the US proletariat, which Dean recruits as her revolutionary subject, can hardly solve the left's problems of collective desire and action. Tight ranks and tactical and organisational coherence are the *result* of a highly politicised and radicalised social group actively invested in the revolutionary fantasy, not its causes, and especially so when the potential revolutionary agent is a North-American population uninterested in left politics.[5] Leninist organisation would be, in fact, anathema to any 'people' seduced by the liberal ideals of difference, individual freedom, and diversity.

Even if we confine the discussion to the academic level, which we shouldn't since it makes a discussion of the revolution useless, is it really desirable to frame anti-capitalist tactics in the problematic language of 'sovereignty' (of the people), as Dean does? Before proposing sovereignty as a response to liberal biopolitics, we should remember Wendy Brown's (2010, 117–133) argument that sovereignty is the supreme masculine political fantasy of mastery: penetration, pluralisation, or interruption of sovereignty represent this fantasy's literal undoing. A fantasy of complete sovereignty is nothing but an offshoot of the hyper-masculinist fantasy of complete control over the body, self, population, and borders whose worst enemy is contamination by the *other*. Can we, as Dean suggests, dissociate the fantasy of State or individual sovereignty from the fantasy of the 'economic sovereignty of the people', as if the latter represents a fundamentally different, revolutionary form of power that has no connection to traditional bourgeois understandings of the (male) individual and of autonomy? Or is, as the present analysis suggests, this fantasmatic longing for the severe form of power associated with a sovereign master (king, father, leader, nation, etc.), with an order, hierarchy, self-control, and self-transparency ineradicably bourgeois and masculinist? Moreover, if the people as wholeness is an impossibility, as Dean (2012, 69–119) insightfully argues, what does it mean to define the people in this language of sovereignty that connotes homogeneity, tight in/out boundaries, and (often military) discipline, unless, of course, the communist militantism that she invokes remains, despite all the caveats she provides in the text, a fantasy of fullness and perfection? We shall see that this dilemma extends to Dean's discussion of the people's 'collective desire'.

This contrast between Dean's nuanced theorising of bourgeois politics and her communist tactics displays the incompatibility between the non-totalising theorising of subjectivity, people and truth in post-Marxist thought (Lacan, Foucault and so on), and a Marxist-Leninist framing of the political fantasy in which self-transparency, rationality, unity, and totality are crucial. For example:

> … communism … designates the sovereignty of the people, and not the people as the whole or the unity but the people as the *rest of us*, those whose work, lives and futures are expropriated, monetized, and speculated on for the financial enjoyment of the few. (Dean 2012, 70)

This assertion starts by refusing a totalising description of the people and ends up describing the people as a totality constituted through the old trope of the 'objective social location' (discovered and certified by the university discourse). The classical definition of the proletariat in relation to ownership over the means of production is replaced with a definition in relation to the— Weberian?—criterion of wealth (the 99 %); with a blunt positioning of the people as the tool of the enjoyment of the 'few' which refuses to engage in a discussion of how the people itself enjoys capitalist dispositifs on one hand and of the theorist's own fantasy of the 'theft of enjoyment' on the other; and with the people's axiomatic ability to obtain sovereignty.

In order for Dean (ibid. 215) to make the rather plain argument that capitalism is a system that does not fulfil adequately the capacities, needs, demands, and collective will of the people, she must assume that such capacities, needs, demands, and will of people exist and, by extension, that a unified people defined by these capacities, needs, and demands also exists. These needs, demands, and so on of the people are invoked as if they precede their environment, as if they exist outside of the governing technologies that shape them and outside the 'people's' collective practices. Dean forgets the rather useful Foucaultian insight that the population's needs, demands, and capacities, as well as our ideal of how they are adequately met, result from the operations of various liberal dispositifs and are therefore highly consonant with capitalism. And that, if it ever assumes any existence, a people is brought into being by its collective action and thus does not pre-exist nor survive such action; therefore, its various capacities, needs, and so on can only be identified during such collective action. While the fascist fantasy of the nation/people portrays it as an eternal entity, the 'German people' assume existence in the fascist regime only when subjects collectively enact the Nazi politico-economic regime, war, genocide, pogrom, and so on. In this particular case, the element that brings the people into existence as a collectively acting entity is the fascist ideology that makes enjoyment depends on the destruction of the non-Aryan *other*. Ignoring such insights ends up precisely with the concept of 'we' that Dean tries to avoid, the 'people' of the nationalist and fascist fantasies of common being and desire.

At the level of tactics, Dean engages in a passionate Leninist rhetoric of the necessity of the party and of proletarian dictatorship. The party, interestingly, is presented as an analyst-like organisation that can resolve the conditions of non-knowledge of the revolution; a Lacanian 'subject supposed to know' on which the masses can project their love and desires in exchange for working through their symptoms:

> As it learns from the struggling masses, the party provides a vehicle through which they can understand their actions and express their collective will, much as the psychoanalyst provides a means for the analysand to become conscious of her desire ... Leninist revolutionaries take on themselves the demands and the conflict of the revolution ... the Leninist party cannot make demands on the people; it is a party that makes present to the people the demands they are already making on themselves, but can't yet acknowledge. (Dean, 240–244)

How exactly can we organise a party so that it fills up the empty space of the Other's desire? What type of situation must be engineered so that the relationship of transfer takes place between the people and party? Who are the people in this case, and since they seem to occupy the position of the analysand in Dean's scheme, should we assume a fundamental psychic commonality between them? Finally, are we to assume, as already mentioned, that the members of this party that can act as the figure of the analyst will be selected from the radical academic elite, who will guide the sacrificial bodies and souls of the masses from above? These are all questions left unaddressed and, I would suggest, unanswerable from within Dean's paradigm.

Faithful to her 'materialist' outlook, Dean (37) plainly sets the revolutionary goals to consist of redressing poverty and redistributing risks and rewards. But, if the revolution restructures the symbolic framework, thus enjoyment and desire, isn't the real revolutionary task to extricate our notions of 'poverty', 'risk', and 'reward' from the bourgeois framework? The transformation of the bourgeois regime must be performed not in order to enrich the poor or to distribute capital and commodities more equitably, but to restructure the liberal-capitalist symbolisation of phallic objects (richness, poverty, worth, success, inclusion, or indeed, needs, and capacities) as possessions so as to dephallicise this libidinal economy. Let us remember that for Marx, the gradual increase in workers' alienation does not refer to their awareness of poverty or exploitation, but to the realisation that works in capitalism is debasing, crippling, and enslaving. Only with this realisation will the proletariat develop the consciousness of their common identity and revolutionary task. I find it hard to believe that the proletariat, or 99 %,[6] or unions, or members of the Occupy movement which Dean considers as the spearhead of the communist revolution come anywhere near to critiquing work in capitalism as debasing per se. On the contrary, most of these groups militate for their State-granted right to work to be respected, in other words for a chance to participate more actively in the capitalist production or to improve the conditions of this participation (wages, health benefits, working hours, employment stability, and so on).

Which brings me to the main point of this discussion: while Dean mobilises a psychoanalytical language throughout her text, she systematically ignores the issue of the 'people's' desire. Wright Mills (1962, 81–94) argued some time ago that being a Marxist involves maintaining the strict distinction between the economic base (forces and relations of production) and the superstructure (including ideology and the psychological structure of the proletariat) it determines. In this account, there is no Marxist thought proper that does not accept the determination of the superstructure by the basis, that is, that does not posit the psychosocial conflict of capitalist society to be a reflection of the objective economic conflict between capitalist relations and forces of production. As mentioned, Dean does maintain the Marxist dichotomy between a material, economic field (structure) and non-material, discursive field (superstructure). However, if we take Marx literally when he argues that revolutionary proletarian consciousness is the inevitable outcome of the objective economic conflict of capitalism, then all post-Marxist thought is irrelevant for the revolution and first and foremost that of Lacan, for whom 'consciousness' has a radically different meaning and for whom the psyche is shaped by radically different mechanisms than the conflict between forces and relations of production. I fail to understand how a Lacanian like Dean, focused on the ideological fantasy as that which spurs political action, can place the determinant of social transformation in the realm of the monetary economy rather than in that of the economy of jouissance. By arguing that other political struggles of the late twentieth century are subaltern fights in relation to anti-capitalism, Dean, like all the other academic neo-communists, chooses to ignore that this century's most pernicious power relations were structured by bourgeois castration, desire, enjoyment, guilt, anxiety, and identification rather than by money, which is but a metonym for the phallic object[7] (see Goux 1990, 112–122).

Lacan places the communist post-revolutionary rejection of an ethics of desire in favour of an ethics of work (of the 'sphere of goods') in direct genealogy of the Western tradition of power, a tradition itself founded on the fantasy that this 'sphere of goods' will at some point embrace the whole universe (see Stavrakakis 2003, 121). And, it seems to me, Lacan's remark applies perfectly to Dean's reduction of political fantasy and action to the 'servicing of goods', which in fact rejects the libidinal field as relevant for revolutionary politics. The irony being that the very issue which prompts Dean to write her pamphlet is the (absence of) popular desire for the left. At no point, however, is this lack of popularity considered a symptom of the Western bourgeoisie's lack of desire for radical transformation. And when Dean indulges in the pleasures of imagining revolutionary violence as the people's capacity to 'wipe out and remake' (60), I am afraid that she is ignoring how difficult it is to wipe and remake precisely the crucial element that needs revolutionising, bourgeois jouissance. Dean's account ends up in a difficult position where her Weberian theory of the revolutionary class comes in conflict with Marx and her Marxian theory of consciousness comes in conflict with Lacan, leaving out the crucial questions. For example, going back to

Dean's relocation of the relationship between the people and the party in the clinical boudoir of the psychoanalytical session where the 'people' are the analysand and the 'party' the analyst, I wonder what are the symptoms, projections, identifications, enjoyment, desire, and trauma of the analysand? What are the processes of resistance at work in the psyche of the analysand, their passionate desire 'a ne rien savoir', and how can these be overcome through party activity?

Dean dedicates a chapter to desire without really engaging with any of these questions: she prefers reducing the problematique of bourgeois desire to the invocation of the Marxist truism that individualized bourgeois desire has to transform into collective, communist desire (191, 197): 'the lower classes have to want in a communist way. If they are to overthrow capitalism and begin establishing a communist society, they have to desire as communists. Without collective, communist desire, revolutionary upheaval moves in counterrevolutionary directions' (198), or 'communist desire is the collective desire for collective desiring' (199). If communist desire consists solely of the desire to desire collectively, then I personally fail to see how it differs from neoliberal desire, where part of the irresistible appeal of commodities is the fact that everyone else desires them, that is, that we are disciplined towards the collective fetishising of specific objects. Or, going back to Badiou's dilemma, how communist desire will differ from fascist desire. 'Collective' is not equivalent to either anti-capitalist or revolutionary.

Such assertions also fail to solve the issue of attributing collective desire to the people without transforming them into the whole of the nationalist fantasy and, more importantly, give no account of the means of transforming the closely governed forms of capitalist desire into communist desire, whatever that is. Dean's repeated and somehow vague invoking of the mechanism of the drive to describe what the capitalist subject needs to overcome is not enough to clarify the issue, leaving us unable to understand the fairly systemic bourgeois hostility to any anti-capitalist activity, or how to break out of these circuits of the drive.

As a note on collective desiring that reiterates a discussion commenced above, despite Dean's justification of her tactical use of 'Us' as a rallying pronoun throughout the text, I would be considerably more hesitant before including myself or any other Western academic among those whose lives are expropriated by capitalism. As privileged State employees and propagandists of the current neoliberal order—to the extent that any radical discourses emanating from elite institutional podiums strengthen the mystique of this institution rather than rupturing it—academics are vessels and handles of liberal power, as Foucault would put it, or profiteers of the neoliberal war machines as Lenin might have.

While Dean does not engage with these issues, I suggest that the majority of Western subjects are quite satisfied with the bourgeois forms of enjoyment, so that their main fear is not that they will have their lives expropriated by the 1 % but that they will lose the liberal-capitalist dispositifs of jouissance. Libidinally, the current situation in the West is more reciprocally advantageous than suggested by Dean's description of 1% of us enjoying, financially and otherwise, at the expense of the 99% others: both the financial elites and the rank-and-file bourgeoisie are enjoying capitalism, in ways that are aligned rather than antagonistic. It is self-defeating for the left to refuse considering that a very important proportion of the 'people' identifies with the 'rich' and more generally with the neoliberal regime at deep levels, that is, at the levels where subjectivity is anchored. Thus, while it is nice to think that in the revolutionary aftermath the population that would regret bourgeois order would only consist of the richest 1 %, I imagine it as being considerably more sizeable.

The Western bourgeois resents revolution—or, more modestly, change—much more than they do capitalism, letting us assume that the revolution will have to be imposed on a majority hostile to it. And while it is equally nice to think that post-revolutionary arrangements will develop new forms of desiring simply by changing the parameters of capitalist production and reward, this fantasy does not address in any way the nagging question of the intractability of bourgeois desire. Or, reversely, does not addres the question of the mechanisms that could tether our bourgeois pleasure and desire to different symbolic orders, an important question since—if the revolutionary experiences of the twentieth century are anything to go by—the socialisation of the means of production is hardly enough to effect this rewiring of desire. This means that the neo-communist revolutionary fantasy persistently ignores the population's possible reaction to the 'No!' of the Father/party in the revolutionary aftermath, especially if we consider that interdiction spurs desire rather than eliminating or radically transforming it. This fantasy seems to imagine a post-revolutionary reality predicated on replacing the current disciplinary training of bodies for capitalist production with their disciplinary training for communist production.

Acting out under the Father's Gaze

The remainder of this chapter takes issue with 'protest' as an anti-bourgeois political tactic, starting from the idea that a protest always implies the persistence of protester's faith in the dominant framing of politics, truth, social justice, or more generally reality and in the authority supposed to safeguard them (State, government, democracy, modernity, and so on). It has been a leitmotif of the left that the failure of its post-war experiments is due to capitalism's unparalleled ability to 'co-opt dissent'. However, this assertion needs further explanation: what precisely makes capitalism so able to digest resistances? I have proposed above that this ability is due to the forms taken by our resistances, which in many cases are a symptomatic enactment of the enjoyment that modern subjects derive from their submissive relationship with to authority. This section expands on this proposal's implications.

As already mentioned, I am not as big an admirer of capitalism as some of the neo-communist academics are and therefore remain unconvinced by the argument that capitalism's ability to phagocytise resistance is due to its revolutionary spirit, its unprecedented ability to destroy the old and constantly create new forms of being and enjoying. I consider capitalism a rigid system based on compulsive, ritual repetition, and its ability to co-opt dissent must be understood in relation to these looping forms of jouissance. What might be acknowledged about capitalism is that it stubbornly and systematically spreads its dispositifs, trying to crush all resistances to bourgeois jouissance, to submit all the spaces available to its libidinal-disciplinary economy. The governing of the bourgeois population is achieved through the idiotic stubbornness of capitalist dispositifs. These dispositifs promise to fill—or at least hide—lack with mass-produced phallic objects and to represent the bourgeois comforts of submitting to symbolic authority as being self-determination. My point, then, is that capitalism co-opts resistances so easily not because it has amazing adaptive powers or because the economy of enjoyment it deploys is irresistible, but because it makes this economy of enjoyment seem like the only one able to appease bourgeois anxiety. Otherwise phrased, capitalism smoothly co-opts dissent only when this dissent is built on a bourgeois libidinal core, that is, on the resisters' commitment to the modern fantasy.

The 'real-socialist' ideal is a good example: built on a fantasy of industrialism, modernisation, technology, and progress; and of a rational, self-transparent subject whose strong ego is shaped by identifications with authority, work, career, patriotism, nationalism, gender, race, heterosexism, or family, socialism was from its inception premised on bourgeois enjoyment. Since the socialist ideals so closely resembled bourgeois ones, socialism remained locked in a relationship with capitalism as the specular *other* that embodies the traits making one's self desirable. This identificatory relationship partly explains the inability of most socialist subjects to decolonise their desires from the fantasy of Europe as phallus, perfectly encapsulated in the 'catching up with the West' motto. In the end, if not even from its troubled beginnings, these fraught identifications transformed capitalism into both the ego-ideal of socialism and the Other whose gaze defines one's worth, an irresistible combo. After a protracted struggle, this shabby foundation brought its collapse in just a few months between 1989 and 1990.

Similarly, the ineffectiveness of contemporary anti-capitalist tactics and their inability to innovate partly result from a repressed demand to be recognised by the bourgeois Other. This reduces contemporary anti-capitalism to a sort of acting out for the benefit of the Father's gaze:

> Acting-out always occurs on a stage, while the authentic act and authentic enjoyment—the radical break from the constraints of symbolic authority—occurs unstaged, without reference to the Other's look. (McGowan 2004, 125)

To the extent that one's political acts aim to attract the attention and desire of the adversary—State, government, businessmen, bourgeois public, the North, and so on—one's political imagination remains confined to the symbolic framework set by this adversary and her enjoyment to the martyr's display of powerlessness in relation to authority. This is why a lot of anti-capitalist tactics take today the form of spectacle politics, tying their success and the activists' enjoyment to the gaze of authority— petitions, demos, protests, marches, occupations of public spaces, hunger strikes, performances, information campaigns, charity, social network campaigns, and so on. Such political acts, which we could subsume under the name 'protests', are not designed to directly intervene upon reality but to convince the authority figure to fulfil our demand; in other words, they preserve the position of the Father as desired, hated, and feared figure that distributes resources, love, and recognition.

When one is protesting, then, she protests the authority's failure to respect its self-imposed ethical-political principles. In the case of holding liberal authorities accountable according to the liberal notions of democracy, freedom, equality, prosperity, peace, and so on, this leaves outside the aims of political action what I consider to be its most important targets, namely the governmental deployment of the notions of truth and the good, and, related, the continuing appeal authority has for the people gathering under its gaze. Thus, 'protesting' continues a liberal line of political action initiated by the myth of the social contract, that is, by the surrendering of governing responsibility to the State/Father in exchange for individual well-being.

The rationale of non-violent action that Judith Butler proposes in an interview to the Guernica magazine (https://www.guernicamag.com/interviews/a_carefully_crafted_fk_you/) seems to confirm my point:

> Effective nonviolent action amounts to a "carefully crafted f[**]k you". Nonviolence has to phrase this claim more perfectly than violence, since it only works if the unjust party *hears* and *is moved*.

On the contrary, I would argue, the real 'fuck you' is to remain impervious to the interpellations of the 'unjust party' while surreptitiously dismantling its governing systems.

Judith Butler (2015, 99–123) is, I think, right to re-focus the political problem around bodies and space, or rather around bodies in space. Intervening in the spatial organisation of power, disrupting the dominant regime's regulation of spaces, and unsettling its ordering of temporality and architecture (106) are tactically and strategically crucial. I am, however, less convinced that 'protests', which are Butler's exemplary such politics, do justice to this strategy. My reticence stems from an understanding of transformative action, especially when meant to destabilise the dominant regime, as presuming a mass of militants that, at the very least, have the desire to experiment with forms of enjoying outside and to a large extent against bourgeois coordinates. Since, as this book tries to suggest, the connections between liberal-capitalist dispositifs and bourgeois enjoyment are intimate and well protected by the will-to-not-know, such desire for desiring otherwise is 'unnatural' in most subjects and must be developed through creative, sustained, and patient collective efforts. Protests and visceral actions in general do not seem to exhibit this preparation or even a desire for forsaking bourgeois dispositifs or the political leaders whose function is to camouflage these dispositifs with the spectacle of their paternal aura; more often they enact demands for perfecting these dispositifs, so that they can offer the full jouissance they promise.

Butler (108–112) argues that the protesting bodies' occupation of space (the street, the plaza, or the park) and persistence in it without protection, facing the risk of violence, create a corporeal challenge to the legitimacy of authorities. This is probably so. But are protests able to demand more than the replacement of an illegitimate regime with a legitimate one that would recognise these previously ignored bodies as valuable members of the liberal community? Are such actions able to go further than exhibiting the absence of rights of the protesters; can they achieve political objectives that go beyond placing demands on authority to grant these rights? And, if successful, will the granting of rights address the cause of the problem, that is, will rights be able to dislocate the systems and technologies that affect these bodies' exclusion and the violence they endure (see Brown 2002) and do so without displacing these violences on other bodies?

Butler's insistence is on appearance, on bodies disavowed by the dominant political regime being made visible and audible through their unauthorised presence in public spaces. I find this insistence on voice and visibility close to the liberal pluralist reduction of the political to making visible the excluded and audible the muted, a reduction of politics to the official granting of recognition, according to the rules of the dominant regime, to previously disavowed bodies as yet another identity group in the rainbow of bourgeois 'multiculturalism'. Such focus on the audible and the visible binds political imagination to catching the master's eye and ear, without really contesting the legitimacy of the dominant framework. While Butler does not quite make this liberal point, I do not see how the legitimacy of authority can be contested through a political form that places bodies under the Other's gaze; and I am not discussing here the illegitimacy of a particular reign within liberal-capitalism, say that of a political party, of Khadafy, or of Mubarak. Such reigns can, of course, be delegitimised by a political protest. I am talking about the modern fantasy, with Europe as the phallus, the very regime that makes enjoyment, including in its incarnations as freedom democracy, equality, prosperity, and so on, depend on submission to authority. It is these—disembodied—authorities that protests cannot delegitimise, since protesting necessitates them to function. Protests might contest leaders, but not authority.

This need for authority's recognition comes through in Butler's language. For example, Butler considers the persistence of bodies in the public space, without 'protection', a destabilising factor for the dominant regime; I would consider the absence of protection to be both a goal and a basic political assumption when once engages with the regime as an enemy. Otherwise this lack of protection is made to seem exceptional, a temporary risk that has to be remedied by being offered the protection of another, legitimate this time, authority. Moreover, is the 'persistence' of bodies in the public space a radical potential? Or is this a persistent demand for recognition from the various modern authorities supposed to ratify the illegitimacy of the local leader; and equally a demand of recognition by the illegitimate leaders themselves who must admit their own illegitimacy?

I am therefore doubtful that Butler (117–120) is right when arguing that the simple presence of bodies severs the connection between the existing regime and the public space and takes over the field where the sovereign power's effects are felt; on the contrary, I would argue that in the case of taking over streets, plazas, or parks, the activists are renting out the space from the State, with the clear understanding that at some point, depending on the will of their landlord, they will be summoned to move out or be forcefully evicted, returning that space to its initial signification and control.

Butler's political vision, like that of the Occupy movement, works fine for a social-democratic type of political activity whose aim is to improve the political framework of the current bourgeois regime through a return to the golden age of welfarism: guaranteed full-time employment, pensions, rights for all, free public services provided by the State, and so on. It is intriguing, though, that contemporary social-democratic analyses supporting the making visible and audible of excluded bodies do not perceive the bourgeois community these bodies desire to be integrated in as being fundamentally predicated on exclusions. If one is distrustful, as I am (see Panu 2009), of the side-effects of this nationalist-socialist form of capitalism based on communities delimited by history, blood, borders, birth rights, and citizenship cards and impervious to any other effects of capitalism besides the economic prosperity of the (national) population (and we should not forget that the 'population' is an entity that emerges as a result of liberal governmentality), then performing the political as a 'protest' is not that relevant for transformative action.

Occupying and keeping a space outside the neoliberal circuits is both a difficult feat (suggesting how important the control of spaces is for the dominant regime) and, in my opinion, a fundamental step towards destabilising bourgeois order. I simply do not think that the energy spent in the occupation and keeping of streets, parks, and plazas is energy well spent. I would argue, again, for a politics that experiments outside the gaze and the political scenes this gaze creates, even if these are scenes from which certain bodies are violently excluded but in which these excluded bodies desire to be included. The political issue is precisely this desire for 'inclusion'.

Rather than threatening, then, protests re-suture the dominant regime in the psyche of both activists and spectators, something that Lost Children's School of Cartography (2011, from now on LCSC 2011) also notices:

> Furthermore, in contrast to acting directly to abolish alienation together for ourselves and our desires, as in insurrection, to center activity on indignation and protest implies a continued belief in some authority who can hear and possibly grant our demands.

This is the customary republican narrative of insurrection as legitimate response to our authorities' failure to protect and nurture our needs and desires (see Žižek 2008, 78). I will add that the left's ritualised narrativising of its defeats at the hands of the bourgeois regime—how much riot police there was; how many activists got shot, beaten up, gassed, tasered, or arrested; and so on—symptomatically points at our secret desire for the correction of paternal authority.

I will briefly discuss the Occupy movement as illustrative of these acting-out tactics and of the position of the academic radical left in relation to them. What I am interested in is a critical reading of some left discourses on Occupy, whose enthusiasm expresses a commitment to mistaking forms of resistance that contain from their inception a bourgeois core for the event that will topple up the capitalist symbolic order. Jodi Dean's text discussed above brackets a serious discussion of the libidinal field partly because it assumes that the sovereignty and revolutionary consciousness of the people, the very conditions of the ruptural event, are not hypotheses but processes developing as a result of the Occupy movement in the USA and more generally of protesting through the occupations of public spaces:

> Even more pronounced is the movement against capitalism at work in 2011's Arab spring, European summer, and US fall. Globally occupations put to work an insistent collectivity that struggles towards a new assertion of the common and the commons. (Dean, 178)

> ... people ... installed themselves in the financial heart of New York city. Occupying the symbol of capitalist class power, they ruptured it. The ostensible controllers of the global capitalist system ... appeared to have lost control over their own cement neighbourhood ... As it unfolded in New York City in the fall of 2011, occupation demonstrated itself to be more than a tactic. Occupy became an evental site and political form. I use the term 'evental site' to point to the *event* of the movement, its rupturing of our political setting. (211)

> With Occupy Wall Street, the collective and self-conscious assertion of our collectivity destroys our prior political incapacity, our prior subjection to the terms and frame of communicative capitalism. Now we can and are right to say 'we'. (235)

In the 'Nation' of 6 October 2011, Naomi Klein wrote an article titled 'Occupy Wall Street: The Most Important Thing in the World Now', illustrating the same propensity to subsume each and every anti-capitalist resistance to whatever happens in the USA at the moment. Like Barack Obama's election a few years before, the New York Occupy movement inflamed the revolutionary imagination of the North American Left. But is such excitement enough to make a theorist of the revolution ignore the liberal, and sometimes liberal-capitalist premises of the popular revolts in North Africa, whose ethos rather reminds me of the 1989–1990 'anti-totalitarian' uprisings in the socialist bloc or the more recent anti-corruption popular mobilisations in the same area? On the other hand, can such a theorist ignore that, despite the repeated efforts of the Occupy movement to inscribe them in a common genealogy, the Arab Spring was very different from what was happening simultaneously in the USA or Western Europe, most obviously because a large percentage of the USA and European bourgeoisie that Dean counts as the 99 % is actually part of the 1 % global financial-colonial elite? Such enthusiastic endorsements also ignore the diverse and often nowhere near anti-capitalist position of the groups involved in Occupy worldwide. Or that none of the Occupy tactics in the USA was directly aimed at forging commons, if by that we mean a *permanent* re-appropriation and radical re-signification of spaces, which involves more than holding general assemblies in a park and would necessitate a different tactical engagement with State dispositifs, including the paramilitary police force and the national army.

> The goal of any insurrection is to become irreversible. It becomes irreversible when you've defeated both authority and the need for authority, property and the taste for appropriation, hegemony and the desire for hegemony. (The Invisible Committee 2007, 130–131)

The academic left's lack of tactical analysis and the easiness with which the jargon of the revolution is deployed to describe forms of resistance clearly unable to sustain the weight of revolutionary hope placed on them are a far cry from the revolutionary Leninist language most of them mobilise so enthusiastically. In fact, they probably would've been firmly denounced as anti-revolutionary bourgeois analyses in the *Pravda*. What

I want to point out is that the ability of otherwise perceptive academics to ignore very obvious bourgeois traits of the Occupy movement is a form of will-to-not-know that, by deploying the radically demobilising effects of its unjustified revolutionary enthusiasm, uses the fantasy of the revolution to keep bourgeois society unchanged.

The general form taken by Occupy in New York and the North American occupations related to it is illustrative enough to include this act among the spectacle or acting-out politics mentioned above. Occupation comes in various forms, some of which desire a liberation of spaces from liberal-capitalist control and some to become a spectacle for the Other's gaze. When Jodi Dean declares occupation movements as the most radical political tactic of the moment and embraces with unbridled enthusiasm Occupy Wall Street as one of them, she is confusing these two types of occupation, one that plans to cut off the Father's head and one that plans to secure better living conditions in the Father's house. Occupy Wall Street started as a thousands-strong march against austerity in the New York financial district. The police successfully pushed the demo in the small Zuccotti Park, privately owned by an estate company, where a couple of hundred people decided to remain overnight (Aaron et al. 2012). Both marching against austerity and the occupation of a small park are spectacle, not revolution. The movement grew in part as a response to the disproportionate police repression during the subsequent marches organised through New York, but never gained a more revolutionary form than that.

The first organisations to start participating in the Zuccotti Park assemblies were members of the Transport Workers Union, at that moment engaged in contract renewal negotiations with the employer; and subsequently telecommunication, healthcare, and construction union workers. And, to my mind at least, contemporary unions are hardly revolutionary organisations. While Dean (44–45) is happy to present unionism, welfarism, and Keynesianism as anti-capitalist political activities that have 'established a "moral economy", a set of expectations of equity, solidarity and fairness with broad social, cultural, and political resonance' (64), the Bolsheviks she upholds as revolutionary ideals would have considered such arguments a lowly form of bourgeois rhetoric worthy of traitors of the movement and lapdogs of the ruling class like Bernstein and Kautsky.

Even a sociologist of non-revolutionary inclination like C. Wright Mills did not fail to notice that by the 1960s, the labour movement in the USA was operating in synchronicity with the business-promoting dispositifs:

> Insofar as labour unions represent 'classes' and labour-management contro-versy 'class struggle', the object of the struggle has become to receive a greater share of the product, rather than to change capitalism as a social structure ... [In the USA, the unions'] function has come to be part of the management of the labour force, a disciplining agent in the plant, in the firm and even in the industry. They have become bureaucratic organizations which in the main work to stabilize relations between wageworkers and owners and man-agers of the means of production. (Wright Mills 1962, 108–109)

Labour unions are by now an important stabilising element in the US electoral dispositifs:

> Every election year, unions spend millions on [Democratic Party] political contributions, direct mail and advertising, while enlisting their staff and rank-and-file activists for nightly phone banks, weekend door-belling, and worksite leafleting. Unions and their PACS spent an estimated $400 mil-lion in 2008 on campaign contributions and independent expenditures, plus many thousands of paid and volunteer hours, aimed mainly at electing Democrats ... Centrists, including Obama, have chosen a different path, working to incorporate union leaders as partners in implementing auster-ity. (Aaron et al. 2012)

At the time it was felt that one of the major threats to the Occupy move-ment, which was endorsed officially by Obama and some prominent members of his party, was its transformation into electoral capital for the Democrats. The movement was already rife with the 'citizens values' intro-duced by the middle class, that is, with the customary liberal-capitalist discourse of non-violence, rights, freedom of speech, and democracy and with a social critique focused not on anti-capitalism but on the much more innocuous 'corporate greed'—Occupy participants have been holding signs saying 'We're not anti-capitalism; We're anti-greed' (LCSC 2011)—whose immediate solution is 'corporate responsibility'. This is what Occupy rep-resented: an anti-austerity, not an anti-capitalist resistance; in the same manner, the majority anti-austerity vote in the 2015 Greek referendum was not an anti-capitalist vote and the subsequent actions of the Syriza party demonstrated that the referendum was never intended to measure anti-capitalist sentiment in Greece but rather the population's desire to 'return to normality', that is, to its previous acquisitive capacity. And this despite the thrill of the European radical left who once again had found its revolutionary agent and event in the 'people of Greece' led by the Syriza.

It was rather obvious from the beginning that if anything radical was to happen in the wake of Occupy Wall Street, it would have gone directly against the political desires and enjoyment of the majority of the participants, whose focus was hardly on a decapitation of the symbolic Father. When one chooses to occupy a public park or a plaza—a visible and exposed position that cannot be held long enough for any serious political experiment to take place—as a valid tactic, she exhibits her desire for a temporary, fleeting occupation whose organisational innovations derive from the participants' awareness of its imminent demise.[8] The political fantasy of Occupy stages the 'people' protesting under the authority's gaze and has to fail as an occupation in order to attract the Father's attention and affections. Isn't suicide according to Lacan the supreme form of narcissism? This is the opposite of the classical planning of a revolutionary occupation that aims to do away with the master's gaze and whose success depends on remaining hidden from this gaze, at least until the master can be safely decapitated.

The organisational forms taken by the Occupy Wall Street movement, despite their pretence of horizontality, illustrate the bourgeois desire for authority camouflaging itself as participative democracy: 'The People's Mic, like the news, or the internet, relies upon the subject's passivity, while at the same time presenting the dangerous illusion of participatory action … The reliance upon a distanced intake of information, and the conclusion of respect for the authority of a speaker behind a podium or at the occupied park, hints at the *authority of the event*' (LCSC 2011). Some of the Montreal militants, involved in student protests that lasted more than seven years, strongly dissociated themselves from the General Assembly form, which they interpreted as a passivising form of organisation whose function is to avoid engagement with any risky transformative tactics:

An Occupy-style assembly was called for Berri Square that night, with the organizers appealing for calm and promising people a chance to 'express their indignation.' Instead, when people gathered, angry militants who wanted nothing to do with the organizers' pacifying rhetoric told them to shut the fuck up. (http://www.crimethinc.com/texts/recentfeatures/montreal1.php, 23 December 2015)

Maybe on the contrary, Occupy was an exercise in revitalising, if that was ever necessary, the US populations' faith in the Father's power to take care of all its children:

As diverse as the context of the occupations may have been … the organizing committees were united by a central theme: insistence upon lawfulness. The official calls to 'Occupy' were thick with the language of the law, going so far in New York as to insist 'the sovereign people of any nation have the right to guide the destiny of their nation and may do so by respecting the law.' September 17th was to be a peaceful day of rage. The internet overflowed with 'how to' manuals designating appropriate, and legal, demonstrator tactics. (LCSC 2011)

LCSC's diagnostic, written at the time when Dean was writing her book on communism and Žižek was giving public talks in the occupied parks of New York, is incomparably sharper and starker, supporting the point that the luminaries of neo-communist revolution mistook Occupy for the event only because the movement was representative of their own bourgeois desires. Another long quote from them is, I feel, justified:

While the occupations were perhaps first populated by the same cliques of activists who had championed the previous failed American social movements, the encampments and demonstrations have grown because they have attracted the self-identified American 'middle class.' As American society comes under further blows of the so-called 'crisis' of capitalism, the illusion of middle class comfort dissipates, revealing its previously hidden, but now more apparent, dispossession. The Occupy movement is an opportunity for the middle class to protest the 'unfairness' of their *proletarianization* … Of course, regardless of its active decomposition, the middle class carries its values into the movement — the ideological values of the *good citizen*. One could characterize the Occupy movement as a citizens' movement for the survival of capitalist democracy in a moment ripe with potentials for true rupture. Here, self-described radicals, anti-authoritarians and in some cases even anarchists may play the most critical but hidden roles in recuperation, if in their well-intentioned attempt to 'build the new world in the shell of the old' they actually succeed at *protecting the core of the old world in the shell of the new.* (LCSC 2011, original italics)

And here is how CrimethInc. comments on the relationship between Occupy USA and Occupy Montreal:

As people sought to identify the specific ways that capitalist exploitation was intensifying in Montréal, Occupy Montréal embraced a simplified analysis needlessly imported from the United States. When militants were strategizing about *occupying something,* Occupy Montréal had the unfortunate effect of making many people shy away from that word lest they be associated with the 99% rhetoric. No matter the richness of Montréal's own traditions of resistance—they couldn't compete with a mass-produced cookie-cutter protest culture imported from south of the border. What *would* be truly inspiring is if the situation was turned completely around: if the crowds refused this ventriloquism in favor of the hundreds of conversations waiting all around them. Imagine the occupation flipped on its axis, its inhabitants *acting* together based upon true affinity and setting their spectator role alight ... (http://www.crimethinc.com/texts/recentfeatures/montreal1.php, 23 December 2015)

The LCSC, and I agree with their reading, goes as far as suggesting that movements like Occupy, to the extent that they fail to seriously threaten capitalism, actually work to facilitate capitalism's adaptation and thus insure its survival. The progressive liberal media, including such pro-capitalist productions as the International Business Times, applauded the experiments of the Occupy movement as paving the road to a less greedy, more local, credit union-based, and population-responsive capitalism that in the future would prevent crises like that of 2008.

The now defunct Occupy, which in the USA lasted for a few months between autumn 2011 and spring 2012, has left no major impact on the North American or global bourgeois system or on the popularity and tactics of the left. The movement's slogans retain today the same revolutionary potential as those from Paris 1968 or the saddened face of the Che on a T-shirt. And the forms of political organisation that continued the Occupy movement—workshops, general assemblies, community programmes, and worker's union struggles—are the routine tactics that the left has been using since the 1960s, if not since the late 1800s.

The radical academic's inability to restrain her revolutionary enthusiasm often results in spurts of overexcited heralding of the event fired in the four winds. And what are such spurts if not a sign of the willed political conservatism of an elite otherwise unafraid of dismissing any political act that does not fit their communist template or of demanding sweeping destruction, righteous bloodshed, and revolutionary terror? I will also refer the reader to the short discussion of the academic radical left's dubious open letter supporting the Maidan movement discussed in Chap. 3 before concluding with a critique of Žižek's politics—Žižek was one of the signatories of said open letter—by Claudiu Gaiu (2015), which illustrates how conservative such academic interventions are when experienced by the subjects they talk about from afar. Gaiu argues that the philosopher strategically justifies certain aspects of the Western imperialist interventions in Kosovo and traces these tactical errors to Žižek's remoteness from local politics.[9] This remoteness, combined with Žižek's desire d'épater the left academic establishment, results in his erasure of fundamental antagonisms that the radical left should rather emphasise and use as the front lines (Gaiu's argument for anti-colonial political Manichaeism echoes Fanon's in the *Wretched of the Earth*). Žižek's usual shock performance of trying to reverse the accepted view on events so as to condemn the Western left's conservatism ends up, in Gaiu's view, supporting the imperial ideological positions and political actions Žižek is otherwise critiquing and reduces radical transformative action to vague sloganeering:

> The trajectory from Václav Havel to Slavoj Žižek is that from the stiff proclamation of the politics of civicness and humanism to the denunciation of the depoliticising of life performed by this former dissident movement's programme centred around human rights and enlightenment values. It is only going half way, since it refuses any attempt at re-politicising. At times, this refusal of the political takes place through adopting the media-dominating position of the Western military propaganda. At others, through boasting his

Eurocentrism, which is supposed to mean a tradition of radical egalitarian-ism without however being able to point out the European agents that still carry this message. And it is always in search of some undefined 'transnation-alism' that absolves one from involvement in any local action and which differs from that comfortable internationalism where no one feels a duty to think the Revolution only by its relocation in television studios and the pages printed by the large media trusts. (Gaiu 2015, my translation)

Leaving the Asylum

For the contemporary academic radical, the fantasy of the revolution ful-fils the promise of a garden of delights (even if these delights are the pro-letarian terror), access to which will be granted at an indefinitely deferred future moment. This indefinite deferral makes possible the radical bour-geois' enjoyment, just like the mystical-religious fantasy of the afterlife fuels the believer's everyday pleasures.[10] Like this religious fantasy, the rev-olution-qua-paradise does not require a radical transformation of every-day libidinal flows but, on the contrary, makes 'sinful' everyday bourgeois enjoyment into a vital tool for steeling and perfecting the self in prepara-tion for the final judgement, insofar as such sins prompt various 'revolu-tionary rituals of purification' equivalent to the religious ones of attending mass, confession, prayer, donations to the church, charitable activities, and so on. This religious fantasy of the revolution also yields additional enjoyment from the establishment of the boundary between the believer and the non-believer, where the believer's purity, irrespective of her acts, is permanently renewed through emphasising and punishing the impurity of the non-believer. Compared to the prudent bourgeois that do not utter the world revolution for fear of making it happen, the revolutionary bour-geois feels like a mythical radical. The connection between academic radi-cal discourses and the population's fetishising of the figure of the Father as embodied by political leaders is well captured by the Invisible Committee:

Thus it should come as no surprise that in their deliriums psychiatric patients are always confusing themselves with political figures, that we agree that our leaders are the roots of all our ills, that we like to grumble so much about them and that this grumbling is the consecration that crowns them as our masters ... That's also why intellectuals here tend to talk so loud when they're so meek, and why they always fail at the decisive moment, the only moment that would've given meaning to their existence, but that also would've had them banished from their profession. (The Invisible Committee 2007, 87–88)

To the extent that it relies on the promise of a ruptural event occurring ex nihilo, the neo-communist academic narrative imports its libidinal mysticism into the theory of radical anti-capitalist transformation. This mysticism implies that resistance is futile: our libidinal circuits cannot be modified from within the symbolic order that shapes them. For new forms of desiring and enjoying to emerge, we need the divine and accidental intervention of an event that belongs to a space outside the political proper, in the sense that it is independent of subjective political acts. Only once this event effects the symbolic rupture can the work of reshaping enjoyment begin.

This scenario begs multiple questions: what is the correlation between the new symbolic order, or the newly created possibility of a radically different symbolic order, and the form that fantasy, enjoyment, and thus the post-revolutionary reality will take? Is the new fundamental fantasy a result of the new order, or vice versa? And if our libidinal circuits cannot be modified from within the current symbolic order, as the theory of the event implies, will they be as impossible to modify from within the new symbolic order? Will thus the subjectivities of the post-event society be fully determined by a symbolic order that the subjects cannot affect, since these subjects seem to remain in the same condition of uncertainty about their aims before and after the event? How will subjects shaped by bourgeois dispositifs and with no experience of enjoying otherwise react to an impossible to suture breach in the bourgeois order? How can the event determine a desire for, say, communism to emerge from a desire for authority that protects itself through willed blindness to the Other's lack? Or are we to assume that the Party will guide these processes through carefully distributed disciplinary dispositifs so that we shall exit the capitalist terror to enter the post-revolutionary one?

Articulating critique in the form of a string of questions, as I did at various points in this last chapter, is no doubt irritating; I use it because it reflects my own irritation at any revolutionary rhetoric that feels justified in ignoring such questions. Continuing to enjoy like a bourgeois while waiting for the revolutionary subject to emerge fully formed from the head of the bourgeois order keeps us comfortably tethered to this order's dispositifs and masters. If the event accidentally happens, the day after will confront the revolutionary leaders with a 'people' whose mechanisms of desire and enjoyment are still resolutely bourgeois. We should be careful not to obscure the fact that Žižek's (2008, 174–175) examples of small reforms that yielded a systemic revolutionary change—Chinese State capitalism, perestroika—mobilised fantasies shaped by the dominant bourgeois apparatuses, pushing change in the direction of liberal-capitalism, not away from it. They are examples of successful co-option, not revolution. I would go as far as proposing that in its present form, the academic revolutionary fantasy fuels the fascism Foucault was discussing not long after the 1968 events in Paris:

> not only historical fascism, the fascism of Hitler and Mussolini – which was able to mobilize and use the desire of the masses so effectively – but also the fascism in us all, in our heads and in our everyday behavior, the fascism that causes us to love power, to desire the very thing that dominates and exploits us. (Foucault in Deleuze and Guattari 2000, xiii)

a fascism that will transform its devotees into 'bureaucrats of the revolution and civil servants of Truth' (Foucault, ibid.).

While Jacques-Alain Miller's fantasy of a psychoanalytical revolution is both funny and rather scary, considering how passionately many of the analysts supposed to be its leaders embrace fascism, at least it suggests that revolutionary labour on bourgeois enjoyment can and should be performed. Irrespective of its outcomes, which are indeed unpredictable, such labour would experiment with actively intervening on the modern fantasy and will-to-not-know, on our ritual and submissive enjoyment.

I have been arguing in this work that the bourgeois is committed to enjoying her submission to a master; it is expected that getting rid of the master needs to pass through moments of 'subjective destitution'. Such moments of desubjectivation would help the bourgeois renounce her obsession with the secret treasure that is her individual uniqueness, with the 'agalma' that hides somewhere deep in her special soul and that only these master-figures can dig out. Only by repeatedly confronting the bourgeois mechanisms of enjoyment harboured by all of us on the left with the Other's lack might we learn to dissociate jouissance from the search for fullness and from the masculinist modern fantasy. As far as I see, these will be risky and fiercely resisted experiments that cannot be brought upon by an event, by an epiphany, but only by tenacious, combative, collective, and local experiments. Such experiments are the conditions that might give the anti-capitalist militant the necessary courage and enjoyment to acknowledge the lack. I think that the radical tear in the symbolic fabric can arrive when the militants are a collective ready to engage in enjoying and desiring otherwise, indifferent to the summoning of the bourgeois dispositifs. To me, whatever accidental effects such revolutionary labour might produce, they are much more appealing than waiting for the accidental effects of the global event promised by the sacerdotal premonitions of the neo-communist academe.

No one can give revolutionary tactical advice, simply because there is no possibility of predicting a revolutionary template. We can only know what we fight against, the symbolic regime and the dispositifs of our time in their positivity. But this is more than sufficient: it is within these fights that the de-phallicising of enjoyment can happen. And while the work of the militants must remain attuned to theory, to the extent that theory is a tool for constructing the alternative political fantasies we need, such experimental collectives cannot pursue their activity in any of the strongholds of the bourgeois order, despite the comforts and the love to be obtained within. Especially not in the seductive thought asylum of the bourgeois university, where provocative discourse is produced exclusively to cover up for docile enjoyment.

Notes

1. This focus on the (fantasmatic) representation of the political act has another justification, one that has deeper implications for political tactics but that I also do not want to discuss in this context: the idea that the transformative political act cannot be defined by academics, since it is an unintended consequence of political experimentations with ways of enjoying otherwise, experiments which cannot be performed within the academic framework.

2. It is interesting that in his discussion of the university discourse, Žižek (2004, 504) underlines precisely the loops of power hidden behind academic truths, without for this reason applying it to his own revolutionary blueprint: 'At a more common level, suffice it to recall the market expert who advocates strong budgetary measures (cutting welfare expenses, and so on) as a necessity imposed by his neutral expertise devoid of any ideological biases: what he conceals is the series of power relations (from the active role of state apparatuses to ideological beliefs) which sustain the "neutral" functioning of the market mechanism.'

3. Wright Mills (1962, 115) argues that the utilitarian and rationalist view of class-consciousness in Marx is too close for comfort to Bentham and that class-consciousness might indeed be the Marxian equivalent of the liberal myth of 'man as citizen'.

4. In an interview given to *Counterpunch*, immediately after pronouncing a rather ungrounded universalist aphorism: 'communism ... [is] the only condition under which a politics adequate to the needs, demands, and common will of the people is possible', Dean squarely places the communist struggle in the academic terrain, by celebrating at length the fact that most academics seem to migrate from Foucaultian, Deleuzian, or Derridian arguments to 'communist' ones.

5. The imminent symbolic rupture seems to be heralded by strong signs: 'As a Pew Research Center poll found, 66 percent of Americans think that division between rich and poor are strong or very strong, an increase of 19 percent since 2009' (Dean 2012, 219).

6. The New Age slogan of the 99 % operates to mask fundamental antagonisms in the US society, including the bourgeois alongside those they exploit into a fake collective: 'In fact we would like to point to the divisions within this 99% that are irreparable, unalienable and inexorable. This slogan functions in favor of control through inclusion. It is an ideological position prevalent throughout liberal democratic society, that of multiculturalism and the insistence upon tolerance, which has emerged as a right-hand-man to Order, intent on wiping out any agitational forces within the movement, even calling in back up forces of control, that is the police' (LCSC, 2011).

7. Including in its relation to the anus, if we take Freud's association of money with faeces seriously.

8. Closer to enacting a proper occupation were the movements of occupation of neighbourhoods, Occupy the Barrio, Decolonize the Barrio, or Occupy the Hood, which attempted to reorganise the spaces where people live and

work on models of self-reliance. These movements were, unfortunately, not very prominent in the commentaries of the academic left, which preferred to comment on the occupation of parks and plazas (see Aaron et al. 2012).

9. Gaiu (2015) perceptively ironises the Western academic elite's unabashed propensity to emit verdicts on each and every local struggle: 'Far away from the events, like an F-16 fighter jet which, flying at hundreds of meters from the ground, can confuse a civil hospital or the embassy of China for a military objective, Slavoj Žižek makes the cynical exploitation of Albanian suffering by one Western camp equivalent to the protests of the political left against NATO crimes' (my translation).

10. We can think here of Kant's theory of freedom, which according to Zupančič (2000, 82) establishes the co-ordinates of time and space outside of time and space and thus enables an endless progress towards moral perfection.

References

Aaron, M., Davis, W., Feeley, D., Finkel, D., & Wainer, K. (2012). The politics of austerity, occupy and the 2012 elections. http://www.solidarity-us.org/site/2012elections. Accessed 12 Mar 2014.

Agamben, G. (1998). *Homo sacer: Sovereign power and bare life.* Stanford: Stanford University Press.

Badiou, A. (2003). Lack and destruction. *UMBR(a): Ignorance of the Law.*

Boteels, B. (2014). *The actuality of communism.* London/New York: Verso.

Brown, W. (2002). Suffering the paradoxes of rights. In B. Wendy & H. Janet (Eds.), *Left legalism/left critique* (pp. 420–434). Durham: Duke University Press.

Brown, W. (2010). *Walled states, waning sovereignty.* New York: Zone Books.

Butler, J. (2015). *Notes towards a performative theory of assembly.* Cambridge: Harvard University Press.

Butler, J., Laclau, E., & Žižek, S. (2000). *Contingency, hegemony, universality: Contemporary dialogues on the left.* London/New York: Verso.

Dean, J. (2010). Drive as the structure of biopolitics: Economy, sovereignty and capture. *Krisis, 2,* 2–15.

Dean, J. (2012). *The communist horizon.* New York/London: Verso.

Deleuze, G., & Guattari, F. (2000). *The anti-Oedipus. Capitalism and schizophrenia.* Minneapolis: University of Minnesota Press.

Foucault, M. (1977). *Discipline and punish: The Birth of the prison.* Hammondsworth: Penguin Books.

Foucault, M. (2003). *Society must be defended*. London: Penguin Books.

Gaiu, C. (2015). Amurgul intelectualilor: Stingerea disidentei in umanism. *Critic Atac.* http://www.criticatac.ro/27832/amurgul-intelectualilor/. Accessed 6 June 1015.

Goux, J.-J. (1990). *Symbolic economies: After Marx and Freud*. New York: Cornell University Press.

Lenin, V. I. (1982). *On the dictatorship of the proletariat*. Moscow: Progress Publishers.

Lost Children's School of Cartography. (2011). Lost in the fog: Dead ends and potentials of the occupy movement. http://theanarchistlibrary.org/library/lost-children-s-school-of-cartography-lost-in-the-fog. Accessed 13 June 2015.

Mbembe, A. (2003). Necropolitics. *Public Culture*, Winter, 11–40.

McGowan, T. (2004). *The end of dissatisfaction? Jacques Lacan and the emerging society of enjoyment*. Albany: State University of New York Press.

McGowan, T. (2013). *Enjoying what we don't have: The political project of psychoanalysis*. Lincoln/London: University of Nebraska Press.

Panu, M. (2009). *Contextualizing family planning: Truth, subject and the other in the US Government*. London/New York: Palgrave.

Procacci, G. (1991). Social economy and the government of poverty. In G. Burchell, C. Gordon, & P. Miller's (Eds.), *The Foucault effect: Studies in governmentality*. Brighton: Harvester Wheatsheaf.

Stavrakakis, Y. (2003). The lure of Antigone: Aporias of an ethics of the political. *Umbr(a): Ignorance of the Law, 1*, 117–129.

Stavrakakis, Y. (2007). *The Lacanian left: Psychoanalysis, theory*. Politics: Edinburgh University Press.

Stoler, A. L. (1995). *Race and the education of desire: Foucault's "history of sexuality" and the colonial order of things*. Durham/London: Duke University Press.

The Invisible Committee. (2007). *The coming insurrection*. Semiotext(e).

Wright Mills, C. (1962). *The Marxists*. New York: Dell, Laurel Edition.

Žižek, S. (2003). "What some would call…" A response to Yannis Stavrakakis. *Umbr(a): Ignorance of the Law, 1*, 131–5.

Žižek, S. (2007b). Trotsky's "terrorism and communism", or, despair and utopia in the turbulent year of 1920. In T. Leon (Ed.), *Terrorism and communism*. London/New York: Verso.

Žižek, S. (2008). *In defense of lost causes*. London/New York: Verso.

Žižek, S. (2004). 'From politics to biopolitics….and back'. *Southern Atlantic Quarterly, 103*(2/3), 501–521, Spring/Summer 2004.

Zupančič, A. (2000). *Ethics of the real: Kant, Lacan*. London/New York: Verso.

Index[1]

---

[1] Note: Page numbers with "n" denote notes.

CPI Antony Rowe
Chippenham, UK
2017-01-09 21:33